Christ's Eucharistic Presence

American University Studies

Series VII
Theology and Religion
Vol. 157

PETER LANG
New York • San Francisco • Bern • Baltimore
Frankfurt am Main • Berlin • Wien • Paris

Paul H. Jones

Christ's Eucharistic Presence

A History of the Doctrine

PETER LANG
New York • San Francisco • Bern • Baltimore
Frankfurt am Main • Berlin • Wien • Paris

Library of Congress Cataloging-in-Publication Data

Jones, Paul H.
    Christ's eucharistic presence: a history of the doctrine/ Paul H. Jones.
      p.   cm. — (American university studies. Series VII, Theology and
  religion; Vol. 157)
    Includes bibliographical references.
    1. Lord's Supper—Real presence—History of doctrines. I Title.
  II. Series.
  BV823.J66   1994   234'.163—dc20   93-2970
  ISBN 0-8204-2174-X   CIP
  ISSN 0740-0446

Die Deutsche Bibliothek-CIP-Einheitsaufnahme

Jones, Paul H.:
Christ's Eucharistic presence: a history of the doctrine/ Paul H. Jones.
- New York; Berlin; Bern; Frankfurt/M.; Paris; Wien: Lang, 1994
  (American university studies: Ser. 7, Theology and religion; Vol. 157)
  ISBN 0-8204-2174-X
NE: American university studies / 07

BV
823
.J66
1994

The paper in this book meets the guidelines for permanence and durability of
the Committee on Production Guidelines for Book Longevity of the
Council on Library Resources.

© Peter Lang Publishing, Inc., New York 1994

Printed in the United States of America.

TO

the *past* generations of Christians,
who passed on the faith and practice of the church, especially
my parents:
G. Curtis and Sybil Jones

the *present* generation of Christians,
who embody Christ's presence in the world, especially
my wife:
Merry Pratt Jones

the *future* generations of Christians,
in whom God's promises and our hopes reside, especially
our children:
Zachary Peter Chastain Jones and Natalie Caroline Nettleton Jones

ACKNOWLEDGMENTS

Writing a book is paradoxical. It is both a uniquely independent process and one which is profoundly dependent on others. Those significant others deserve recognition. Several teachers and colleagues read the manuscript during different stages in its preparation: David Buttrick, Peter Hodgson, Phil Points, J. Hill Hamon, and Asa Humphries. Each reader offered valuable insights for which I am grateful.

This book was written while I was employed by Transylvania University, Lexington, Kentucky. Special appreciation is extended to President Charles Shearer and Dean James Moseley for their encouragement. Support from the David and Betty Jones Faculty Development Program was most helpful. Jonathon Jensen and Michael Delk, Transylvania students, assisted with the indices. Nancy Dunnavant provided invaluable assistance in the preparation of the text.

I am also grateful for permission to reprint material previously published by: Augsburg Fortress Publishers (Reprinted from *Selected Writings of Martin Luther*, edited by Theodore G. Tappert, copyright © 1967 Fortress Press. Used by permission of Augsburg Fortress.); Cambridge University Press (Thomas Aquinas, *Summa Theologiae*, vol. 58. New York: Blackfriars; McGraw-Hill Book Company, 1965. Reprinted by permission of the publisher. All rights reserved.); Epworth Press (Geoffrey Wainwright, *Eucharist and Eschatology*. New York: Oxford University Press, 1981. Reprinted by permission of the publisher. All rights reserved.); The Liturgical Press (Nathan Mitchell, *Cult and Controversy*. New York: Pueblo Publishing Company, 1982, and Willy Rordorf *et al*, The *Eucharist of the Early Christians*. New York: Pueblo Publishing Company, 1978. Copyright © by The Order of St. Benedict, Inc. Published by The Liturgical Press, Collegeville, Minnesota. Used with permission.); Oxford University Press (Eugene R. Fairweather, *The Oxford Movement*. New York: Oxford University Press, 1964, and James Hastings Nichols, ed., *The Mercersburg Theology*. New York: Oxford University Press, 1966. Reprinted by permission of the publisher. All rights reserved.); Sheed and Ward (Edward Schillebeeckx, *The Eucharist*. New York: Sheed and Ward, 1968. Reprinted by permission of the publisher. All rights reserved.); SPCK (Yngue Brilioth, *Eucharistic Faith and Practice*. London: The Society for Promoting Christian Knowledge, 1934. Reprinted by permission of the publisher. All rights reserved.); and Westminster/John Knox Press (From Calvin: *Institutes of the Christian Religion*, edited by John T. McNeill and translated by Ford Lewis Battles [Volume XX & XXI: The Library of Christian Classics]. Copyright © MCMLX W. L. Jenkins. Used by permission of Westminster/John Knox Press., From *Table and Tradition*, by Alasdair I. C. Heron. © Alasdair Heron 1983. Used by permission of Westminster/John Knox Press., and From *Zwingli and Bullinger*, translations with introductions and notes by G. W. Bromiley [Volume XXIV: The Library of Christian Classics]. Published simultaneously in Great Britain and the United States of America by the S.C.M. Press, Ltd., and The Westminster Press. Used by permission of Westminster/John Knox Press.).

Although I am indebted to the above people for their many contributions, the sole responsibility for errors of commission and omission resides with the author.

TABLE OF CONTENTS

PREFACE

The claim that the divine life exhibits particular presence as well as omnipresence constitutes one of the most perplexing and profound problems for Christian theology.

This apparent contradiction surfaces dramatically with the doctrine of the incarnation. On the one hand, both God, as Creator and Sustainer, and Christ, as the divine Logos or Second Person of the Trinity, are attributed universal presence. On the other hand, the central Christian affirmation that God was in Christ "in a particular way at a particular time in a particular place" seems irreconcilable with the concept of omnipresence. Nonetheless, the tradition has steadfastly defended these apparently contradictory claims by insisting that Christ's life represents a special mode of presence.

The constitutive yet controversial nature of Christ's special mode of presence surfaces distinctively in the eucharistic rite. The ecumenical document *Baptism, Eucharist and Ministry* is unequivocal.

> The words and acts of Christ at the institution of the eucharist stand at the heart of the celebration; the eucharistic meal is the sacrament of the body and blood of Christ, the sacrament of his real presence. Christ fulfills in a variety of ways his promise to be always with his own even to the end of the world. But Christ's mode of presence in the eucharist is unique. Jesus said over the bread and wine of the eucharist: 'This is my body . . . this is my blood. . . .' What Christ declared is true, and this truth is fulfilled every time the eucharist is celebrated. The Church confesses Christ's real, living and active presence in the eucharist.[1]

Without the conscious, communal awareness of Christ's living presence there is no church. We should not be surprised, therefore, that the mode of Christ's eucharistic presence has been a topic of continuing discussion and debate. It is, however, astonishing to realize that the development of an adequate doctrine of Christ's eucharistic presence is virtually absent in Protestant theology and is currently undergoing critical revision in Roman Catholic theology.[2]

This book addresses this serious lacuna in Protestant doctrine and the uncharacteristic irresolution in Roman Catholic doctrine by tracing the historical development of the church's formulations of Christ's eucharistic presence. Recommendations for further development of an ecumenical interpretation follow in an epilogue.

A chronological survey is an essential prelude to any constructive proposal since it is prerequisite for both the proper understanding of the theological issue and the proper framing of a contemporary interpretation. It is, however, doubly important for this topic because no single comprehensive study of the mode of Christ's eucharistic presence exists.[3]

Our historical treatment—or archaeology—employs two interrelated steps. The first procedure, an *eidetics* of the eucharist, discussed in chapter one, uncovers four constitutive features of eucharistic celebrations. These features are: the communal context of the eucharist, connection of ritual and material elements, past-future dialectic, and presence-absence dialectic. The second procedure, an *empirics* of the eucharist, investigates chronologically the church's formulations of Christ's eucharistic presence.

Beginning in chapter one with the New Testament eucharistic texts and continuing over the next five chapters, the survey examines and evaluates each designated time period with respect to its treatment of the communal character and the three requisite features of the eucharist.

In chapter two it is argued that the concept of ecclesial presence dominated the discussion from the time of the Christian Scriptures to the beginning of the Carolingian Age.

In chapter three it is argued that the concept of substantial presence dominated the discussion from the Carolingian Age to the dawn of the Reformation.

Chapter four is a presentation of the various Protestant Reformation concepts of Christ's eucharistic presence and the relevant conclusions of the Council of Trent. In this chapter it is argued that the Protestant Reformation produced diverse but incomplete interpretations of Christ's eucharistic presence, while the Catholic Reformation reaffirmed the doctrine of transubstantiation.

Chapter five is a survey of both Protestant and Catholic pronouncements over the last four centuries and it is concluded that these proposals are, for the most part, reiterations of the various Reformation models.

Chapter six details the emergence of the new "Interpersonal-Encounter Model." In particular, this chapter depicts the eucharistic theologies of the model's principal advocates, Edward Schillebeeckx and Piet Schoonenberg. Both theologians locate the doctrine of the mode of Christ's eucharistic presence in human consciousness and personal communication. Schillebeeckx pursues a phenomenology of human meaning, while Schoonenberg develops a phenomenology of personal presence. Their contributions include the reappropriation of the early church's concept of ecclesial presence and their respective articulations of the concept of transignification.

A final, cautionary note is necessary. Any study of the theology of the eucharist must recognize that the sacrament, at its essence, is a mystery. Indeed, the Greek word *mysterion* was later translated into the Latin *sacramentum*. In the New Testament *mysterion* refers "to the secret purposes of God revealed and worked out in the world through the mission of Jesus as the Christ."[4]

The eucharist is, therefore, an "ineffable sacrament." Although believers will never comprehend with any completeness the mode of Christ's eucharistic presence, we can come to comprehend better the voices of the tradition. Although communicants will never exhaust the reality of Christ's eucharistic presence, we can exhaust the available alternatives in our efforts for clarity. Theologians strive neither to "prove" nor to "solve" the mystery of Christ's eucharistic presence; instead, we seek intelligibility. That is a major task of theology and the goal of this study.

Notes

1. *Baptism, Eucharist and Ministry*, Faith and Order Paper 111 (Geneva: World Council of Churches, 1982), #13, p. 12.

2. See David N. Power, *The Eucharistic Mystery* (New York: Crossroad, 1992), especially Part I. Because of space limitations, a treatment of the Orthodox Church's formulations will not be pursued.

3. The most recent history of the doctrine of the eucharist is Darwell Stone's *A History of the Doctrine of the Holy Eucharist*, 2 vols. (London: Longmans, Green, and Co., 1909). Although it was once the definitive treatment, it is now both antiquated and inadequate. To the author's knowledge there exists no single, contemporary treatment of the mode of Christ's eucharistic presence.

4. Robert L. Browning and Roy A. Reed, *The Sacraments in Religious Education and Liturgy: An Ecumenical Model* (Birmingham: Religious Education Press, 1985), 28.

CHAPTER ONE

THE CONSTITUTIVE FEATURES

Before we can investigate the tradition's formulations of the mode of Christ's eucharistic presence, prior methodological issues must be addressed. Consequently, this chapter will concentrate on three methodological concerns. The first section will set forth the rationale and procedure for the overall project. The second section will conduct an *eidetics* of the eucharist which will uncover four constitutive features of eucharistic celebrations. The final section will examine the New Testament eucharistic texts and will confirm the findings of our *eidetics*.

Methodology

The goal of this book is to survey the unfolding meaning of Christ's eucharistic presence. However, prior methodological questions confront us: What is the eucharist? What are its constitutive features and where do we go to find them? This section will address these issues and provide a rationale for the over-all procedure.

Because the eucharist has been a central rite of Christianity from its inception, diverse procedures have been employed to determine its meaning. Nonetheless, a typology emerges.[1] On the one hand, the Roman Catholic Church generally secures the meaning of the eucharist and eucharistic presence via the Magisterium. That is, the essence of the eucharist is uncovered by listening to dogmatic definitions that have been advanced by various church councils, especially the Council of Trent. On the other hand, Protestant churches generally secure the meaning of the eucharist through variations on one biblical route. Some Protestants argue that the meaning of the eucharist is reducible to the intention of Jesus that night in the Upper Room as presented in the biblical text. Others argue a variation of this method by claiming that the meaning is synonymous with the originating event or, at minimum, the uncovering of the earliest stratum of the church's understanding of the eucharist as found in scripture. This book will argue that neither of these routes is acceptable, and that an alternate method must be devised in order to establish a genuinely ecumenical meaning of the eucharist and of Christ's eucharistic presence that maintains continuity with the tradition.[2]

The Protestant Route of Intention

We begin by analyzing the Protestant methodology. The proposal that the meaning of the eucharist is reducible to the intention of Jesus as presented in the biblical text proves to be inadequate for at least two reasons. First, recent hermeneutical theory argues that the meaning of a text or an event should be derived primarily from the text or the event, and not from the intention of the author. Words and actions have a meaning independent from either the intentions of the author(s) or the participant(s).

Second, Jesus' intentions are not presented in the biblical text. Although the gospels are the vehicles by which we gain access to Jesus' intentions, these narratives have a meaning independent from the historical Jesus. Because they were not written by him and because they are kerygmatic in nature and not historically reliable biographical portraits, no direct access to Jesus' intentions is available. Textual criticism reveals layers of interpretation and we cannot get behind the layers to Jesus' thoughts.

Thus, the route of intention proves inadequate for two reasons: the meaning and intention of the eucharist are different and the nature of the gospel materials precludes access to Jesus' intentions.

The variation of this method seeks to determine the meaning of the eucharist by claiming that the meaning is synonymous with the originating event or, at minimum, the uncovering of the earliest stratum of the church's understanding of the eucharist as found in scripture. This proposal proves to be inadequate for at least three reasons.

First, the meaning of the eucharist transcends the originating event since the consequences of an action belong to its meaning. Future receptions of an event have direct bearing on the event's interpretation. For example, the disciples who gathered with Jesus in the Upper Room understood neither the events of that night nor the events of that weekend. In addition, they were not cognizant that a sacrament was being instituted. Furthermore, an argument could be advanced that Jesus himself did not know the full consequences of that meal! As part of an unfolding event, the meaning of the eucharist is part of a continuum that extends into the future.

Second, the meaning of the eucharist transcends the originating event since redemption is only partially experienced or actualized in the originating event. Because an eschatological or *transempirical telos* attends all historical manifestations of redemptive presence, meaning is neither exhausted by nor limited to the founding event.

This is not to suggest, however, that the originating event is superfluous. On the contrary, the founding event is causally indispensable. The eucharistic rite that evolved from the originating event maintains continuity through the collective memory of its origin. However, no *a priori* relation exists between the origin of the eucharist and the way it endures through time.

Yet, the first eucharistic celebration is normative to the degree that redemption was mediated. That is, events that effect a new condition of redemptive existence are attributed by the church to God's activity in Christ. Consequently, divine presence becomes identified as a distinctive element of all eucharistic celebrations.

Third, the meaning of the eucharist transcends the originating event since the earliest, historically retrievable stratum of the church's understanding of the eucharist resists systemization and harmonization. As we shall discover in the last section of this chapter, the New Testament sources that record the originating event present diverse and sometimes conflicting interpretations. Hence, the New Testament itself does not present a single, authoritative account of the eucharist.

We dismiss, therefore, the predominantly Protestant route of securing the meaning of the eucharist through the originating event for three reasons. First, the consequences of an action belong to its meaning. Second, redemption is only partially realized in the originating event. Third, the New Testament eucharistic texts do not furnish a single, authoritative interpretation.

Thus, the Protestant route of securing the meaning of the eucharist through intentionality or the originating event proves inadequate. We now turn to an analysis of the Roman Catholic position.

The Roman Catholic Route of Magisterium

In general, the Roman Catholic Church secures the meaning of the eucharist through the authoritative teaching of the councils and papal encyclicals. Clearly, they operate as legitimate guidelines for determining the meaning of the eucharist.

On the positive side, this method values postorigin developments of eucharistic interpretation. It realizes that the restricted focus on the originating event falsely presupposes that the origins are exhaustive sources and norms. Furthermore, it realizes that the ongoing celebrations of the eucharist constitute the *transempirical telos* of the eucharist being historically actualized. Hence, the meaning of the eucharist extends beyond the study of its origins.

On the negative side, this method does not go far enough. The selection of representative council statements as normative for eucharistic understanding does not do full justice to the ongoing tradition. Although the Roman Catholic Church values tradition, in practice it merely substitutes a designated time period of the church for the originating time period. An advantage results only from an expanded understanding that might have accrued over that time span.

Parenthetically, many Protestant denominations practice a similar methodology when they invoke, in addition to the Bible, the interpretation of their respective founder(s) as definitive. Consequently, Protestants and Catholics apparently embrace at this point a similar methodology, but because they select different authoritative statements, they disagree on eucharistic interpretation.

In spite of valuing postorigin developments of eucharistic interpretation, what we have designated the Roman Catholic method fails to satisfy the criteria of continuity and ecumenicity. Continuity is not preserved since only selective interpretations are highlighted from the ongoing tradition. Ecumenicity is not possible since this method, whether practiced by Roman Catholics or Protestants, intentionally ignores alternative voices of interpretation.

The Method of Discernment

We have argued that neither the two Protestant methods of securing the meaning of the eucharist (by discerning Jesus' intentions or by uncovering the originating event as recorded in the biblical text) nor the single Roman Catholic method of selecting definitive statements from within the tradition satisfies our criteria of continuity and ecumenicity. It is the thesis of this book that a new method is required to secure the meaning of the eucharist and Christ's eucharistic presence. We propose a twofold method of discernment through which the constitutive features of the eucharist are revealed by an *eidetics*[3] of the eucharist, and the actual attempts by the tradition to make sense of Christ's eucharistic presence are surveyed by a subsequent "historical archaeology" or *empirics*.[4]

Both of these steps are necessary. Because the tradition involves continuity and not simply an itemized succession of events, we need to understand the eucharist *diachronically*. That is, we need to examine the ongoing meaning of the eucharist as it is received by, and makes an impact upon, successive generations within the church. Since the meaning of the eucharist and Christ's eucharistic presence involves the history of its reception, our *empirics* will survey the diverse "concretizations" of the eucharistic rite and its attendant understandings of Christ's eucharistic presence throughout the history of Christianity.

Although we have argued against an *a priori* relation between the origin of the eucharist and the way it endures through time, we have claimed that the originating event is normative since it mediates redemption. Divine presence is active in that initial event. Therefore, a historical archaeology should start with the New Testament eucharistic texts.

Yet, we also need to locate criteria of continuity or the enduring features of the eucharist. An *eidetics* would uncover the essential eucharistic structures through a phenomenological analysis of the eucharist. It will be argued that four constitutive features attend eucharistic celebrations. These features are: the communal context, connection of ritual and material elements, past-future dialectic, and presence-absence dialectic.

We have thus argued that the method of discernment involves two inter-related steps. First, an *eidetics* of the eucharist would uncover its constitutive features, and second, an *empirics* of the eucharist would examine and evaluate the tradition with respect to its treatment of these essential features. We proceed with step one.

An *Eidetics* of the Eucharist

The Communal Context

Human meaning operates within a comprehensive network or social world of meaning. That is, objects in the everyday world collect "an aura of meaning." They impact upon, are evaluated by, and, in turn, are integrated into our personal fields of meaning. In short, each person participates in a structure of meaning that we call a social world or unified structure of meaning.

The meaning of the eucharist also operates within this larger network of significations. Like all objects in the world, bread and wine evoke many different meanings. They are the products of nature and of human labor. Their meaning is related to our personal history as well as to a world that has already been shaped by human meaning. Consequently, the full meaning of bread and wine can be discerned only within this broader nexus of meanings.

When Christians declare, therefore, that in the eucharist the body and blood of Christ are somehow identified with bread and wine, they are speaking of a reality charged with unique significance. Indeed, the world of meanings connected to bread and wine are "transignified," i.e., bread and wine become signs of Christ through a change in the sign-reality of the bread and wine. To understand properly the particular meaning of this change, we must examine the broad nexus of significations that compose the world of church.

Because human beings in the world are constituted by both subjectivity and intersubjectivity, we, as individuals, have consciousness of our situation in life, of our strengths and weaknesses, of our temporality and spatiality, as well as consciousness that these elements of existence are shared with and dependent upon other individuals. Consciousness is, then, a prerequisite of meaning and meaning is a requisite of social existence. The meaning of the eucharist is discerned, therefore, only as the communal faith-consciousness of Christian existence is explored.

The church is a particular way humans relate together in the world. It is a corporate historical existence which shares a determinate intersubjectivity. This means that a specific structure of cointentions, or ways of "meaning" each other, unifies the participants. The distinctive reality that is mediated by the Christian corporate faith-consciousness is redemptive consciousness or redemptive intersubjectivity.

Participation in church or *ecclesia* means to share this common world of meaning or this determinate way of being in the world together with others before God. Consistency is possible since ecclesial existence bridges the generations by means of corporate memory and celebrations of the originating and normative events of this community. Continuity of the present with the originating event that first occasioned redemptive transformation is preserved primarily through ritual acts of identity formation. Worship functions, then, as one of the principal vehicles through which the Christian community transmits and shapes its communal faith-consciousness. In turn, "proclamatory" and "sacramental" activities comprise the core of the worship experience.

As the church's dramatic activities, the sacraments invite participation. By requiring people to act out the reciprocal intentions of the community, sacraments intentionally communicate this distinctive ecclesial intersubjectivity and thereby restructure individual consciousness. In particular, the eucharist, through the distribution of the elements, the passing of the peace, and the eucharistic prayers, enables participants to act out the intentions of the community members toward each other, the world, and the divine. Sacramental activities are, then, formative communal rites in which the community's intentions are expressed and the individual is drawn into the community's intersubjectivity.

Because human meaning occurs within a social world of meaning and because the eucharist is a communal and not a private rite, an adequate interpretation of the eucharist and of Christ's eucharistic presence must always include its communal context.[5]   In addition, the intersubjective network that attends Christian consciousness permits our methodology to satisfy both the criteria of continuity and ecumenicity. The structure of ecclesial faith-consciousness bridges the generations as well as the diversity of Christian communal expressions.

Connection of Ritual and Material Elements

To participate in rituals is to be human. Starting at birth with patterns which develop around feedings, people of every age discover the meaning and purpose of life through ritual celebrations. Perhaps the common meal, where people recognize most vividly their dependence upon persons and forces other and greater than themselves, functions as the most basic ritual experience for humanity.

Clearly, every Jewish meal with its blessings of bread and wine, and thanksgiving prayers is a ritual occasion. In the Upper Room Jesus did not, therefore, "institute" a ritual meal as much as he transformed the meaning of an existing ritual practice. Without question, the eucharistic celebrations through the centuries have been and continue to be ritualistic.

Because sacramental activity entails a visible and tactile symbolic act of incorporation into a distinctive corporate intersubjectivity, the material components of the eucharist are indispensable for at least two reasons. First, the material elements of bread and wine are a traditional part of the eucharist and distinguish themselves from other modes of divine presence. Yet, we must first acknowledge that the use of a "medium" in God's self-disclosure is not peculiar to the eucharist. On the contrary, the "naked," transcendent God never directly appears, since

God's self-revelation always occurs in and through earthly media. The presence of God, therefore, is always mediated "symbolically" or a "mediated immediacy." In the incarnation it is the human Jesus who serves as the symbolic mediator. In baptism it is the water, and in the eucharist it is the material elements of bread and wine. Theologically, material elements are requisite for God's self-disclosure.

Second, human consciousness requires an object in order to invoke presence. Bread and wine serve as the focal points for personal and communal consciousness. Within the determinate Christian consciousness, these elements invoke a constellation of human meanings that attend Jesus and table fellowship. Besides the Passover, covenant rites, and messianic banquets from the Jewish tradition, possible images would also include Jesus eating and drinking with tax collectors and sinners, the feeding of the multitudes, the marriage at Cana in Galilee, the last supper, and the resurrection meal appearances. What becomes immediately clear is that the single event of eucharistic ritual and its material elements of bread and wine encompass an immensely wide field of meaning.

The meaning of the eucharist and Christ's eucharistic presence necessarily involves a ritual celebration that includes material elements. Without the ritual activity, the eucharist would sever its association with Jewish and Christian ritual meals as well as impair its ability to incorporate participants into a distinctive corporate intersubjectivity. Without the material elements of bread and wine, human consciousness would lose its focal points by which Christ's presence is invoked. Thus, the connection of ritual and material elements is constitutive to eucharistic celebrations.

Past-Future Dialectic

A determinate intersubjectivity, which structures the cointentions of members toward each other within a society, includes temporal meanings. The past persists in the collective memory of a society and the future is anticipated by its members. Yet, what persists as memory is neither the total of time past nor even the total past of a specific people. Nor is the future open to an infinite number of possibilities. Rather, the past is remembered in the present in determinate ways and the future is anticipated in the present in determinate ways. The past is governed by the originating and normative events of the community, and the horizon of the future is established by the selective memory of the past. Thus, a society limits the range of its memory and its hope by its determinate intersubjectivity or unifying meaning structure.

In ecclesial existence, the social reality is corporate redemptive existence. Through the proclamatory and sacramental activities of the church, believers remember the originating event of Christ and anticipate the salvific end of his work.

"Memory and hope," according to Dietrich Ritschl, *"are the dimensions of faith in the Christus praesens* and it is only because of the *Christus praesens* that these dimensions are open to our perception."* The church invites its members to "'hope backward' into the realm of memory and to 'remember forward' into the realm of hope."[6] The former, in the knowledge of forgiveness, removes any past elements which burden the present and destroy hope for the future, while the latter, in the knowledge of promise, assures the fulfillment of the future.

Through the celebration of the eucharist, the present is not only filled with the presence of the risen Christ but it is also filled with the presence of the past and the presence of the future. The mnemonic Christ comes to human consciousness in historically defined ways. Explicit images and meanings attend his memory. The repetitive character of the eucharist re-presents the death and resurrection of Jesus, which, in turn, orders the present and the future. Yet, his pastness is recalled in the midst of the affirmation of his risen Lordship.

The presence of the risen Christ in the eucharist is also presence of the future. Present in human consciousness as hope or anticipation, the expected Christ is wrapped in the symbols of fulfillment. The ultimate future or completion of Christ's saving work "comes out of the future and into the present without however ceasing to be future." The eucharist contains the "pre-presentation of the parousia." Jesus' coming to the community through the eucharist involves a "not yet" character "which establishes a real presence but one which does not rule out a real absence at the same time."[7]

This anticipatory character of the eucharist summons to corporate consciousness the eschatological community of the end-time. Although this future assembly is both really present in and really absent from the historical assembly, it genuinely and creatively shapes the current eucharistic community. Through the symbols of bread and wine the Christian community "finds in the future as made present eucharistically nourishment and sustenance for . . . life in the present."[8] Because of the eucharistic presence of Christ in the mode of futurity and the anticipatory presence of the ultimate future, Christian corporate consciousness expects hope instead of despair.

Succinctly, participants in ecclesial existence live "from the future" and not "for the future." "The Christian lives from the future in the sense that the eschatological future of God's kingdom, which has already been announced in and through the resurrection of Jesus, is the ground of his present piety and politics, his suffering and his activity."[9]

We have argued that the eucharistic rite encompasses temporal dimensions. Christ's presence is related to the incarnation of Jesus as the Christ, which belongs to the past, and to the eschatological presence of Christ at the parousia, which belongs to the future. A backward referent to the crucified and risen Lord as well as a forward referent to the coming Christ attends each eucharistic celebration. Therefore, the past-future dialectic is constitutive for eucharistic celebrations.

Presence-Absence Dialectic

In order for ecclesial existence to be redemptive, divine presence must be active. This is not to suggest that proclamatory and sacramental activities "cause" divine presence, but it is to claim that they announce its availability.

Throughout the centuries, the Christian tradition has affirmed that the risen Christ is present at the celebration of the eucharist. Yet, Christ's eucharistic presence is not an immediate presence. Although the tradition refers to Christ's presence in the eucharist as "Real Presence," it is in actuality situated between a memory and a hope. The historical Jesus is past and the expected Christ is future. Christ's eucharistic presence is "presence-in-absence."

Inherent in the church's claim of Christ's eucharistic presence is, then, a dialectic of presence and absence. Christ is present because redemption occurs and only divine presence can effect it. Christ is absent because the historical Jesus is dead and the expected Christ is not yet. Paradoxically, Christ's absence is signaled by the symbolic elements of bread and wine which in turn act as focal points for the consciousness of Christ's redemptive presence.

The presence-absence dialectic is, therefore, constitutive for Christ's eucharistic presence. Without the reality of Christ's presence, redemption would be unavailable to the faith community. Without the reality of Jesus' absence, the assertions of Christ's death, resurrection, ascension, and parousia would be undermined. Both presence and absence are required simultaneously.

Conclusion

Our *eidetics* of the eucharist has uncovered four constitutive features. Because individual human meaning operates within a social world of meaning and because the eucharist is a communal and not a private rite, an adequate interpretation of the eucharist and of Christ's eucharistic presence must always include its communal context. In addition, three requisite features attend eucharistic celebrations: the connection of ritual and material elements, the past-future dialectic, and the presence-absence dialectic. Each constitutive feature is indispensable. Whenever one feature is absent or a dialectic is severed, the range of meaning that attends eucharistic celebrations is reduced. Whether it be communal cointentions or temporal meanings, the more perfectly the features are actualized, the more efficaciously Christ's eucharistic presence is invoked.

New Testament Sources

A historical archaeology or *empirics* of the doctrine of Christ's eucharistic presence should begin with the major New Testament sources for the Lord's Supper.[10] This starting point is indispensable for at least two reasons. First, these accounts contain the earliest written records of the eucharistic practices of the early church. Second, an examination of these accounts and their attendant controversies will yield the requisite features of the doctrine of Christ's eucharistic presence.

Most scholars agree that the Pauline description of the Lord's Supper as recorded in I Corinthians 11:23-26 not only represents the earliest New Testament account but also contains a pre-Pauline formula in verses 23-25.[11] The priority of Paul over the synoptic accounts, and especially Mark, rests on the belief that the incongruence of the Pauline version of the "words of interpretation" has been harmonized by Mark, and thus points to a later Markan formula.[12] The claim that verses 23-25 are a pre-Pauline formula hinges on the phrase "after supper." This designation indicates that the two individual actions of eating the bread and drinking from the cup were once separated by the meal. Yet, in Paul's description of the current Corinthian practice the communal meal precedes the celebration of the Lord's Supper. Although the phrase "after supper" is retained by Paul, it no longer reflects actual practice. This incongruence of word and action strongly suggests that Paul was employing an earlier formula. It is, therefore, easy to understand why this phrase becomes superfluous and is omitted from the Markan account. For the above reasons, the Pauline rendering of the Lord's Supper as found in I Corinthians 11:23-26 is listed first.[13]

> For I received from the Lord what I also handed on to you, that the Lord Jesus on the night when he was betrayed took a loaf of bread, and when he had given thanks, he broke it and said, 'This is my body that is for you. Do this in remembrance of me.' In the same way he took the cup also, after supper, saying, 'This cup is the new covenant in my blood. Do this, as often as you drink it, in remembrance of me.' For as often as you eat this bread and drink the cup, you proclaim the Lord's death until he comes.

Mark's version of the eucharist is recorded in chapter fourteen, verses 22-25.

> While they were eating, he took a loaf of bread, and after blessing it he broke it, gave it to them, and said: 'Take; this is my body.' Then he took a cup, and after giving thanks he gave it to them, and all of them drank from it. He said to them, 'This is my blood of the covenant, which is poured out for many. Truly I tell you, I will never again drink of the fruit of the vine until that day when I drink it new in the kingdom of God.

Besides dropping the phrase "after supper" (discussed above), Mark also omits the instruction of Jesus to "repeat" this eating and drinking "in remembrance of me." This omission reinforces our earlier observation that Mark harmonizes Jesus' "words of instruction." In addition, Paul's phrase "this cup is the new covenant in my blood" is altered to read "this is my blood of the covenant. . . ." Thus, Paul's incongruence between "my body" and "this cup" is rendered by Mark into parallel phrases of "my body" and "my blood."

Since Matthew's account of the Lord's Supper as told in chapter twenty-six, verses 26-29, is highly dependent on Mark, it is listed next.

> While they were eating, Jesus took a loaf of bread, and after blessing it he broke it, gave it to the disciples, and said, 'Take, eat; this is my body.' Then he took a cup, and after giving thanks he gave it to them, saying, 'Drink from it, all of you; for this is my blood of the covenant, which is poured out for many for the forgiveness of sins. I tell you, I will never again drink of this fruit of the vine until that day when I drink it new with you in my Father's kingdom.'

Two changes are evident. First, Matthew alters verse 27 to read "Drink from it, all of you" so that it may conform more closely to the phrase "take, eat" of verse 26. Second, and more important for the history of the doctrine, the phrase "for the forgiveness of sins" is added to verse 28.

Although references to the "breaking of the bread" are located in the second and twentieth chapters of the Acts of the Apostles, Luke's primary description of the Lord's Supper is found in the gospel, verses 15-20 of chapter twenty-two.[14]

> He said to them, 'I have eagerly desired to eat this Passover with you before I suffer; for I tell you, I will not eat it until it is fulfilled in the kingdom of God.' Then he took a cup, and after giving thanks he said, 'Take this and divide it among yourselves; for I tell you that from now on I will not drink of the fruit of the vine until the kingdom of God comes.' Then he took a loaf of bread, and when he had given thanks, he broke it and gave it to them, saying, 'This is my body, which is given for you. Do this in remembrance of me.' And he did the same with the cup after supper, saying, 'This cup that is poured out for you is the new covenant in my blood.'

Even a casual reading of Luke raises significant problems. Immediately, we notice that the giving of the cup precedes the giving of the bread. To compound the problem, the giving of a second cup occurs after the meal. It appears on first reading that the Lukan description has conflated both the Pauline and Markan traditions.

Before the entangled traditions can be unraveled, the parameters of the text must be set. We now confront the central issue of Lukan eucharistic scholarship. Do verses 15-20 (the longer text) or do verses 15-19a (the shorter text) represent the original Lukan narrative? If the shorter version is primary, then the account presents a third version of the Lord's Supper that resembles Mark more than Paul but is, nonetheless, too different from both to be considered a variant of either.[15] If the longer text is primary, then the Lukan description can be considered a variant of Paul with a second cup. Recent scholarship concurs with this second view.[16]

So far we have listed the four major New Testament source texts for the Lord's Supper. However, we would be remiss if mention were not made of the Gospel of John. Clearly, a formal account of the eucharist is absent and scholarship is sharply divided over whether or not sacramental references are even present in the Johannine gospel.[17]

One group of scholars, composed mostly of Protestants, maintains that the Gospel of John is anti-sacramental since the evangelist's overemphasis on the Word nullifies any viable sacramental system. Consequently, the identification of Johannine sacramental references represents eisegesis.

Another group of scholars, composed of both Catholics and Protestants, affirms the presence of sacramental symbolism in John while concurrently acknowledging the dangers of eisegesis. Regardless of the motive for John's veiled references, broad sacramental interest is apparent throughout the gospel and primary eucharistic elements are evident in chapter six.

Since the controversy over sacramental imagery in John is tangential to our historical archaeology, a resolution need not be pursued. However, the Reformation concepts of Christ's eucharistic presence presuppose sacramental references.

The primary New Testament narratives of the Lord's Supper are now before us. At best, they are fragmentary and diverse. Not surprisingly, they reveal neither a systematic theology of the eucharist nor a comprehensive doctrine of Christ's eucharistic presence. In spite of these failings, the New Testament sources have supplied the tradition with ample material for endless controversies. Because the constitutive elements of doctrine elicit the most attention, the major disputes can direct us to the requisite New Testament features of the Lord's Supper.

The Communal Context

Although consensus among scholars avers that the eucharist is derived from a Judaistic prototype, those same scholars are sharply divided when asked to identify what kind of meal it was. Was it a Passover seder, a chaburah meal, a kiddush, an Essene meal or perhaps another rite entirely?[18]

Without question the synoptics and the tradition have associated the Lord's Supper with the Passover seder. Joachim Jeremias, the most persuasive contemporary advocate of this view, argues that the ancient liturgical formula itself, the eschatological references, the actual description of the meal, and the reported arrangement of the room unanimously substantiate the Passover character of the last meal of Jesus.[19]

In light of the scriptural and traditional evidence for the Passover connection, the burden of proof clearly rests with those scholars who deny this link. Yet, many scholars and much data negate this association.[20] Missing from the scriptural accounts are mention of the Passover lamb and herbs, unleavened bread, and the recitation from the Midrash. Instead of drinking from four cups of wine, only one is used. In addition, women and children, who are normally involved in both the meal and the intermittent dialogue, are absent. Furthermore, the Passover celebration occurs annually while the Lord's Supper occurs weekly. And finally, a different chronology is found in the synoptics and Johannine accounts. These objections to the traditional Lord's Supper-Passover connection have encouraged some scholars to explore other prototypical meals.

If Jesus' Last Supper was not a Passover observance, it could have been a chaburah or male religious fellowship meal.[21] Deriving its name from the Hebrew word *chaber*, which means "friend," this meal would have begun with the blessing of the bread and would have concluded with the blessing of the wine.

For those scholars who contend that the Last Supper was neither a Passover meal nor a *chaber* meal, alternative possibilities include: the weekly Sabbath kiddush meal,[22] an Essene cultic meal,[23] a meal like the one to which the Jewish story of Joseph and Asenath refers,[24] or even an ordinary meal.

Although the above typology evidences more conflict then consensus, on one thing scholars are unanimous: regardless of the type of meal Jesus celebrated with his disciples, it was a meal! Indeed the central feature of the ministry of Jesus, according to Norman Perrin, is the "table-fellowship" which Jesus shared with scribes and disciples, tax collectors and zealots.[25]

The scriptural narratives are replete with thoughts of fellowship and community. The disciples drank of the cup, which was the symbol of the new covenant between them and God. In Acts 2:42, the breaking of the bread is connected to the "apostles' teaching and fellowship." Paul relates the theme of fellowship and community to the body of Christ in I Corinthians 10:16-17.

> The cup of blessing that we bless, is it not a sharing in the blood of Christ? The bread that we break, is it not a sharing in the body of Christ? Because there is one bread, we who are many are one body, for we all partake of the one bread.

Paul unequivocally affirms that fellowship is constituted at the meal. Both eucharistic narratives in chapters ten and eleven of the First Epistle to the Corinthians are cited as theological correctives to the divisions which exist primarily between the rich and poor at the Corinthian table-fellowship. Although Paul's solution to the social conflict is a compromise, he asks the wealthy to have their private meal at home.

More important, the social tensions are placed within a larger eschatological framework.[26] That is, those in the community of faith who have experienced baptism, in which divisions of social and economic status have been replaced by a norm of equality between brothers and sisters of a new humanity, should visibly manifest this new reality at the table. Thus, the common meal experience functioned as an identity formation ritual. In lieu of Jewish dietary restrictions, Paul identified group solidarity in social terms. Those who had not been baptized into the community were excluded from the table of the Lord and those who had been baptized were excluded from the table of demons (I Corinthians 10:21). The one body of Christ and the single loaf ritually symbolize the unity of Christ with the believer and, consequently, the unity of the community in its participation in Christ.[27] Christian identity is, therefore, a corporate identity.

Although the New Testament sources for the Lord's Supper do not clearly identify the type of meal that Jesus celebrated with his disciples, they do agree that the meal was communal and not private. The communal context is salient.

Connection of Ritual and Material Elements

Through the form of a meal, the eucharist expresses not only the communal nature of the new age but also its dependence upon the transcendent God for life.[28] Humanity requires nourishment to sustain its life; likewise, the new humanity requires divine provisions to sustain its life in Christ. In the hands of mortals, ordinary bread and wine provide the necessary food for life. In the hands of Christ, ordinary bread and wine become the necessary food for new life. By identifying his body with the bread and his blood with the cup, Christ blends archetypical symbols for presence and nourishment to convey the new humanity's dependence upon himself for life. In some sense, then, Christians eat and drink in the presence of Christ while, concurrently, they eat and drink of Christ's body and blood. Christ is both host and food at the banquet of the eschatological community.

Although the question of the precise connection between Christ and the eucharistic elements of bread and wine is not directly posed in the New Testament, the tradition has not been discouraged from seeking a precise relationship. Because some kind of connection is assumed in the biblical accounts, the temptation to define that relationship has been irresistible.

The focal point for this continuous debate has been Paul's phrase "This is my body." The controversy between Radbertus and Ratramnus in the ninth century, and Berengar and Lanfranc in the eleventh century, pivoted on the interpretation of this phrase. During the Reformation all parties had to decide whether this identification was literal or symbolic. Currently, the debate centers on whether or not the phrase refers to the elements or to the action of breaking and pouring. Since the idea of eating and drinking Christ's literal flesh and blood would have been abhorrent to a Jew, those who want to maintain the identity are being challenged by those who claim that this connection is a later addition to the tradition.

Regardless as to how one resolves the debate over the meaning of Paul's phrase, one point is undeniable. The tradition has repeatedly affirmed an essential connection between the ritual communal meal and the elements of bread and wine with Christ's eucharistic presence. This linkage is even more pronounced when we realize that, perhaps within the New Testament itself, "the celebration of the Lord's Supper achieved ritual independence from its original context in a community meal."[29] With the gradual separation of the Lord's Supper from its meal context, the detached elements assumed greater and greater prominence.

The disengagement of the eucharist from its original meal context occurred in four stages.[30] Initially, as we have already stated, the earliest eucharist celebrations were complete meals and served to link the pre-Easter table-fellowship of Jesus with the post-Easter table-fellowship of the community of faith with the risen Christ.

However, Paul's reference to the eucharist in First Corinthians already alludes to a shift, or second stage. Instead of the breaking of the bread and the sharing of the cup framing the meal, the entire eucharistic celebration moves to the end of the meal. The Lord's Supper, as Willi Marxsen observes, follows the community meal as a kind of "sacramental appendix or conclusion to the ordinary meal."[31] Although the identity of the eucharist as a complete meal is undercut, the "deep connection between the community's meal-sharing and its supper-sharing remains clear."[32]

In the third stage, which the Gospel of Mark evidences, the shift between the community meal and the Lord's Supper results in a corresponding interpretive shift. As previously mentioned, Mark omits Paul's phrase "after supper" since it becomes superfluous to an independent liturgical rite now separated from the community meal. This shift not only results in a harmonization of Jesus' "words of instruction" but it also tends to attach the presence of the Lord to the material elements. Consequently, the more ecclesial concerns of Paul evolve into more explicit eucharistic concerns for Mark.

> Paul represents a tradition that stresses the community and its new covenant relationship with the Lord. The meal seals and ratifies this

covenant, and in the context of that meal the Lord is experienced
as powerfully present 'eating and drinking along with his people.'
Mark (as interpreted by Marxsen) represents a tradition that stresses
the food itself as the community's point of contact with the crucified
one. The covenant motif has receded a bit into the background, as
seems to be evident when one compares Mark's version of the words
over the cup with that of Paul's. In sum, one tradition emphasizes
community-covenant-covenant-meal; the other emphasizes community-
food-body and blood of Christ.[33]

In the fourth stage, the gradual evolution of the eucharist as an independent
liturgical rite and the gradual identification of the eucharistic elements with
the eucharistic presence of Christ combine to permit the possibility for Christians
to "'make contact' with the Lord even if they are unable to be present at the
assembly's celebration."[34]

This emerging fixation with the eucharistic food, grounded in the New
Testament and clarified in the second century, strengthens the connection between
the eucharistic rite and its material elements with the eucharistic presence of
Christ. Throughout the tradition the reality of Christ's presence at the table
is associated with the eucharistic signs of bread and wine. The precise nature
of that relationship constitutes, however, a continuing controversy. Hence, our
first requisite feature, the connection of ritual and material elements, is clearly
present in the eucharistic source texts.

Past-Future Dialectic

Another debate that emanates from the meal character of the Lord's Supper
is Lietzmann's two types of eucharist theory. Employing a methodology that
was the reverse of the traditional approach to eucharistic source studies, Lietzmann
in his massive work *Messe und Herrenmahl* (1926) began with the liturgical
materials from later centuries and worked backwards through the third and
second centuries to the New Testament era. His conclusions shocked the liturgical
world. Instead of recovering the original, single eucharistic source meal, his
archaeology uncovered two foundational ancient liturgies: one that is attributed
to Serapion in Egypt and another that is attributed to Hippolytus at Rome.
Each of these, in turn, was traced back to two types of meal-celebrations that
existed in early Christianity and are found in the New Testament itself.[35]

The Egyptian liturgy of Serapion, whose themes are evident in the *Didache*,
was identified with the practice of the Jerusalem church as recorded in Acts
and, therefore, called the "Jerusalem type." Continuing the table-fellowship
that Jesus shared with his disciples during his lifetime, the post-Easter Jerusalem

community celebrated the abiding presence of Christ through the "breaking of the bread" (Acts 2:42, 46). Set within the context of apocalyptic gladness, the peculiar character of these meals was the joy of renewed fellowship with the risen Lord. Thus, this version of the Lord's Supper, which is usually associated with the *agape* meal or "love feast," contained neither Words of Institution nor references to the death, cross, or blood of Christ.[36]

The other type, the liturgy of Hippolytus of Rome, whose themes are evident in the gospel accounts, was labeled by Lietzmann the "Pauline type." In this eucharistic celebration, which Lietzmann thought Paul originated on the basis of direct revelation from Christ,[37] the Words of Institution are used and stress is placed on Jesus' death. Reflecting Hellenistic influence, Paul's meal became a memorial of Christ's death ("Do this in remembrance of me.").

In contrast to mainstream scholarship, whose starting point is the *a priori* belief that these different meals can be referred back to Jesus' last meal with his disciples,[38] Lietzmann's dual origin theory has received a hostile reception.[39] Nonetheless, the Lietzmann controversy illustrates the inherent duality present in the biblical descriptions of the eucharist. On the one hand, there exists the communal urge to celebrate the joyful sense of Christ's living presence and the confident expectation of his imminent return. On the other hand, there exists the communal concern to remember the Lord's death and to memorialize his sacrificial death. Both the forward reference to the parousia and the backward reference to the crucifixion are essential to the eucharist and indigenous to the biblical accounts.

Eschatological themes attend the eucharist in three basic groupings. First, as evidenced in I Corinthians 11:26 ("For as often as you eat this bread and drink the cup, you proclaim the Lord's death until he comes") and in Mark 14:25 ("Truly I tell you, I will never again drink of the fruit of the vine until that day when I drink it new in the Kingdom of God"); the early church clearly expected Jesus' coming at the last day.[40] Second, the image of feasting and feeding is often associated with the anticipated day of salvation.[41] Third, the close connection between the Lord's Supper and Sunday, the day of the resurrection and the day of liturgical assembly, reflected the eschatological dimension of the eucharist.[42]

References to the past events of Jesus' life, and particularly his death, are present within the eucharist in all four New Testament accounts and are primarily connected with the term *anamnesis*, which is found only in the Pauline and Lukan Words of Institution. Intense disagreement surrounds the proper translation of this term. Usually the English equivalent is rendered "remembrance" or "memory." However, many scholars are seeking alternative interpretations that will expand its meaning beyond the simple intellectual function of recalling a past event, which remembrance implies. Dom Gregory Dix, author of the immensely influential work *The Shape of the Liturgy*, argues that the cultic commemoration of Jesus occasions both the "re-presentation" of the sacrifice of Christ and its here and now operative redemptive effects.[43] By emphasizing the major scriptural theme of memorial, Max Thurian, author of *The Eucharistic Memorial*, concurs that "the Eucharist is the real 're-presentation' of the unique sacrifice which Christ accomplished once and for all."[44] In contradistinction, Jeremias inverts the referent of remembrance. Instead of celebrating the eucharist in order to remind the disciples of the crucified Lord, the subject of *anamnesis* is God. When God remembers Christ, God acts to cause the kingdom to break in via the parousia.[45] Although no consensus attends the proper translation of *anamnesis*, scholarship universally agrees that the cultic meal contains a backward reference.

Thus, the second requisite feature of the early cultic celebration of the Lord's Supper, the past-future dialectic, points the gathered community backwards to the crucified and risen historical Jesus, and forwards to the coming Christ.[46] Christ's presence in the eucharist functions between the cross and parousia. The presence celebrated in the eucharist is related to both the incarnation of Jesus as the Christ in time and space, which is apprehended as a reality belonging to the past, and the eschatological presence of Christ at the parousia, which is apprehended as a reality belonging to the expected future.

Presence-Absence Dialectic

Our discussions of the connection of ritual and material elements and the past-future dimensions of the eucharistic celebration have both presupposed and prepared us for our final requisite feature, the presence-absence dialectic. Without discounting the embedded past and future references, feasting at the table is clearly understood to occur in the presence of Christ. Like the Emmaus road experience, Christ is known in the breaking of the bread. However, these past and future references also announce the absence of the crucified and risen Lord.

In the face of logical contradiction, the eucharistic texts simultaneously proclaim that Christ is both present among and absent from his people. On the one hand, the New Testament refers to the empty tomb, the ascension, and the parousia as examples of Christ's absence.[47] As the risen Lord, Jesus is "in heaven" or "with the Father" or "at God's right hand." On the other hand, the New Testament testifies to the presence of Christ with his people during the eating and drinking of the Lord's Supper.[48]

Astonishingly, Paul utilizes the symbols of eating and drinking to imply both absence and presence. In I Corinthians 11:26, Paul suspends the eucharistic action between the death of Christ and his anticipated return. These symbols of absence suggest neither the making of an absent one present nor the dining with the risen Lord. Yet, in I Corinthians 10:16, Paul speaks of eating and drinking as establishing *koinonia* with the Lord's body and blood. Fellowship is effected between the community and Christ, and between community members. Thus, eating and drinking signals both absence and presence.[49]

The paradoxical theme of "here but not here" is also evident in the early church's liturgical use of *maranatha*. Originally understood as an imperative, *maranatha* functioned as a liturgical invocation: "Our Lord, come!" Yet, it can also be understood to refer to a present perfect action: "Our Lord has come!" Thus, *maranatha* implies both the congregation's call for the final parousia in the future and for the fulfillment of Christ's promise to be present wherever two or three are gathered in his name.

At the opening of the eucharistic liturgy, this double reference is maintained. It functions as an acknowledgment of the continuing presence of the Lord who has been with the community in the celebration of the Word, and it perceives Christ's eucharistic presence as at least partial anticipation of the parousia.[50] Both present and future references are proclaimed.

Although the theme of Christ's presence pervades Christian worship, an attitude of absence persists. In one sense, the temporal polarities of past and future collapse into an eternal present. In another sense, the distant Christ's absence profoundly alters the mindscape of the community. Yet, the early church refused to entertain a dichotomy between presence and absence. Life in the spirit meant concurrent celebrations of Christ's presence and calls for consummation. Fundamentally, it meant Christ was present to the community at the hearing of the Word and the receiving of the eucharist, while spatially absent. Clearly, the New Testament sources evidence a presence-absence dialectic as indispensable for eucharistic celebrations.

Conclusion

Our historical archaeology of the doctrine of Christ's eucharistic presence has begun with the major New Testament sources. Our survey of the narratives and their attendant controversies has yielded the four constitutive features and has confirmed the *eidetics*. The subsequent five chapters will employ these requisite features as criteria by which we shall examine and evaluate the unfolding interpretation of the mode of Christ's eucharistic presence through the tradition.

Notes

1. Our typology is necessarily painted in broad strokes. Although the study which follows does not always conform to these trends, the typology serves as a guide to the contours of the field of eucharistic study.

2. Our methodology is suggested by Edward Farley and Francis Schuessler Fiorenza. That is, their work shows a direction which we now employ for the eucharist. See Edward Farley, *Ecclesial Reflection* (Philadelphia: Fortress Press, 1982), especially Part Two, and Francis Schuessler Fiorenza, *Foundational Theology: Jesus and the Church* (New York: Crossroad, 1984), especially chapter 5.

3. Appropriating the phenomenological method of Edmund Husserl, a phenomenological analysis proceeds by means of a rigorous discipline to identify the essential structures or invariant features, called "essences," of any state of affairs. The quest for such structures or its "essence" (*eidos*) is called *eidetics*. See Edmund Husserl, *Ideas: General Introduction to Pure Phenomenology I* (New York: Macmillan, 1952), *passim*.

4. On the experiential level, the description of any state of affairs which no longer deals with the abstracted essential features but how such "essences" are actually manifest in historically determinate forms.

5. This point is persuasively argued in David N. Power, *The Eucharistic Mystery* (New York: Crossroad, 1992), 27-32 and William R. Crockett, *Eucharist: Symbol of Transformation* (New York: Pueblo Publishing Co., 1989), 1-8.

6. Dietrich Ritschl, *Memory and Hope* (New York: Macmillan Co., 1967), 13.

7. Donald Gray, "The Real Absence: A Note on the Eucharist" in *Living Bread, Saving Cup*, ed. R. Kevin Seasoltz (Collegeville: The Liturgical Press, 1982), 194.

8. Ibid., 195.

9. Ibid., 196.

10. There are five traditional English names, four of which are derived from the New Testament, by which this event is identified. One of the most common terms is "Holy Communion." Its scriptural usage is found in I Corinthians 10:16: "the cup of blessing that we bless, is it not a *koinonia* in the blood of Christ? The bread that we break, is it not a *koinonia* in the body of Christ?" Although traditional translations (King James Version) render *koinonia* "communion," more recent translations use "participation" (Revised Standard Version and New International Version), "sharing" (New Revised Standard Version and Today's English Version) or "means of sharing" (New English Bible). A second term, "Lord's Supper," represents the usual translation (King James Version, Revised Standard Version, New Revised Standard Version, New English Version) of Paul's phrase *"kyriakon deipnon,"* which describes the church's common meal that in Paul's view is being defiled by the Corinthians: "When you come together, it is not really to eat the Lord's supper" (I Corinthians 11:20). A third term, "the breaking of the bread," is found in Acts 2:42 and Luke 24:35. The corresponding verbal form "to break bread" is employed by Paul when referring to the Lord's Supper in I Corinthians 10:16 and also by Luke in Acts 2:46; 20:7,11; 27:35. The fourth term, "eucharist," is derived from the Greek word *eucharistia* which means "thanksgiving." Although the noun form is not found in the New

Testament, except as a variant reading in I Corinthians 10:16; its verbal form, "to give thanks," may be found in Mark 14:23, Luke 22:17, 19 and I Corinthians 11:24. Within a short time it became the favorite expression which the early church used to designate its communal meal. The fifth term, used almost exclusively by the Roman Catholic Church and not a biblically-based term, is the "Mass." It is derived from the use of the Latin term *missio*, which refers to the dismissal of the non-members and catechumens prior to the celebration of the ritual meal. We shall use the terms "Lord's Supper" and "eucharist" interchangeably.

11. Willi Marxsen, *The Lord's Supper as a Christological Problem*, trans. Lorenz Nieting (Philadelphia: Fortress Press, 1970), 6.

12. Joachim Jeremias argues that the Markan tradition is "linguistically" the most ancient and belongs to the "first decade after the death of Jesus." See Joachim Jeremias, *The Eucharistic Words of Jesus*, trans. Norman Perrin (New York: Scribner, 1966), 6-7 & 189.

13. All scripture passages are taken from the New Revised Standard Version of the Bible unless otherwise noted.

14. On the basis "of the laws of evolution toward symmetry and conciseness of expression which govern liturgical formulations" Edward Kilmartin argues that the Pauline and Lukan accounts are the most ancient traditions. See Edward J. Kilmartin, *The Eucharist in the Primitive Church* (Englewood Cliffs, NJ: Prentice-Hall, 1965), 32-34.

15. Alasdair I. C. Heron, *Table and Tradition* (Philadelphia: Westminster Press, 1983), 5.

16. Jeremias, *Eucharistic Words*, 144; Marxsen, *Lord's Supper*, xi-xii; and Edward Schweizer, *The Lord's Supper According to the New Testament*, trans. James M. Davis (Philadelphia: Fortress Press, 1967), 19.

17. Raymond E. Brown, *The Gospel According to John*, vol. 1 (Garden City: Doubleday and Co., 1977), cxi-cxii.

18. Alexander Schmemann, *Introduction to Liturgical Theology*, trans. Asheleigh E. Moorhowe (London: The Faith Press, 1966), 45.

19. Jeremias, *Eucharistic Words*, 61-62 and Angus J. B. Higgins, *The Lord's Supper in the New Testament* (Chicago: Henry Regnery Co., 1952), 13-23.

20. Hans Lietzmann, *Mass and Lord's Supper: A Study in the History of the Liturgy*, trans. Dorothea H. G. Reeve (Leiden: E. J. Brill, 1979), 172; Tad W. Guzie, *Jesus and the Eucharist* (New York: Paulist Press, 1974), 47; Schweizer, *Lord's Supper*, 29-31; Geoffrey Wainwright, *Eucharist and Eschatology* (New York: Oxford University Press, 1981), 158-159, ft. 51; and Heron, *Table and Tradition*, 9.

21. Dom Gregory Dix, *The Shape of the Liturgy* (New York: Seabury Press, 1982), 50; Lietzmann, *Mass and Lord's Supper*, 185; and Felix L. Cirlot, *The Early Eucharist* (London: Society for Promoting Christian Knowledge, 1939), 44.

22. Yngue Brilioth, *Eucharistic Faith and Practice: Evangelical and Catholic*, trans. A. G. Hebert (London: Society for Promoting Christian Knowledge, 1934), 10.

23. George H. Kehm cites K. G. Kuhn, "The Lord's Supper and the Communal Meal at Qumran" in K. Stendahl, ed., *The Scrolls and the New Testament*.

24. I. Howard Marshall, *Last Supper and Lord's Supper* (Grand Rapids: Eerdmans, 1981), 26-27.

25. Norman Perrin, *Rediscovering the Teaching of Jesus* (New York: Harper and Row, 1976), 107-108. Also see Guenther Bornkamm, *Jesus of Nazareth*, trans. Irene and Fraser McLuskey (New York: Harper and Row, 1960), 80-81.

26. The following argument is taken from Wayne A. Meeks, *The First Urban Christians* (New Haven: Yale University Press, 1983), 159-160.

27. This dual theme is prominent in scholarship. See Wainwright, *Eucharist and Eschatology*, 115-116; Schweizer, *Lord's Supper*, 5-6; Higgins, *Lord's Supper*, 69-70; Robert P. Roth, "Meaning and Practice of the Communion in the New Testament Period," in *Meaning and Practice of the Lord's Supper*, ed. Helmut T. Lehmann (Philadelphia: Muhlenberg Press, 1961), 29-30; Oscar Cullmann, *Early Christian Worship*, trans. A. Stewart Todd and James B. Torrance (London: SCM, 1953), 18, 34; Arthur Voeoebus, "The Eucharist in the Ancient Church," in *Meaning and Practice of the Lord's Supper*, ed. Helmut T. Lehmann (Philadelphia: Muhlenberg Press, 1961), 50; Jeremias, *Eucharistic Words*, 237; Guzie, *Jesus and the Eucharist*, 50; and Brilioth, *Eucharistic Faith*, 27.

28. See Wainwright, *Eucharist and Eschatology*, 58-59 for a more elaborate treatment.

29. Nathan Mitchell, *Cult and Controversy: The Worship of the Eucharist Outside Mass* (New York: Pueblo Publishing Co., 1982), 196.

30. The following argument is based on Mitchell, *Cult and Controversy*, 19-33.

31. Ibid., 22.

32. Ibid., 23.

33. Ibid., 26-27.

34. Ibid., 27.

35. Marxsen, *Lord's Supper*, xiii-xiv.

36. Ibid., xiv-xvi and Lietzmann, *Mass and the Lord's Supper*, 204-207.

37. His argument is based on parallel formulas found in I Corinthians 15:3-5 ("For I handed on to you . . . what I in turn had received") and I Corinthians 11:23 ("For I received from the Lord what I also handed on to you").

38. Oscar Cullmann and F. J. Leenhardt, *Essays on the Lord's Supper*, trans. J. G. Davies (London: Lutterworth Press, 1958), 6-7.

39. Representative scholars opposed to Lietzmann include: Brilioth, *Eucharistic Faith*, 23; Cullmann, *Essays*, 7; George H. Kehm, "The Lord's Supper in the New Testament, 1962" (photocopy): 2; Higgins, *Lord's Supper*, 25-26, 59; Marxsen, *Lord's Supper*, xvi; Schweizer, *Lord's Supper*, 25; Charles Francis Digby Moule,

The Origin of Christology (New York: Cambridge University Press, 1977), 25-26; Heron, *Table and Tradition*, 8; and Dix, *Shape of the Liturgy*, 236-237.

40. See Wainwright, *Eucharist and Eschatology*, 135, ft. 188 for reference texts.

41. Wainwright, *Eucharist and Eschatology*, 26-27 cites MT 8:11 & LK 13:29; LK 6:21a & MT 5:6; MT 25:14-30 & LK 19:12-27; LK 12:35-38.

42. Wainwright, *Eucharist and Eschatology*, 74-75 and A. H. Couratin, "Liturgy" in *Historical Theology*, vol. 2, The Pelican Guide to Modern Theology series (Baltimore: Penguin Books, 1969), 145.

43. Dix, *Shape of the Liturgy*, 161-162.

44. Joseph M. Powers, *Eucharistic Theology* (New York: Herder and Herder, 1967), 119.

45. Jeremias, *Eucharistic Words*, 247-249.

46. This dual temporal feature of the meal is cited by numerous scholars: Cullmann, *Early Worship*, 35; Higgins, *Lord's Supper*, 54; Roth, "Communion in the New Testament Period," 33; Dix, *Shape of Liturgy*, 4; Marshall, *Last Supper*, 113; Kilmartin, *Eucharist in the Primitive Church*, 143; Scott McCormick, *The Lord's Supper: A Biblical Interpretation* (Philadelphia: Westminster Press, 1966), 104; and Jeremias, *Eucharistic Words*, 205.

47. Acts 1:6-11 and Luke 24:50-51.

48. See Luke 24 and I Corinthians 10:16-17. Matthew 28:20b claims that Christ is continually present.

49. This discussion is based on Mitchell, *Cult and Controversy*, 390-391.

50. Wainwright, *Eucharist and Eschatology*, 70; Cullmann, *Essays*, 14-15; and Roth, "Communion in the New Testament Period," 23-24.

CHAPTER TWO

THE CONCEPT OF ECCLESIAL PRESENCE

This chapter begins our historical survey of the mode of Christ's eucharistic presence through the tradition. Because the official sanction of Christianity by Constantine in 312 C.E. constitutes a watershed event for the early church, this chapter will be subdivided into two historic periods: from the post-New Testament to Constantine, and from Constantine to 800 C.E. Our overall thesis is that the concept of ecclesial presence dominates both time periods.

Post-New Testament to Constantine

Although the doctrine of the eucharist in general and the doctrine of the mode of Christ's eucharistic presence in particular were not thematized during this first period, fragmentary evidence indicates that the early church understood the ecclesial community to be the locus for eucharistic celebration and Christ's presence. The importance of the communal context will become clear as we examine representative documents and early church apologists.

The Communal Context

In chapter nine of the *Didache*, an ancient instructional text dating perhaps from the apostolic period, but certainly no later than the beginning of the third century, an image of the church's unity emerges.

> Just as the bread broken was first scattered on the hills, then was gathered and became one, so let your Church be gathered from the ends of the earth into your kingdom.[1]

Solidarity as the one people of God has, even at this embryonic stage, dual referents. On the one hand, the local community affirms its oneness in Christ as the body of Christ when it partakes of the one loaf. "On the other hand, it is conscious that it is but a small fragment of the entire body, and it prays fervently for the visible unity of all Christians."[2] Through the image of bread, the church expressed its present oneness as well as its eschatological hope for unity.

Cyprian, the Bishop of Carthage and author of *Letter 63*, the only ante-Nicene writing that deals exclusively with the eucharist, offered an eloquent testimony to the interrelationship of ecclesial community and eucharist. In this letter Cyprian treats the issue of "aquarianism," the practice of using water alone, instead of wine mixed with water, for the eucharistic celebration. Although Cyprian admonished the church to follow the Master's instruction, he used the occasion to express his conviction for the inherent inseparability of Christ, eucharist, and church.

> Since Christ carried us all and bore our sins, we can see that the water rightly symbolizes the people, and the wine the blood of Christ. When the water is mixed with the wine in the cup, the people are being mingled with Christ, and the throng of believers are brought into union with him in whom they believe. The mingling and union of wine with water in the cup of the Lord is indissoluble, just as the Church, that is, the people who are in the Church and who faithfully and courageously persevere in the faith can never be separated from Christ but will remain bound to him by a love that makes of the two one.[3]

Through the symbolism of the water and the wine, Cyprian eloquently conveyed the ecclesial dimension of the eucharist. It is the eucharist that "makes" the church. Just as the bread and wine are inseparable, so are the symbolic forms and realistic effects of the eucharistic celebration. To receive Christ's body under the forms of the eucharistic elements is to be united in reality to the body of Christ. The body of Christ is both eucharistic and ecclesial. They are different yet inseparable.

In *Letter 59* Cyprian multiplied the imagery already found in the *Didache*:

> When the Savior takes the bread that is made from the coming together of many grains, and calls it his body, he shows the unity of our people, which the bread symbolizes. And when he takes the wine that is pressed from many grapes and grains and forms a single liquid, he shows that our block is composed of many who have been brought into unity.[4]

Clearly the eucharist is for Cyprian "the *sacramentum unitatis*, the sign and manifestation of the reality it contains and continuously effects, so that there is a ceaseless reciprocal action between Christ, the Church, and the eucharist. . . ."[5] Thus, the unity symbolized for Cyprian by the eucharistic ceremony becomes real for the community.

Ignatius, early Bishop of Antioch and a martyr, was equally passionate in his conviction that the sacrament of the eucharist is the sacrament of the unity of the church. In his letter to Philadelphia he urged:

> Be careful then to participate in only the one eucharist, for there is only one flesh of our Lord Jesus Christ and one cup to unite us in his blood. . . .[6]

Irenaeus also witnessed to the solidarity between Christ and the church via the eucharist. In *Adversus Omnes Haereses* he indirectly discussed the eucharist in order to refute the Gnostics. Through a reference to I Corinthians 10:16, Irenaeus reflects Paul's view that *koinonia* is constituted by the partaking of the body and blood of Christ. Furthermore, he cites Ephesians 5:20 to express his belief that we become members of the one ecclesial body of Christ by partaking of the eucharistic body.[7] Thus, to Irenaeus, the community's identity as the people of God and body of Christ was inseparably connected to the eucharist and Christ.

The interrelationship of Christ, eucharist, and church was clearly present in the texts of representative ante-Nicene writers. Although the eucharist had ceased to occur within a meal context (as previously discussed), its independent ritual observance was not divorced from its communal context. As the liturgy of the church evolved, the communal dimension was intentionally retained.

The first full description of the celebration of the eucharist is provided by Justin Martyr in his work, *First Apology*, written in Rome about 150 C.E.

> After we have baptized him who professes our beliefs and associates with us. . . . After finishing the prayers, we greet each other with a kiss. Then bread and a cup of water and wine mixed are brought to the one presiding over the brethren. He takes it, gives praise and glory to the Father of all in the name of the Son and of the Holy Ghost, and gives thanks at length for the gifts that we are worthy to receive from Him. When he has finished the prayers and thanksgiving, the whole crowd standing by cries out in agreement: 'Amen.' 'Amen' is a Hebrew word and means, 'So may it be.' After the presiding official has said thanks and the people have joined in, the deacons, as they are styled by us, distribute as food for all those present, the bread and the wine-and-water mixed, over which the thanks had been offered, and also set some apart for those not present.

> And this food itself is known amongst us as the Eucharist. No one may partake of it unless he is convinced of the truth of our teaching and is cleansed in the bath of Baptism. . . .

> . . . After the end of the [readings, address and] prayers, as has already been remarked above, the bread and wine mixed with water are brought, and the president offers up prayers and thanksgivings, as much as in him lies. The people chime in with an Amen. Then takes place the distribution, to all attending, of the things over which the thanksgiving had been spoken, and the deacons bring a portion to the absent. Besides, those who are well-to-do give whatever they

will. What is gathered is deposited with the one presiding, who therewith helps orphans and widows. . . .[8]

Through this double window, the eucharist following a baptism and the eucharist on Sunday following the celebration of the Word, the early church's stress on corporate worship is clearly visible. In particular, Justin cites communion as the chief expression of the community's oneness.

In Justin's first complete description of the eucharist as well as in other liturgical accounts, one theme persists: because Christ has united us to himself through the eucharistic elements, we are also united to the ecclesial body of Christ and, thus, to one another.

Connection of Ritual and Material Elements

Although the eucharist stood at the center of the early church's life, few writings existed on this celebration. Two reasons surface. First, there were neither controversies nor councils that generated literature and, second, the ante-Nicene church was a secret society that deliberately shielded knowledge of its liturgy from all but its members. However, there exists a surprising amount of writings which address the connection of ritual and material elements with respect to Christ's eucharistic presence.[9] Yet, we dare not forget that the primary ethos of the ante-Nicene church was experiential and not theological. Consequently, no efforts were made to define systematically the way in which "the elements (were) ontologically related to the life-giving body and blood."[10] A preoccupation with that set of questions would not appear until the ninth century.

Because the doctrine of Christ's eucharistic presence was not thematized and the early church's liturgical celebrations were deliberately private, rumors quickly spread concerning the treasonous and immoral practices that attended these assemblies. In correspondence between Pliny and Trajan, for example, accusations extended beyond social and political concerns to doctrinal issues. That is, the realistic manner in which the early Christians spoke of the presence and consumption of the body and blood of Christ elicited charges of cannibalism. Thus, for practical reasons the doctrine of the real presence of Christ in the eucharist surfaced in accusations, although early church theologians did not elaborate a distinct doctrine of real presence.[11]

Without inquiring into the exact manner of Christ's eucharistic presence, the ante-Nicene church presupposed some form of real presence. In response to external accusations of cannibalism and to internal needs for catechesis, there exist ample references to Christ's eucharistic presence. It would, however, be an error to consider the references as evidence for either strict realism or bare symbolism. Instead, it would be more plausible to assume that none of the second or third century orthodox theologians of whom we have record "either declared the presence of the body and blood of Christ in the eucharist to be no more than symbolic (although Clement and Origen came close to doing so) or specified a process of substantial change by which the presence was effected (although Ignatius and Justin came close to doing so)."[12] Operating within these parameters, the early church avoided bare symbolism and strict realism. Thus, the oscillation between these extremes evidenced a mix of positions within the period as well as by most theologians of the period.[13]

The overlapping of the symbolic and realistic interpretations is particularly evident in the following six representative theologians.

Justin Martyr, drawing a parallel between the divine Logos in the incarnation and the eucharist, argued almost exclusively for a realistic interpretation. In his *First Apology* he wrote:

> For not as common bread and common drink do we receive these; but in like manner as Jesus Christ our Saviour, having been made flesh by the Word of God, had both flesh and blood for our salvation, so likewise have we been taught that the food which is blessed by the prayer of His word, and from which our blood and flesh by transmutation are nourished, is the flesh and blood of that Jesus who was made flesh.[14]

In this passage a realistic tone and an explicit suggestion of change are clearly present. Yet, Justin does not indicate whether the eucharistic elements have been changed into the actual body of Christ, or into the sacramental body of Christ. Furthermore, he does not declare whether "the bread and wine, now metabolized in our bodies," serve to join partakers with Christ in a spiritual manner. Because explicit answers are not provided, and since these are later questions and not his, we cannot automatically eliminate any spiritualizing tendency. Rather, we must posit that Justin conveys a strong sense of eucharistic realism, though not exclusively.

Echoing Justin's concern for the authenticity of Christ's human nature in the incarnation and in the eucharist, Ignatius of Antioch, in his letter to the Smyrnaeans, criticized those who would deny the flesh of Christ.

> They abstain from the eucharist and from prayer, because they do not confess that the eucharist is the flesh of our Lord Jesus Christ, the flesh that suffered for our sins, and that the Father in his goodness raised this flesh up again.[15]

Because the reality of Christ's flesh in the incarnation is for Ignatius inseparable from its reality in the eucharist, he tenaciously protects the scandal of the cross. As a result, Ignatius' language sounds emphatically realistic. Yet, in his letter to the Romans he weaved a symbolic interpretation into his identification of the eucharistic elements with the body and blood of Christ.

> I have no pleasure in the food of corruption or in the delights of this life. I desire the 'bread of God,' which is the flesh of Jesus Christ, who was 'of the seed of David,' and for drink I desire his blood, which is incorruptible love.[16]

Although the tone of this passage is realistic, the reference to Christ's love excludes an absolutely literal interpretation. Intentional or not, Ignatius' statements avoid the dual pitfalls of affirming the bodily eating of Christ, and thus the charge of cannibalism, and of succumbing to a mere memorial theory of Christ's remembrance, and thus the charge of subjectivism. Ignatius' realistic language includes symbolic interpretation and, therefore, falls between the extremes of bare symbolism and strict realism.

The predominantly realistic language of Justin Martyr and Ignatius was counterbalanced by the predominantly symbolic language of Clement and Origen, both of Alexandria.

Like the other ante-Nicene theologians, Clement identified the eucharistic elements with Christ's eucharistic presence. In one passage, he employed the analogy of a mother feeding her infant from her own body to make his point.

> The young brood which the Lord Himself brought forth with throes of the flesh, which the Lord Himself swaddled with precious blood. O holy birth, O holy swaddling clothes, the Word is all to the babe, father and mother and tutor and nurse. 'Eat ye My flesh' He says, 'and drink ye My blood.' This suitable food the Lord supplies to us, and offers flesh and pours out blood, and the little children lack nothing that their growth needs.[17]

Yet, Clement made it clear that this identification was not literal.

> The Lord expressed this by means of symbols in the Gospel according to John when he said, 'Eat My flesh and drink My blood,' depicting plainly the drinkable character of faith. . . .[18]

Although Clement professed a symbolic interpretation of Christ's eucharistic presence, he did not deny or exclude "real presence." Rather, we find a tendency to blend the two positions.

> And the blood of the Lord is twofold. For there is the blood of His flesh, by which we are redeemed from corruption; and the spiritual,

that by which we are anointed. And to drink the blood of Jesus, is to become partaker of the Lord's immortality; the Spirit being the energetic principle of the Word, as blood is of flesh.[19]

As with Clement, doubts have surrounded Origen's adherence to the reality of Christ's eucharistic presence. And like Clement, Origen identified the eucharistic elements with Christ's body and blood.

If you go up with him (the Lord) to celebrate the Passover, he gives you the cup of the new covenant; he also gives you the bread of blessing. In short, he gives you the gift of his own body and his own blood.[20]

The interpretation of this identification, Origen acknowledges, is varied. However, his Platonic categories insist upon a split between the material and the spiritual. Thus, in his commentary on John, he stated his spiritual bias.

Let the bread and the cup be understood by simpler people according to the general teaching about the Eucharist. But those who have learned a deeper comprehension ought also to observe what the sacred proclamation teaches concerning the nourishing Word of truth.[21]

This bias is further elaborated in his commentary on Matthew.

In respect of the prayer which is added to [the eating of the bread], it becomes profitable 'according to the proportion of faith' (Ro. 12.6), and is the cause of spiritual discernment in the mind which looks to its spiritual advantage. It is not the material bread that profits the person who eats the bread of the Lord, and does so not unworthily; rather it is the word which is spoken over it.[22]

Origen's preference for the spiritual understanding excludes neither the eucharistic presence of Christ nor the relationship of the material elements to the eucharistic body and blood of Christ.

Both Tertullian and Irenaeus represent a kind of *via media* between the two extreme tendencies of crass realism and bare symbolism.

Reflecting the Platonic tension between the material and the spiritual, Tertullian's consistent use of the term "figure" places him closer to the symbolic side of interpretation. Yet, he sometimes used vivid materialistic language. "Against the Gnostics he stated that 'the flesh feeds upon the body and blood of Christ in order that the souls may fatten on God.'"[23]

Similar to other ante-Nicene theologians, he also presupposed a doctrinal correlation between the incarnation and the eucharist.

The bread which he (Christ) took and gave to his disciples he turned
into his body with the words 'This is my body,' which means 'This
is the figure of my body.' There would have been no figure had the
body not been real, for a phantom is an empty thing and there can
be no figure of it. In addition, if Christ has only pretended to make
the bread his body, because in fact he had no real body, then it is
also bread he must have handed over for us; in other words, he catered
to Marcion's docetism by causing bread to be crucified! But then
we should go a step further and ask why Christ called bread his body
and not rather a melon which Marcion put in place of the heart?
No, Marcion did not understand that bread was an ancient figure
of the body of Christ. . . .[24]

Thus, Tertullian's Platonic sensibilities preclude a crass literalism, but his
correlative doctrines of the incarnation and eucharist preclude a mere symbolic
interpretation of "figure." Since the interpretations of his texts and the language
of his treatises are varied, his theology represents middle ground.

Preoccupied with repelling the fundamental Gnostic error of separating the
spiritual and the material realms, Irenaeus' middle position also reflected the
doctrinal correlation between the incarnation and the eucharist, although it leans
to the realistic side.

If the 'flesh' is not the object of salvation, then neither did the Lord
redeem us by His blood, nor is the cup of the Eucharist the
communication of His blood, nor is the bread which we break the
communication of His body. . . . The cup of created wine, from which
He redeems our blood, He acknowledged as His own blood, and the
created bread, from which He increases our bodies, He affirmed to
be His own body.[25]

Although Irenaeus took for granted eucharistic realism, he left room for
the symbolic.

For as the bread, which is produced from the earth, when it receives
the invocation of God, is no longer common bread, but the Eucharist,
consisting of two realities, earthly and heavenly; so also our bodies,
when they receive the Eucharist, are no longer corruptible, having
the hope of the resurrection to eternity.[26]

Irenaeus' failure to inform us of the nature of the "heavenly" reality suggests
more than a sheer realistic interpretation. Is the body of Christ "physical,

undefined heavenly in a spiritual modality, or a mystical participation in the body of Christ?"[27] Regardless, Irenaeus articulates a middle position.

Our brief survey of the ante-Nicene period has uncovered no systematic explication of how the material elements of the eucharistic rite are "ontologically" related to the body and blood of Christ. Rather, there appears a mix of positions that oscillates between the two extremes of strict realism and bare symbolism.

These varied formulations reflect, for the most part, the church's adoption of the Platonic dialectic relationship between the world of sense-experience and the world "beyond" sense-experience. When applied to the sacraments, two levels are identified: the material level perceived by the senses and the reality level perceived by faith. For the eucharist, bread and wine are "symbols" that signify a deeper "reality," the body and blood of Christ. Because in Platonism the relationship between the visible or material symbols and the "spiritual" or "heavenly" reality is one of dialectical participation, both sides are simultaneously united yet separate. Consequently, the oscillation between realism and symbolism suggests different points of emphasis or different modes of expression within the same philosophical conceptual framework. In short, the ante-Nicene formulations are complimentary, not conflicting, ways of expressing the eucharistic presence of Christ.[28]

Past-Future Dialectic

Although there are only a few extant examples of early eucharistic liturgies, and although there occurred no controversies that would have isolated the past-future dialectic, all the liturgies contain both a backward and a forward reference. This should not surprise us, since the themes of *anamnesis* and parousia were already present in the Last Supper tradition.

The *Apostolic Tradition* of Hippolytus represents the earliest extant example of the technical *anamnesis*. Like the Jewish thanksgiving for bread, which offers praise to God for the food and not a prayer for blessing on the bread, the *anamnesis* concentrates on what God has done and not upon the bread and wine.

> Remembering therefore his death and resurrection, we offer to you the bread and the cup, giving thanks because you have held us worthy to stand before you and minister to you.[29]

Fairly quickly then, the eucharistic prayer became an *anamnesis* for all that God has done on behalf of humankind. That is, the prayer presented a sweeping narrative from creation to Christ's incarnation and resurrection. These prayers even included an *anamnesis* of the second advent!

> Remembering therefore his passion and death, his resurrection and
> his ascension into heaven, and his future second parousia in which
> he is coming to judge the quick and the dead and to reward every
> man according to his works. . . .[30]

Soon, however, the liturgies were altered to reflect the idea of "looking for"
the second coming instead of "remembering" it. Thus, the presupposed themes
of past and future were retained but separated.

The future referent of early Christian eucharistic worship was evident in
at least five different forms.[31] As mentioned in the previous chapter on the
New Testament sources, the *maranatha* prayer had a double reference: it
expressed the desire for Christ's final parousia as well as his immediate coming
to the congregation. This double intentionality is clear, according to Lietzmann,
in a liturgical dialogue between the president and the people found in the *Didache*.

> President: Let grace come and this world pass away.
> People: Hosanna to the Son of David.
> President: If anyone is holy let him come. If any is not, let him
>   repent. Maranatha.
> People: Amen.[32]

At the point of the elevation of the species, the phrase *Benedictus qui venit
in nomine Domini* (Psalm 118:26 and Matthew 21:9), which means "Blessed
is the one who comes in the name of the Lord," found its place in eucharistic
liturgies. Like *maranatha*, it indicates a visit of the Lord to the eucharistic
community that prefigures the final advent.

Although the precise origin of the early summons *Sursum corda*, located
at the opening of the eucharistic prayer, remains unknown, it anticipates both
the cultic epiphany of Christ and the rapture of the church. It may have drawn
its parallel from the apocalyptic words of Christ found in Luke 21:27-28:

> Then they will see the 'Son of man coming in a cloud' with power
> and great glory. Now when these things begin to take place, stand
> up and raise your heads, because your redemption is drawing near.

Testimonies from the second century verify that the early church continued
the New Testament practice of observing the eucharist on Sunday.[33] The
connection between Sunday and the eucharist has strong eschatological
implications. As the day of our Lord's resurrection, Sunday inaugurates the
new age as well as witnesses to the promised general resurrection. With the
advent of the new age, creation is, in principle, renewed. Hence, the first day
of the week was often referred to as the "eighth day," or the day that prefigured

the future age. It is, therefore, appropriate that on Sunday the new humanity should meet the Lord and partake of the feast of the new life. There is also evidence that the early church expected the parousia to take place on Sunday.

The church's preoccupation with the second coming was also expressed in the liturgical mannerisms of early Christians. In patristic literature, worshiping Christians faced East for reasons that had eschatological significance. Since Christ ascended into heaven towards the East and his expected return will occur "in like manner," the proper orientation for prayer was towards the East. From the Syriac *Teaching of the Apostles* we read:

> The apostles therefore appointed: Pray ye towards the east: because, 'as the lightening which lighteth from the east and is seen even to the west, so shall the coming of the Son of Man be'—that by this we might know and understand that He will appear from the east suddenly. . . .[34]

These five references underscore the early church's anticipation of the imminent return of Christ. Although the church gradually acknowledged the delay of the parousia, the sense of expectation was not lost. Furthermore, the delay of the parousia was counterbalanced by persecutions and martyrdoms. Martyrs could not do without the eucharist, and the church interpreted these deaths as the prelude to the approaching end of this age. For example, the vision of James just before his death connected martyrdom and the eucharist.

> 'Good,' said James. 'I am on my way to the banquet (*convivium*) of Agapius and the other blessed martyrs. Last night, brethren, I saw Agapius happy amid all the others who had been in prison along with us at Cirta, sitting at a solemn and joyful banquet (*convivium*). When Marianus and I hurried there in the spirit of love and charity, as if to a love feast, there ran up to meet us a boy, who was clearly one of the twins who had suffered martyrdom with their mother three days ago. He was wearing a garland of roses round his neck and held a green palm-branch in his right hand. "Why do you rush?" he said, "Rejoice and be glad, for tomorrow you also will dine (*cenabitis*) with us."'[35]

In addition, the early church's practice of observing the eucharist at martyrs' tombs (particularly on the anniversary of their death) kept the eschatological dimension of the eucharist ever present in the church's consciousness.

Thus, the early church retained both the backward and the forward references which were already present in the New Testament eucharistic texts. The dialectic tension between the themes of *anamnesis* and parousia remained prominent.

Presence-Absence Dialectic

Living between the decisive past event of Christ's crucifixion and resurrection, and the future anticipation of Christ's second coming, the community of faith gathered for praise and worship. Although the ascension witnessed to Christ's absence from the assembly of believers, the community was not bereft of Christ's divine presence. The early church emphatically believed that "where two or three are gathered in (Christ's) name, (he is) there among them" (Matthew 18:20). Hence, the primary locus for experiencing Christ's divine presence was the assembled communion of believers.

The early Christian community's experience of Christ's presence can be characterized as bipolar. That is,

> the *assembled community* is the necessary presupposition for actualizing the salvific presence and communion with Jesus (through the Eucharist, baptism, gifts, etc.), while at the same time the *presence of Christ* in the community is the necessary presupposition for the efficacious gathering of the community.[36]

Contrary to contemporary assumptions, the primary mode of conceptualizing the presence of Christ to the early community was neither the eucharist nor the proclamation of the Word. Rather, the early church perceived these indispensable features of Christian worship as "epiphenomena," which owed their respective significance to the still more basic concept of communal Christian experience.

Thus, the fundamental conviction of the early church was its irreducible belief that the community itself operated as "the sacrament *par excellence*" and, therefore, functioned as the primary context in which the other constitutive features of worship were located.[37]

The presence of Christ was neither tied to some magical transformation of the elements nor to some ecstatic experience of the believers. Christ's presence was inextricably connected with the ecclesial body.

Yet, the presence of Christ to the community required more than the assemblage of like-minded people. Although the gathering of believers anticipated Christ's presence, it was Christ himself who called the community into existence. Thus, the church's coming together as community was not an expression of the voluntary actions of individual persons. Rather, it was the expression of individual acceptances of Christ's prior call to build this community of new humanity. If human initiative replaced Christ's call to faith, then Christ was displaced as the head of the church and the ecclesiological character of the eucharist was undermined.[38]

This bipolar dimension of Christ's eucharistic presence conveys the distinctive experience of early Christian worship. Although the gathered community of believers, on the horizontal plane, is the necessary presupposition for actualizing Christ's eucharistic presence, the risen Christ's call to community, on the vertical plane, pre-dates the community.[39] Whenever one side of this dialectic is excluded or an epiphenomenon is elevated, we must conclude that a radical perversion of the early Christian worship experience has occurred. In short, the concept of Christ's eucharistic presence is undergirded by the concept of ecclesial presence and is celebrated despite his admitted absence via the ascension.

Conclusion

Our survey of the mode of Christ's eucharistic presence from the post-New Testament to Constantine period has uncovered two significant findings. First, the early church retained the New Testament church's emphasis on the communal character of the eucharist and the three requisite features. Second, and more important, the concept of ecclesial presence permeated every phase of the discussion of Christ's eucharistic presence. Because *koinonia* is constituted by the partaking of the body and blood of Christ, the connection between Christ, eucharist, and church is indissoluble.

Constantine to 800 C.E.

With Constantine's identification of the Christian God as protector of the empire in 312 C.E., and with the period of the great councils, beginning with the Council of Nicaea in 325, the history and liturgy of Christianity were drastically altered. Instead of an imperial attitude of indifference or hostility, collaboration between church and state became the norm. The dangers to the faith shifted from the threats of persecution to the allure of assimilation. Gone was the age of the apostles, and present was the possibility of systematic reflection. The four ecumenical councils of Nicaea, Constantinople, Ephesus, and Chalcedon, in particular, shaped theological expression.

Although Christological controversies dominated formal discussions, the liturgy and the eucharist did not go unaddressed. The expansion of worship was evident in attention given to the "external ceremonial of worship," the "liturgical cycles," the growth of hymnody, and "the extraordinary development of the Sanctoral—the reverencing of the tombs of the saints, relics, etc."[40] The shape of the liturgy was forever altered with the fusion of the synaxis and the eucharist. The proclamation of the Word and the celebration of the Lord's Supper were now inseparable.[41]

Augustine of Hippo

Without question the preeminent Christian thinker of this period and the architect of Western theology was Augustine, Bishop of Hippo. His early devotion to rhetoric, Manichaeism, and Neoplatonism well equipped him to defend the faith against the three great heresies of Manichaeism, Donatism, and Pelagianism.

Although Augustine, like other church theologians, did not construct a systematic theology of the eucharist, he more than any other patristic author shaped the direction of eucharistic theology. Therefore, we must give attention to his formulations before we describe the eucharistic landscape of this period.

Credited with the first serious theological exploration of the concept of sacrament, Augustine's greatest contribution to liturgical theology was the distinction he drew between the outward sign (*signum*) and the inward reality (*res*). "For him a sign is essentially an object that, over and above its own distinctive and characteristic form which it imprints upon the sense, evokes some further reality beyond itself in the mind of the beholder."[42]   Drawing from Neoplatonism as well as Origen and the Alexandrians, Augustine concluded that a sacrament was a sacred sign that evoked a religious reality of which the sign is its image.   He summarized his view in a sermon:

> Brethren, these things are called sacraments because in them the appearance is one thing but the reality is another. What appears to the senses is one thing, a material object, but what is grasped by the mind is a spiritual grace.[43]

A sacrament, the standard translation of the Greek *mysterion*, required the dual sign character of a "visible sign" and a "visible word." As the former, a sacrament resembled in some way what it signified. Augustine wrote:

> If the sacraments had not a kind of likeness to those things of which they are sacraments, they would not be sacraments at all. From this likeness, further, they are generally given the names of the things themselves. So the sacrament of the body of Christ is, in a sense, the body of Christ, and the sacrament of Christ's blood is Christ's blood. . . .[44]

As the latter, a sacrament must be identified as a sign by the word spoken over it, which in turn consecrated and elevated the material element to the rank of a sacrament. In his commentary on the Gospel of John, Augustine penned this classic expression:

> The word comes to the element and it becomes a sacrament, itself a kind of visible word.[45]

Hence, genuine partaking of a sacrament involves the apprehension and participation in the invisible reality that is made present through the purely visible sign. In the eucharist, the visible signs are the bread and wine, and the invisible reality is the body and blood of Christ.

This distinction between the sign and the thing signified has, not surprisingly, given rise to both realistic and symbolic terminology within Augustine's discussion of the eucharistic presence of Christ. Although he clearly adheres to the belief in the real presence of Christ, he is a proponent of neither transubstantiation nor bare symbolism. Rather, his complex and sophisticated treatment of the eucharist demonstrates the importance of the material dimension of the sacrament as well as the insistence on a spiritual interpretation.

In a commentary on Psalm 98, Augustine made these observations:

> He (Jesus) took earth from the earth; because flesh is of the earth, he took flesh from the flesh of Mary. And because he walked here in this flesh, he also gave us this flesh to eat for our salvation. But no one eats this flesh unless he has first adored it. . . . 'It is the spirit that gives life; the flesh profits nothing.' . . . He himself instructs us and says, 'It is the spirit that gives life; the flesh profits nothing: the words I have spoken to you are spirit and life.'[46]

Augustine then has Jesus say:

> Understand what I have said spiritually. You will not eat this body that you see, nor will you drink the blood that will be shed by those who will crucify me. A sacrament is what I have given to you: understood spiritually, it will give you life. Even if it is necessary to celebrate (this sacrament) visibly, it should be understood invisibly.[47]

Augustine's insistence upon the essential connection between the material and the spiritual accounts for the presence of realistic language. Yet, his theology of a sacrament, the distinction between the *signum* and the *res*, militates against a materialistic interpretation. On the contrary, the eucharist for Augustine can be interpreted only "spiritually."

However, a dilemma emerges. If the "sign" of the eucharistic sacrament consists of the material elements of bread and wine, and the "reality" of the eucharistic sacrament consists of the spiritual body and blood of Christ, Augustine must explain the relationship between the historical and eucharistic bodies of Christ. If the eucharistic presence of Christ is merely subjective, then Augustine undermines a real sense of Christ's eucharistic presence. If the eucharistic presence of Christ is purely objective, then he undermines a real distinction between the historical and eucharistic bodies of Christ. In reply, Augustine relied on his dualistic scheme to affirm both the real and true presence of Christ's body and blood in the eucharist, and the distinction between the historical and eucharistic bodies of Christ.

To be succinct, Augustine believed that Christ's body was present in the eucharist as *ad modum Ideae*. That is, Christ's body was present in the eucharist somewhat in the same way that the Platonic Idea was present in the phenomenon.[48] Constituted by material elements, the eucharist was not the historical body of Christ, although it was the sign of that body. Beneath the appearance of the sign, however, lay an unseen reality that was evoked by the consecration. This reality, the eucharistic body of Christ, was identical to the historical body of Christ. Therefore, the distinction between *signum* and *res* collapsed into an identity, while retaining their differences.

Both the identification and distinction of Christ's historical and eucharistic bodies was grounded in Augustine's theology of sacraments. However, the distinction was reinforced by Augustine's view of the ascension.

> [Jesus] suffered persecution at the hands of the Jews; he hung from the cross. He was taken down from the cross and buried; on the third day he rose again and on the appointed day he ascended into heaven. That is where he raised his body and from there he will come to judge the living and the dead. He is there now sitting at the right hand of the Father. How then can bread be his body or how can the contents of the chalice be his blood?[49]

For Augustine, the ascension referred to the disappearance of Christ's historical body. Thus, the ascension marked Christ's bodily absence and, consequently, the distinction between the historical and eucharistic bodies. Yet, in the midst of Christ's absence Augustine confidently and consistently affirmed Christ's eucharistic presence.

> In respect of his majesty, his providence, his ineffable and invisible grace, his own words are fulfilled, 'Lo, I am with you always, even to the end of the world' (Matt. 28.20). But in respect of the flesh he assumed as the Word, in respect of that which he was as the son of the Virgin, of that wherein he was seized by the Jews, nailed to the tree, let down from the cross, enveloped in a shroud, laid in the sepulchre and manifested in his resurrection, 'you will not have him always' (cf. John 12.28). And why? Because in respect of his bodily presence he associated with his disciples for forty days and then, having brought them forth for the purpose of seeing him rather than of

immediately following him, he ascended into heaven, and is no longer here. ... In other words, in respect of his *divine* presence we always have Christ; but in respect of his presence *in the flesh* it was rightly said to his disciples, 'Me you will not have always.' In this respect, the church enjoyed his presence only for a few days; now it possesses him by faith, without seeing him with the eyes. (In Ev. Joh. Tract. L.13)[50]

Augustine's theology of the sacraments in general and of the eucharist in particular constitutes the major contribution to sacramental theology in the first millennium. Through his category of sign he was able to hold in tension the physical and the spiritual, the visible and the invisible. Yet, this precarious correlation had the inherent danger of compromising one or the other component. In one sense both the Medieval and the Reformation formulations of Christ's eucharistic presence are merely footnotes to the inability of sacramental theology to hold this correlation together.

Augustine's sacramental theology also included a strong communal motif. Sacraments were not intended just as a sign of individual sanctification. They were visible bonds that united women and men who sought a common goal. Thus, Augustine viewed sacraments as indispensable to the corporate religious life.

Men cannot be brought to unite in the name of any religion, be it true or false, unless they are brought together by the communion of visible signs or sacraments.[51]

The eucharist for Augustine played a prominent role as both creative and expressive of unity. It was creative because we are turned into the (ecclesial) body of Christ by partaking of the (eucharistic) body of Christ. Augustine conveyed this understanding in a sermon.

If you have received well, you are what you have received; for the Apostle says 'we many are one bread, one body.' ... There is commended to you in that bread in what manner you ought to love unity. For was that bread made from one grain? Were there not many grains of wheat? But before they came together into bread, they were separate: through water they were joined. ... You have been made the bread which is the body of Christ. And in like manner unity is signified.[52]

Because the eucharist also expressed the unity of the body of believers, Augustine considered it "the sacrament of unity." This is clear when he wrote:

If, then, you are the body of Christ and his members, then that which is on the altar is the mystery (sacrament) of yourselves; receive the mystery (sacrament) of yourselves. You hear what you are, and you answer 'Amen,' and confirm the truth by your answer; for you hear the words 'The body of Christ,' and you answer 'Amen.' Live as a member of the body of Christ, that your Amen may be truthful.[53]

As both a creative and an expressive agent of the one church, the eucharist links for Augustine the ecclesial body and the eucharistic body. The two are interdependent and inseparable. The eucharist both presupposes the communal body and sustains it. Yet, that union does not consist of individuals with Christ. Rather, it is constituted by individuals together united in Christ. As host of the table and head of the body, Christ is mystically and eternally identified with eucharist and church. Thus, the reality of Christ's sacramental presence is grounded in the prior identity of eucharistic and ecclesial bodies.

The Communal Context

Although the assimilation of the church into the affairs of the empire had severe consequences for the corporate nature of the church, which will be detailed shortly, Augustine's articulation of high ecclesiology was not by any means a lone voice. Though rival bishops, John Chrysostom, Patriarch of Constantinople and an Antiochene, and Cyril, Patriarch of Alexandria, shared a similar understanding of the fellowship nature of the eucharist.

In an interpretation of I Corinthians 10, John Chrysostom eloquently stated the priority of the ecclesial body over the individual member, and the grounding of all in Christ.

What makes the *koinonia* is not the same as that with which the *koinonia* is made. Even this apparently trifling difference he (Paul) sets aside. By speaking of the 'koinonia of the body' he strives for an even closer description, and so adds, 'Because it is one bread, we many are one body.' (Here he goes over to v. 17.) 'What do I mean with *koinonia*?' he says. 'We are that selfsame body.' For what is the bread? The body of Christ. What do they become who partake of it? The body of Christ: not many bodies but one body. . . . In the same way we are also bound up with one another and with Christ. You are not nourished from one body and the next man from a different body, but all from one and the same body. For this reason he adds, 'We have all partaken of one bread. If of one and the same bread, then we are all become the same thing.[54]

Equally compelling was Cyril's commentary on John 17:21:

> In order, then, that we ourselves also may come together and be
> blended into unity with God and with each other, although through
> the actual difference which exists in each one of us we have a distinct
> individuality of soul and body, the Only-begotten has contrived a means
> which his own due wisdom and the counsel of the Father have sought
> out. For by one body (that is, his own), blessing though the mystery
> of the Communion those who believe on him, he makes us of the
> same body with himself and with each other. . . . For if we all partake
> of the one bread, we are all made one body; for Christ cannot suffer
> severance. Therefore also the church is become Christ's body, and
> we are also individually his members, according to the wisdom of
> Paul. For we, being all of us united to the one Christ through his
> holy body, inasmuch as we have received him who is one and indivisible
> into our own bodies, owe the service of our members to him rather
> than to ourselves.[55]

Throughout the centuries this dual understanding of unity of communicants
in Christ and unity of communicants with one another through Christ is affirmed.

Also commenting on Paul's statement in I Corinthians 10:16-17, John of
Damascus in the eighth century wrote:

> We say *koinonia*, and so it is, for through it we have *koinonia* with Christ
> and partake of His flesh and deity, but through it we also have *koinonia*
> (among ourselves) and are united with one another. Since we receive
> of one bread, we all become one body of Christ and one blood, and
> members one of another. We are united in one body with Christ.[56]

Although it is important to remember the elevated role of the eucharist
and its communal context for the first millennial Christians, the gradual
disengagement of the eucharist from its ecclesial setting had begun. The flowing
affirmations of *koinonia* continued in spite of a steady and constant erosion
already at work.

Within the New Testament itself and certainly by the fourth century, the
inevitable separation of the eucharist from its meal context had begun. With
the official recognition of the church, the process accelerated.

Several factors contributed to this subtle yet significant shift. By the middle
of the second century Justin Martyr referred to taking the eucharist to members
of the community who were absent from the Sunday celebration. In the third
century, Hippolytus mentioned the practice of weekday communion. Though

intended to strengthen the individual's relationship to the ecclesial body, these practices had the reverse effect.

This period also evidenced two different practices that loosened the connection between Lord's Supper and Lord's Day. The first of these was the custom of celebrating the eucharist on days of the week other than Sunday. By the third century this was a common practice on the anniversary of the death of martyrs. Although these services were public and communal, they had the adverse effect of disassociating the eucharistic liturgy from Sunday. Second, the custom of celebrating the eucharist at funerals and weddings, essentially private affairs, had the dual effect of undermining the communal and Sabbath context of eucharistic worship.[57] Thus, by the fourth century the "ancient rhythm of Lord's Supper on the Lord's Day had become somewhat obscured by a multiplication of eucharistic liturgies on other days for other purposes."[58]

Because of the rapid growth of Christian communities in urban centers like Rome, a new phenomenon also appeared—the multiplication of eucharistic celebrations on the same day. Although the practical need for additional services, or even different church celebrations, stemmed from the inability of local congregations to accommodate all their members, the motive behind multiplying Masses was pastoral. In fact, the fourth century church so feared the divisive potential of this practice that it instituted the *fermentum*, i.e., a fragment of consecrated bread from the pope's celebration was placed in the chalice of presbyters' Masses in order to signify the unity of all who shared in the one body of Christ. Innocent I, Bishop of Rome from 401-417, explicitly referred to this practice and intention in a letter to Bishop Decentius of Gubbio.

> On Sunday the presbyters at the *tituli* are not able to join us because
> of the people entrusted to their care, the *fermentum* consecrated by
> us is therefore sent to them by acolytes, so that they (the presbyters)
> will not consider themselves separated from communion with us,
> especially on that day (Sunday).[59]

Thus, the trend toward multiple celebrations was intended to meet the pastoral needs of an expanding Christian urban community and, most important, precautions were taken to ensure the oneness of the ecclesial body. However, the increased number of eucharistic celebrations on Sunday indirectly encouraged the growing "devotional motives" of the multiple Masses. By the seventh and eighth centuries, private Masses for personal motives rivaled communal celebrations.

These modifications in eucharistic practice paled in comparison to the dramatic shift that occurred, during the New Testament era, when the Lord's Supper achieved ritual independence from its original community meal context.[60] As stated earlier, this realignment caused the eucharistic presence of Christ to be more directly associated with the food itself. Thus, the earlier emphasis on "community dining" changed to an emphasis on the ritual elements of bread and wine.

The ramifications of this shift for eucharistic theology[61] are most clearly found in Theodore of Mopsuestia. In his fourth *Baptismal Homily* he wrote:

> They bring up the bread and place it on the holy altar to complete the representation of the passion. So from now on we should consider that Christ has already undergone the passion and is now placed on the altar as if in a tomb. That is why some of the deacons spread cloths on the altar which remind us of winding-sheets, while others after the body is laid on the altar stand on either side and fan the air above the sacred body and prevent anything from settling on it. . . . This shows us the importance of the body on the altar; for it is the custom among the great ones of this world that at their funerals . . . attendants fan the body as it is carried on its bier. The same practice must be observed now that the sacred bread and incorruptible body submits to being laid out on the altar, soon to rise again with an immortal nature.[62]

The eucharistic liturgy is no longer an expression of communal symbols of unity. Instead, the eucharist, through ritual allegory, "reenacts the events of Jesus' passion, death, burial, and resurrection." A *category shift* occurs, whose ramifications are enormous. The communal symbols of eating and drinking are replaced by the ritual drama of passion and death. The tensive richness of symbols is replaced by univocal expressions of allegory. According to Nathan Mitchell:

> The movement from symbol to allegory is thus a movement from ambiguity to clarity, from multiple meaning to single meaning, from revelation to explanation. The ambiguous strategy of symbols provokes action; the reductive strategy of allegory provokes passivity. Whereas symbols require one to search and struggle for meaning, allegories explain meaning.[63]

With Theodore of Mopsuestia's allegorical interpretation, the liturgy of the eucharist undergoes a second radical shift. In the first shift, the eucharistic celebration is separated from the communal meal and a resultant shift of emphasis from meal to sacred food occurs. Now a shift occurs at the level of *root metaphor*. That is, the metaphor of table fellowship, which carries with it the image of the new humanity of God partaking of, and rejoicing in, the presence of Christ, is replaced by the image of table as tomb.

... the holy table becomes an allegorical figure of Jesus' tomb; the bringing of gifts to the altar becomes a funeral procession in which deacons solemnly bear the Lord's body for mystical burial; the action of sacrifice (praise and thanksgiving, eating and drinking) becomes a dramatic rehearsal of historical events from the past (Jesus' death, resurrection). In this process, symbols are perceived as historical allegories (commemorations); actions are regarded as objects; and liturgical verbs become nouns (things to be contemplated).[64]

This shift in liturgical sensibilities is far ranging. The link of table fellowship with experiences of sharing food and drink is replaced by the link of tomb with experiences of burying the dead. The present experience of Christ at fellowship with the community gives way to the remembered past events of Christ's life. Instead of the table drawing people together in participatory acts of breaking bread and sharing cup, the contemplation of the death and burial of Jesus drives them inward and, thus, distances people from one another. The action metaphor of table, which focuses on the present, is replaced by a passive metaphor of tomb, which focuses on the sacred past. This decisive shift in liturgical interpretation, beginning in the fourth century, encouraged important changes in ritual practices.

The most prominent and direct evidence of this metaphorical shift in eucharistic theology was the act of elevating the elements and uttering "language of terror." During the first few centuries of the empire's embrace of Christianity, the following communion invitation was popular.

Come, people, celebrate the holy and undying mystery—the offering. Approach with fear and faith. With clean hands let us grasp the fruit of repentance: for the Lamb of God is offered in sacrifice to the Father on our behalf. Let us adore and glorify him alone, and with the angels let us sing: Alleluia![65]

The language of terror was not totally absent from the early church's eucharistic liturgy. Then, the pronouncement of terror was attached to an unworthy reception of the elements (I Corinthians 11:27-32). With the fourth century, however, the language of terror is attached to the elements. "Cyril of Jerusalem calls the time when the Eucharistic prayer is being said 'that most terrifying hour' and the elements themselves 'the holy and most terrifying sacrifice.'"[66]

The Christological disputes, especially Arianism,[67] also attributed to the development of this eucharistic language of terror. So strongly was the church determined to eradicate Arianism that the heresy elicited an overreaction. Emphasis upon the divinity of Christ became so pronounced that Christ's humanity was virtually forgotten. Christology lost its dialectic balance between divinity and humanity and, therefore, Jesus became "enshrined in the absolute and abstract Trinity"—very God and emperor-like. Removed from the human realm, Jesus was transformed into a "fearsome imperial divinity."

Reflecting this Christological shift, the eucharist was gradually transformed into "something of awe, mystery, and distance." In Chrysostom's words, the eucharist was identified as that "shuddering hour" with the "terrible and awful table."

The heresy of Arianism was defeated, but at a high cost to the eucharist. The table of fellowship was now shrouded in mystery and fenced by the language of terror.

The reception of the elements in fear and dread, instead of thanksgiving and joy, shaped not only the liturgy but also the place of worship. Modifications in the basilica reflected this new model of eucharistic worship: "the reception ritual of the king."[68] The apse became the royal throne and a canopy served to protect the throne. Around the fourth or fifth century, curtains were added to prevent the congregation from viewing the terrifying mystery of the liturgy. Gradually, the veils became screens or *balustrades* which separated the bishop and clergy from the communicants. The theological character of the eucharist as the *mysterium tremendum* found its ultimate architectural expression in the permanent picture wall or *iconostasis*.[69] This solid screen with three sets of doors, the middle one leading to the altar, dominated Eastern Orthodox worship of the Middle Ages and was not unknown in the West.

The development of these screens resulted concurrently from, and gave rise to, other liturgical changes. As a terrifying mystery, the eucharist was best performed by professionally trained clergy out of eye and ear contact from the congregation. Hence, the post-Nicene church witnessed a significant increase in the role of the celebrant in the liturgy of the eucharist. Not only did the spoken roles of the celebrant increase but, correspondingly, the participatory roles of the laity decreased. In the East, for example, the people's offertory disappeared.

Starting in the fourth century, Rome desired the use of Latin as standard in all liturgies. The stress on the "awfulness of the holy" also gave rise to a "great silence reign." "Let all mortal flesh keep silence" even meant that the celebrant had to hush his voice.[70]

The shift away from the vernacular, the silence of the liturgical action, and the intrusion of screens inevitably prevented the people from understanding, let alone hearing, the liturgy. It is small wonder that the exclusion of the laity from the liturgical action resulted not only in two simultaneous services—one conducted outside the screen by the deacon for the people, and the "real" one conducted inside the screen by the celebrant—but also in the rapid decline in the frequency of lay communions.[71]

Unable to be heard or seen, the liturgical mysteries were gradually withdrawn from the ordinary people. The passive receptivity that characterized the laity's role in the synaxis now extended to the core of the worship experience—the eucharist. The fusion of the synaxis and eucharist, like all the other factors, led to the creation of two classes of worshiping Christians: the elevated and educated (in Latin and the proper liturgical rituals) clergy, and the ordinary people.

The one body of believers who shared the one baptism, the one faith, the one bread and the one cup was now irreparably divided by ecclesiological rank. The shift in root metaphors gave impetus and legitimacy to the rise of a special class of Christians. Many liturgical modifications altered the original context and content of early eucharistic worship. However, none was more devastating than the gradual but steady erosion of Augustine's inseparable union between the eucharistic body and the ecclesial body of Christ. During the last half of the first millennium the ecclesial meaning of the body gradually receded.

However, the metaphorical shift from table to tomb effected a change in the ethos of worship even more than in the content of worship. A study of the eucharistic prayers, for example, reveals continuity.[72] Yet, the framework by which the eucharistic liturgy was interpreted was fundamentally altered. The early church's concept of the gathered *ecclesia* as the necessary pre-condition for the eucharistic celebration gradually dissolved. Instead, the cultic worship was viewed as "a mystery performed for the sanctification of those participating."[73] That is, the sacrament of the eucharist was celebrated on behalf of the people by the clergy. No longer the experience of constituting the people of God, the eucharist reflected a radical shift in the Christian consciousness. Borrowing from the mystery cults, the churches presented a system of sanctification whereby the profaneness of the people could be transformed into sacredness. In short, the Roman Empire's reconciliation with the church led to a diminution at best and a total break at worst with the eschatological dimension of salvation history. The first century's anticipation of the restoration of the old order in time was now replaced by the longing for deliverance from this order.

This change is best seen in the fourth century with the rise of monasticism as an instinctive reaction against the worldliness of the church and the loss of the eschatological character of worship.[74] Intended as a movement to retain the ideals of the church, it nevertheless introduced new features which would in time alter the landscape of Christian worship. In particular, monasticism's emphasis on renunciation of the world and withdrawal into private life greatly modified the "ecclesiocentricity" of the early Christian cult. Inevitably, then, this movement led to radically new liturgical practices.

Born out of the church's inability to unite the two fundamental antinomies of "in this world" but "not of this world," monasticism did not understand itself to be a church movement with perfunctory liturgical rites. However, to the extent that it was removed from the common ecclesiastical cult and that it desired to retain the centrality of the eucharistic celebration, new forms of celebration were required.

Obviously, the life of a hermit precluded a communal context for worship. It was natural, therefore, to progress toward self-administration of the eucharistic elements. St. Basil the Great wrote:

> All the hermits who live in the desert, where there is no priest, reserve the communion where they live and communicate themselves.[75]

The early church's practice of receiving the elements at home, when participation with the community became impossible, was now extended to the hermits. Yet, the motive was different. Although the connection with the gathered community was ever present in the early church's private communion, this connection was severed by early monasticism. As a result, the reception of communion was subordinated to individual piety.

With asceticism, the eucharist became an "instrument" of piety. The change was not, then, in the centrality of the eucharist, but in the way it was experienced. Early monasticism's reaction against the worldliness of the church produced a profound upheaval in liturgical practice. Not only was the eschatological character of worship shifted to renunciation, but the ecclesiological framework of worship was also removed.

In conclusion, theory and practice of the post-Nicene church retained the communal character of the eucharist. Through the eucharistic rite, *koinonia* with Christ as well as with communicants was established. Oneness in the body of Christ meant unity of the believers with Christ and with one another.

Yet, the gradual erosion of the eucharist from its original ecclesial context, already begun in the New Testament texts, was accelerated during this period. In particular, the shift in root metaphor from table fellowship to tomb accounted for a series of changes that diminished the ecclesial meaning of the body of Christ. The movement from symbol to allegory, and the exclusion of the laity from the liturgical action, also eroded the communal character of the eucharist. Even the rise of monasticism undermined the ecclesiological framework of the eucharist. The concept of ecclesial presence was still intact but the seeds of its disintegration were now sown.

Connection of Ritual and Material Elements

Ever since Jesus uttered the Words of Institution, the tradition has incorporated the bread and the cup into its liturgical ritual. Yet, the shift in root metaphor from table to tomb resulted in an inordinate fixation on the elements. This is most apparent in the change in meaning of the *epiclesis*.

In the early church the *epiclesis* was an invocation of the Holy Spirit upon the congregation. The *epiclesis* in the Jacobite Liturgy of Mark reads:

> Hear, O Lord, the prayer of Thy people . . . on account of mine own sins and the defilements of my heart do not withhold from Thy people the descent of Thine Holy Spirit.[76]

The invocation of the Holy Spirit to descend upon the worshipers was intended to enable them to realize the presence of the Lord in the service.

In contrast, the advent of the tomb metaphor and the institutionalization of the church occasioned a shift in focus from the worshipers to the elements. Consecration of the elements now assumed a more prominent place in the liturgy of the eucharist.

Beginning with the eucharistic theology of the fourth century, the tradition sought to connect a particular moment in the rite with the consecration of the elements. The two most available candidates were the invocation of the Holy Spirit and the recitation of the Words of Institution.

In several passages in the *Catechetical Lectures* of St. Cyril of Jerusalem, the descent of the Holy Spirit was described as the miraculous moment of change.

> Then having sanctified ourselves by these spiritual hymns (by which he means the eucharistic prayer of thanksgiving, praise and affirmation which he has just outlined), we call upon the merciful God to send forth his Holy Spirit upon the gifts lying before him; that he may make the bread the body of Christ, and the wine the blood of Christ; for whatsoever the Holy Spirit has touched is sanctified and changed.[77]

John Chrysostom similarly associated the moment of consecration with the *epiclesis*:

> When the priest stands before the table holding up his hands to heaven and invoking the Holy Spirit to come and touch the elements, there is a great quiet, a great silence.[78]

In the West, the dramatic moment of change was usually connected to the recitation of Jesus' Words of Institution. Predominantly through the influence of Ambrose, who provides us in *De Mysteriis* and *De Sacramentis* the earliest eucharistic liturgical texts in Latin that we possess, the conversion of the elements was effected by the Words of Institution.

> At the consecration this bread becomes the body of Christ. Let us reason this out. How can something which is bread be the body of

Christ? Well, by what words is the consecration effected, and whose words are they? The words of the Lord Jesus. All that is said before are the words of the priest. . . . But when the moment comes for bringing the most holy sacrament into being, the priest does not use his own words any longer: he uses the words of Christ. Therefore, it is Christ's word that brings this sacrament into being.[79]

John Cyrysostom, who associated the moment of consecration with the *epiclesis*, was not reluctant to ascribe the moment of conversion to the Words of Institution as well.

Christ is present, and He who arranged that table (of the Last Supper) the very same even now arranges this table. For it is not man who brings it about that the gifts which are set forth become the body and blood of Christ, but Christ Himself who was crucified for us. The priest stands fulfilling a role and saying these words, but the power and grace are of God. 'This is my body,' He says. This word transforms the elements that are set forth. (Hom. on the Betrayal of Judas, I, 6 [PG, 49, 380])[80]

In his commentary on the Gospel of Luke, Cyril of Alexandria attributed the transformation of the elements into the body and blood of Christ to the words of Jesus.

For lest we be stunned with horror on seeing flesh and blood set upon the holy tables of the churches, God condescends to our weakness and sends the power of life into the elements and transforms them into the power of His own flesh, that we may have and partake of them as a means of life, and that the body of life may become in us a life-giving seed. And doubt not that this is true, since He clearly says: 'This is my body' and 'This is my blood'; rather, in faith receive the Saviour's word, for He is the Truth and does not lie.[81]

The post-Nicene church's desire to fix a precise moment of consecration is a departure from the early church's conception of the consecration as the result of the whole eucharistic event, both the assembled community of faith and the partaking of the elements. This preoccupation with consecration constitutes a significant departure because it moves in the direction of objectivism. Although this tendency was discouraged by the East's stress on the *epiclesis*, it was encouraged by the West's stress on the Words of Institution.

Although Ambrose and Augustine, along with other Latin theologians, reserved a role for the Holy Spirit,[82] the salient role ascribed to Christ's Words of

Institution led to the belief that the elements became the body and blood of
Christ by some miraculous change. The eventual urge to explain and define
this alteration in some systematic fashion resulted in the doctrines of *ex opere
operato* and transubstantiation.

In no way, however, are these doctrines present in the mid-millennium
theologies. Yet, the emphasis on the divinely prescribed formula spoken by
the celebrant, and the change effected by divine power, gradually became
conceptualized in the doctrine of *ex opere operato*. Had the West, like the East,
balanced the danger of confining Christ's presence to the elements by stressing
the role of the Holy Spirit, the steady progression toward transubstantiation
might have been avoided. Without the neutralizing influence of the *epiclesis*,
the Western church's march to objectivism proceeded unchecked.

The church's growing fascination with the precise moment of consecration
invited the corollary issue of relating the presence of the body and blood of
Christ to the elements of bread and wine. Two possible interpretations emerged.
The first interpretation stressed the abiding reality of the bread and wine, while
the second affirmed a change in the elements themselves.

By the end of the fifth century adherents to the first interpretation were
well established. Reacting against Monophysite conversionism, the moderate
Antiochene, Theodoret, argued for the continued existence of the elements
on the basis of his "two natures" Christology. Since the divinity and humanity
of Christ abided without "confusion," their eucharistic counterparts were
no different.

> Our Savior exchanged the names, and gave to the body the name
> of the symbol, and to the symbol that of the body. . . . He did not
> change the nature of the elements but added grace to their nature.[83]

In a dialogue between an Eutychian heretic and an orthodox divine, Theodoret
had the orthodox refute the theory of the annihilation of the elements.

> For even after the consecration the mystic symbols do not depart
> from their own nature. For they remain in their previous substance
> and figure and form; and they are visible and tangible as they were
> before. But they are regarded as being what they have become, and
> they are believed so to be, and they are worshipped as being those
> things which they are believed to be.[84]

By acknowledging the ascendancy of the two natures Christology and affirming
the sensible appearance of the elements, John Chrysostom, like Theodoret, also
averred the continued existence of the bread and wine after consecration.

As before the bread is consecrated we call it bread, but after the grace of God has consecrated it through the agency of the priest it is no longer called bread but counted worthy of the name of the body of the Lord, although the nature of bread remains in it, and we speak not of two bodies but of one body of the Son, so in this case when the divine nature was united to the body the two natures made one Son, one Person.[85]

The second interpretation, advocating a more pronounced change in the bread and the wine, and moving in the direction that would later be identified as transubstantiation, is represented by Cyril of Jerusalem, Gregory of Nyssa, and Ambrose.

Although ante-Nicene theologians like Justin, Irenaeus, and Hippolytus could write that "the food which has been made eucharist is the Flesh and Blood of that Jesus who was made Flesh";[86] the new idea of "transformation" of the elements was given liturgical expression by Cyril of Jerusalem.

Therefore, look not upon the bread and wine as bare elements, for they happen to be, according to the Lord's assurance, the body and blood of Christ; for even though the senses suggest this to you, let faith make you certain and steadfast.[87]

Gregory of Nyssa offered another early attempt to explain more closely how this change should be understood. Believing that the transformation of the consecrated elements paralleled both the ordinary digestive processes of bread and wine being "transmade" into body and blood, and the process of incarnation, Gregory posited an elaborate theory of the transformation of the elements.

If the existence of the whole body depends on nourishment while this consists of food and drink; if, further, bread serves for food, and water mixed with wine for drink, and if the Logos of God, as has been already proved, is united in his character as God and Logos with human nature, and, having entered our body, produced no different or new constitution for human nature, but rather sustained his body by the usual and fitting means and supported life by food and drink, the food being bread; then, just as in our case, he who sees the bread to some extent perceives the human body therein, because when the bread enters the latter it becomes part of it, so in that case the body which conceals God within it, and which received the bread is to a certain extent identical with the bread ... for what is characteristic of all was also admitted regarding the flesh of Christ, namely, that it was also supported by bread, *but the body was by the residence in it of the Divine Logos transformed to a divine sublimity and dignity.* We accordingly are now also justified in believing that the bread consecrated by the word of God is transformed into the body of the God-Logos. For that body was also virtually bread, but was consecrated by the residence in it of the Logos, who dwelt in the flesh. Accordingly as the bread transformed in that body was invested with divine energy we have the same thing happening here. For in the former case the grace of the Word sanctified the body which owed its existence to, and to a certain extent was, bread, and similarly, in the present instance, the bread, as the apostle says, is made holy by God's Word (Logos) and command; not that it is first changed into the body of the Logos by being eaten, but that it is at once transformed into his body by the Logos (by its consecration) in accordance with the saying of the Logos, 'This is my body.'[88]

Although Gregory's explanation suggests neither an identity between the eucharistic body and the transfigured body of Christ nor a change in the "substance" of the elements, the similarities to the later Western doctrine of transubstantiation are remarkable. This parallel is even more astonishing when we realize not only the difference in philosophical schools of thought but also Gregory's relationship to the "spiritualist" Origen!

In the West, Ambrose presented a persuasive argument in his treatise *On the Mysteries* that God can effect a change in the elements from bread and wine to Christ's body and blood.

Now if the word of Elias was powerful enough to bring down fire from heaven, will not the words of Christ be powerful enough to change the specific nature (species) of the eucharistic elements.

The Lord Jesus himself exclaims: 'This is my body.' Before the blessing of the heavenly words a different kind of thing is named; after consecration it is designated as a body. He himself speaks of His blood. Before consecration it is called something else; after consecration it is named blood. And you say: Amen, that is, it is true.[89]

The existence of these two interpretive groups does not imply that the question of continued existence of the bread and wine or change in the elements was now a theological issue. That statement would be too strong. The objectification of the bread and wine was not formalized until the ninth century. However, the post-Nicene church's inordinate fixation on the elements and on the precise moment of consecration would later blossom into objectivism.

Past-Future Dialectic

The middle centuries of the first millennium, and particularly the fourth century, were a time of pronounced readjustment for this new religion, Christianity. Imperial patronage and state provision for worship quickly converted this semi-secret society into a public association. Although the fourth century was, on the whole, conservative in its liturgical forms, it unconsciously generated radical changes in the ethos of Christian worship. As previously mentioned, this was particularly evident in its understanding of eschatology.

In form, the "golden age of liturgical writing," as Dix characterized the fourth and fifth centuries, conserved the past-future dialectic of the ante-Nicene church. Even the liturgical innovator, Theodore of Mopsuestia, gave sufficient expression to the eucharist's connection with the cross and the future heavenly existence that awaits the Christian.

> In every place and at every time we continue to perform the commemoration of this same sacrifice; for as often as we eat this bread and drink this chalice, we proclaim our Lord's death until he comes. Every time, then, there is performed the liturgy of this awesome sacrifice, which is the clear image of the heavenly realities, we should imagine that we are in heaven.[90]

Like the early liturgies, the *anamnesis* for Theodore included an eschatological dimension.

> *The priest, privately:* We therefore, remembering this saving commandment and all the things that were done for us: the cross, the tomb, the resurrection on the third day, the ascension into heaven, the session at the right hand, the second and glorious coming again; (aloud) offering you your own from your own, in all and through all.[91]

Although the radical metaphorical shift from table to tomb, which was first evident in Theodore's writings, did not diminish the eschatological theme of his liturgies, the same factors that elicited the rise of monasticism account for the gradual fading of the eschatological character of the eucharist.

With imperial sanction, Christianity became, almost overnight, the official public religion. Radical adjustments were required in order to assimilate the Hellenistic worshiper into the predominantly Judaeo-Christian worship experience. This adjustment was nowhere more pronounced than in their respective understandings of time.

For the Greek, history was "cyclical." Influenced by Babylonian astronomy and its periodical repetition of the eight "circles of the heavens," the Hellenistic mind could not assimilate the eschatological orientation of the eucharist.[92]

With the beginning and end of history rooted in time, the Jewish view of history was "linear." God had endowed time with a purpose and direction, and the climax of history, the "Day of the Lord," the *eschaton*, would occur both within and beyond history. Thus, the completion of history would be neither an interruption nor renunciation of time, but its fulfillment.

Christianity, nurtured in Jewish eschatological soil, made one alteration in the scheme. To Christians, the telos of history had already been manifest in the life, death, and resurrection of Jesus. Although the decisive moment in history had already occurred, the consummation of time, the second coming, lay in the future.

In the *anamnesis* the early Christian liturgy placed meta-historical and eternal events, viz., the resurrection, ascension, and judgment, alongside historical events, viz., the life and death of Jesus. Thus, the concept of eschatology operated within time. Historical events in the past and meta-historical events in the future were collapsed into the present worship experience. It was precisely this concept of time, and especially the eschatological character of time, that was unconsciously challenged by Hellenism.

The establishment of Christianity as the state religion necessarily led to a more positive evaluation of the present age. On a daily basis, the church encountered the political, economic, and social routines of life. Instead of training Christians for dying, the church found itself training the citizenry for living. Indeed, a strong emphasis on eschatology could be construed as sedition. This gradual process of secularization spawned the monastic movement. But the institutional church could neither escape nor renounce its new responsibilities. So, the liturgy began to reflect a historical interpretation of life without its eschatological character.

This historicizing of the liturgy did not affect the past referent of worship. On the contrary, the advent of the metaphorical shift by Theodore of Mopsuestia refocused the liturgical action upon the earthly life of Jesus. Consequently, the prominence of the death theme in both Paul and Theodore solidified the backward referent of the *anamnesis*.

Regrettably, this historicizing trend gradually displaced the eschatological theme of the *anamnesis*. The fixation on both the eucharistic elements and the question of consecration was but one instance of the effect this change had on the liturgical ethos. There were others.

One of the first examples of eschatological deemphasis was Constantine's decree making Sunday the official holy day and weekly day of rest. This seemingly harmless and highly appropriate pronouncement produced a double effect. On the one hand, it weakened the understanding and experience of the Lord's

Day as the manifestation of new time within the old and, on the other hand, it returned Sunday into the rhythm of the "old" time. In short, the day of the resurrection was "naturalized."[93]

The rise of monasticism and its hermit lifestyle also influenced the eschatological character of the liturgy. Although monasticism's rapid growth can be attributed to its emphasis on the eschatological, it severely undermined the corporate sense of worship. These dual components merged to produce a "vertical and individualized eschatology."[94] Present in the writings of the pseudo-Areopagite, which date around 500 C.E., the vertical and individual references in the New Testament were exaggerated to the detriment of the eschatological orientation.

Furthermore, the loss of a full eschatological perspective in the West can be traced to its inadequate pneumatology. Although the Eastern church developed a strong doctrine of the Holy Spirit, evident in its stress on the *epiclesis*, the Western church's emphasis on the repetition of the Words of Institution severed the Holy Spirit's connection to the "not yet" dimension of faith.

These remarks illustrate the major adjustments in the past-future dialectic that accompanied the church's imperial sanction. The exaggerated emphasis on the past referent and the gradual elimination of the future referent are present only as hints. The radical changes in the ethos of Christian worship would not be visible in liturgical forms for centuries to come. However, the seeds of those revolutionary revisions were planted in the fourth and fifth centuries.

Presence-Absence Dialectic

The abrupt status change of Christianity did not elicit a corresponding conceptual change in the mode of Christ's eucharistic presence. Mid-millennium theologians were not preoccupied with this question. Heresies concerning Christology and ecclesiology dominated theological discourses. Christ's real presence in the eucharist was unequivocally and universally affirmed. Pope Leo I, who occupied the see of Rome from 440-461 C.E. and called the Chalcedon Council, spoke for the age when he said:

> In what darkness of ignorance and what depth of sloth have they hitherto lain that they have neither learnt from hearing nor understood from reading the truth which in the church of God so resounds in the mouths of all that at the rite of the Communion not even the tongues of infants are silent as to the reality of the body and blood of Christ?[95]

Without a prominent eucharistic controversy to sharpen and clarify positions, the church after Constantine adopted the sacramental framework of Augustine.

Consequently, the diversity in expression resulted from an emphasis on either the difference or the identity between the sign and thing signified.

Those articulations that underscored the difference can generally be classified as "symbolic."

In his book *The Theology of the Church*, Eusebius of Caesarea commented on the sixth chapter of John:

> 'The Spirit is the life-giver; the flesh profiteth nothing; the words that I have spoken unto you are spirit, and are life.' In this way He instructed them to understand spiritually the words which He had spoken concerning His flesh and His blood; for, He says, you must not consider Me to speak of the flesh with which I am clothed, as if you were to eat that, nor suppose that I command you to drink perceptible and corporal blood; but know well that 'the words that I have spoken unto you are spirit, and are life,' so that the words themselves and the discourses themselves are the flesh and the blood, of which he who always partakes, as one fed on heavenly bread, will be a partaker of heavenly life.[96]

Cyril of Jerusalem in his *Catechetical Lectures* referred to the presence of Christ associated with the elements in figurative language.

> According to the Gospel His body bore the figure of bread. . . . In the figure of bread is given to thee the body, and in the figure of wine is given to thee the blood.[97]

In a homily ascribed to St. Maearius of Egypt, the word "antitype" was used:

> In the Church bread and wine are offered, the antitype of His flesh and blood.[98]

Likewise, Ambrose in his book *On the Sacraments* used figurative language in describing the words used by the priest at the consecration of the eucharist.

> You have taken the likeness of the death. . . . You drink also the likeness of the precious blood. . . . The priest says, 'make this oblation to us approved, ratified, reasonable, acceptable, because it is the figure of the body and blood of our Lord Jesus Christ.'[99]

Following the contours of Augustine's sacramental theology, these expressions of Christ's eucharistic presence have emphasized the difference between the sign and the thing signified.

In a period with few eucharistic treatises and even fewer systematic treatments, it is not surprising that many of these same theologians, as well as others, also gave expression to the identity between the consecrated elements and the body and blood of Christ.

Cyril of Jerusalem used realistic language in his *Catechetical Lectures*.

> Regard the bread and the wine then not as bare elements; for they are the body and blood of Christ according to the declaration of the Lord.[100]

In his third letter to Nestorius, which received general assent from the Ecumenical Council of Ephesus in 431 C.E., Cyril of Alexandria expressed a preference for identity.

> Proclaiming the death according to the flesh of the only begotten Son of God, that is, Jesus Christ, and confessing His resurrection from the dead and ascent into heaven, we celebrate the bloodless sacrifice in our churches; and thus we approach the mystic blessings, and are sanctified by partaking of the holy flesh and the precious blood of Christ the Saviour of us all. And we receive it, not as common flesh (God forbid), nor as the flesh of a man sanctified and associated with the Word according to the unity of merit, or as having a divine indwelling, but as really the life-giving and very flesh of the Word Himself.[101]

Western theologians were no less willing to declare an identity between *signum* and *res*.

In his treatise *On the Trinity*, Hilary professed unabashed confidence in an identity.

> Concerning the verity of the flesh and blood there is no room left for doubt. For now it is shown both by the declaration of the Lord Himself and by our faith that in truth it is flesh and in truth it is blood.[102]

Chrysostom also spoke of a complete identity—even to the point of cannibalism.

> In proof of his love he has given us the body pierced with nails, that we might hold it in our hands and eat it; for we often bite those whom we love much.[103]

> In order then that the disciples might not be afraid, he drank first, and thus introduced them undismayed into the Communion of his mysteries; therefore he drank his own blood.[104]

The most significant and influential proponent of an identity, and thus realistic language, was Ambrose. Although the doctrine of transubstantiation was not conceptually expressed, the realism which eventually gave rise to the doctrine was clear. In his treatise *On the Mysteries*, Ambrose defended the belief that the eucharistic bread and wine are the body and blood of Christ.

> After an explanation of Baptism and Confirmation (Ambrose) describes how 'the cleansed people, rich with these adornments, hastens to the altar of Christ,' and so goes on to speak of the Eucharist. The Sacraments of the Church, he says, are more ancient than those of the synagogue and more excellent than the manna with which the Jews were fed in the wilderness. . . . because those who ate of the manna died in the wilderness, while 'whosoever shall eat of his bread,' 'the bread that come down from heaven,' 'shall never die,' 'and it is the body of Christ.' Moreover this food is 'in reality,' while the manna and the water from the rock were 'in a shadow;' and 'light is better than the shadow, the reality than the figure, the body of its Giver than the manna from heaven.'[105]

His treatise *On the Sacraments* also presented a realistic interpretation.

> This bread is bread before the sacramental words; when the consecration has taken place, from being bread it becomes the flesh of Christ.[106]

Even Augustine, champion of the spiritualist tradition, used the language of identity when establishing the essential thin line that distinguishes between a sign and its referent.

> If the Sacraments had not any likeness to those things of which they are Sacraments, they would not be Sacraments at all. And from this likeness for the most part also they receive the names of the things themselves. As then after a certain fashion the Sacrament of the body of Christ is the body of Christ, and the Sacrament of the blood of Christ is the blood of Christ, so the Sacrament of faith is faith.[107]

Between the sixth and eighth centuries there existed a paucity of references to the eucharist and fewer still of great importance. What is present, however, is the steady drift toward the belief in Christ's eucharistic presence being tied to the consecrated elements.

Gregory the Great, pope from 590 till his death in 604, implied in numerous writings a realistic view of Christ's eucharistic presence.

The good Shepherd laid down His life for His sheep, that in our
Sacrament He might give His body and blood, and might satisfy the
sheep whom He had redeemed with the nourishment of His flesh.[108]

His body is taken, His flesh is distributed for the salvation of the
people, His blood is poured . . . into the mouths of the faithful.[109]

A younger contemporary of Gregory, Isidore of Seville, related a more sophisticated
view. Reflecting an Augustinian theology of sacrament, which would later be
appropriated by Rabanus Maurus, Ratramnus, and Paschasius Radbertus, he used
spiritualistic categories to convey realistic concepts. Through a transformation of
the elements, which is caused by the power of the Holy Spirit but does not effect
a metaphysical change, the eucharist exhibited the presence of the body and blood
of Christ.[110]

The transformation of the Sacrament, that the oblation which is offered
to God, being sanctified by the Holy Ghost, may be transformed to the
body and blood of Christ. . . . The sacrifice which is offered by Christians
to God, Christ our Lord first instituted as Master, when He gave to the
Apostles His own body and blood. . . . The bread which we break is the
body of Christ. . . . The wine is His blood. . . . The bread . . . is called
the body of Christ; the wine . . . is referred to the blood of Christ. Though
these things are visible, yet being sanctified by the Holy Ghost, they are
changed into the Sacrament of the divine body. . . .[111]

In the seventh century, Bede the "Venerable" was the first Western theologian
to combine Ambrosian realism and Augustinian symbolism into a single system.
Although his voluminous writings did not contain a systematic treatment of the
eucharist, his embrace of realism overshadowed his Augustianian categories.

We celebrate the rite of the Mass, we offer anew to God for the advance
of our salvation the most holy body and precious blood of our Lamb,
by which we have been redeemed from sin.[112]

Although little is known of the life of John of Damascus, his theological tome,
On the Orthodox Faith, was well known as a standard textbook in the Eastern Church.
His interpretation of the mode of Christ's eucharistic presence is, consequently,
representative of Eastern theology until the fifteenth century.

The body, that is the body which was derived from the holy Virgin,
is truly united to Godhead, not that the body which ascended comes
down from heaven, but that the bread and wine itself is transmade

into the body and blood of God. But if you inquire as to the method,
how this comes to be, it is enough for you to hear that it is by means
of the Holy Ghost, as also from the holy Mother of God by means
of the Holy Ghost the Lord took to Himself flesh to be His own.
And we know no more than that the word of God is true and active
and almighty, while the method is inscrutable. But there is no harm
in saying this, that, as in the processes of nature bread through being
eaten and wine and water through being drunk are changed into the
body and blood of him who eats and drinks them, and do not become
a different body from his former body, so the bread that is offered
and the wine and water are by means of the invocation and descent
of the Holy Ghost supernaturally transmade into the body and the
blood of Christ, and are not two things but one and the same thing.
. . . The bread and the wine are not a figure of the body and blood
of Christ (God forbid) but the body of the Lord itself that is filled
with Godhead, since the Lord Himself said, 'This is My'—not
figure of the body but—'body,' and not figure of the blood
but 'blood.' . . .[113]

Untouched by eucharistic controversies, the Eastern theological expression
of Christ's eucharistic presence did not develop beyond John of Damascus.[114]
With virtual unanimity, Eastern theologians taught that before consecration
the elements were the image of the body and blood of Christ, but that after
consecration, effected by the power of the Holy Spirit, the elements became
the body and blood of Christ, and no longer images. This transformation, though
similar to transubstantiation, was not the same. Yet, it was not until the fifteenth
century, in Gennadius' *Homily on the Sacramental Body of our Lord Jesus Christ*,
that the full influence of transubstantiation became evident.[115]

The abrupt change from alien church to imperial church did not alter the
foundational affirmation of Christ's eucharistic presence. Although diversity
in expression existed, it can be attributed to the Augustinian distinction between
the sign and the thing signified. What is evident, however, is the steady
progression in linking Christ's eucharistic presence with the consecrated elements.
As a result, fewer and fewer eucharistic statements reflected the presence-absence
dialectic. Instead of an acknowledged tension, only Christ's avowed presence
was affirmed.

Conclusion

The establishment of Christianity as the state religion did not alter overnight
the eucharistic theology or practice of the post-Nicene church. To be sure, there

were changes, but the communal context and the requisite features were generally and universally affirmed. Christ's eucharistic presence was identified as ecclesial presence.

Yet, the winds of change were stirring. The impending storm, which would not form until the ninth century, centered on the shift in root metaphor from table to tomb. Although this subtle change would never emerge as the direct subject of debate, its impact was pervasive.

This metaphorical shift, along with the rise of monasticism, the movement from symbol to allegory, and the exclusion of the laity from the liturgical action, started the gradual erosion of both the communal character of the eucharist and the concept of ecclesial presence.

This shift in root metaphor also accounted for the inordinate fixation on the elements and on the precise moment of consecration. By deemphasizing the *epiclesis*, the Western church began its inexorable march toward objectivism.

Although the metaphorical shift did not alter the past-future dialectic, the status change of Christianity affected the eschatological side of the dialectic. Once Christianity became the accepted state religion, a more positive evaluation of the present age and a more negative evaluation of the future age evolved. Consequently, the historicizing of the liturgy undermined the eschatological side of the dialectic while leaving the past side intact.

Because theological energies were directed elsewhere, the abrupt status change of Christianity did not elicit a corresponding conceptual change in the mode of Christ's eucharistic presence. However, the increased association of Christ's eucharistic presence with the consecrated elements muted the "is not present" component of the presence-absence dialectic. The presence of Christ in the eucharist was affirmed while his absence was not.

Notes

1. Willy Rordorf, "The Didache," in *The Eucharist of the Early Christians*, Willy Rordorf *et al*, trans. Matthew J. O'Connell (New York: Pueblo Publishing Co., 1978), 18.

2. Ibid.

3. Raymond Johanny, "Cyprian of Carthage," in *The Eucharist of the Early Christians*, Willy Rordorf *et al*, trans. Matthew J. O'Connell (New York: Pueblo Publishing Co., 1978), 162.

4. Ibid., 172.

5. Ibid., 173.

6. Raymond Johanny, "Ignatius of Antioch," in *The Eucharist of the Early Christians*, Willy Rordorf *et al*, trans. Matthew J. O'Connell (New York: Pueblo Publishing Co., 1978), 52.

7. Werner Elert, *Eucharist And Church Fellowship in the First Four Centuries*, trans. N. E. Nagel (St. Louis: Concordia Publishing House, 1966), 26-27.

8. Joseph A. Jungmann, *The Mass of the Roman Rite: Its Origins and Development*, vol. 1, trans. Francis A. Brunner (New York: Benziger Brothers, 1951), 22-23.

9. Direct references to the material elements are commonplace in the early period. See the *Didache*, chapter X, in Henry Bettenson, *Documents of the Christian Church* (New York: Oxford University Press, 1972) 64-65; Justin Martyr, *I Apologia*, 66, 2, in J. N. D. Kelly, *Early Christian Doctrines* (New York: Harper and Row, 1978), 198; and Irenaeus *Against the Heresies* in Heron, *Table and Tradition*, 63-64.

10. G. W. H. Lampe, "The Eucharist in the Thought of the Early Church," in *Eucharistic Theology Then and Now*, R. E. Clements *et al* (London: SPCK, 1968), 36.

11. Jaroslav Pelikan, *The Christian Tradition: A History of the Development of Doctrine*, vol. 1, *The Emergence of the Catholic Tradition (100-600)* (Chicago: The University of Chicago, 1971), 28.

12. Ibid., 167.

13. Egil Grislis, "The Manner of Christ's Eucharistic Presence in the Early and Medieval Church," *Communio* 6 (October 1980): 5; Kelly, *Early Christian Documents*, 440; and Guzie, *Jesus and the Eucharist*, 124-126. Although the secondary literature, as noted, evidences widespread use of the two categories, realism or materialism, and symbolism; according to Schmemann the Greek fathers saw no opposition between these two categories.

14. Grislis, "The Manner of Christ's Eucharistic Presence in the Early and Medieval Church," 5.

15. Johanny, "Ignatius of Antioch," 56. Note Ignatius' effort to identify the crucified flesh and blood of Christ with the risen Christ.

16. Grislis, "The Manner of Christ's Eucharistic Presence in the Early and Medieval Church," 4.

17. Darwell Stone, *A History of the Doctrine of the Holy Eucharist*, vol. 1 (London: Longmans, Green, and Co., 1909), 37-38.

18. Ibid., 25.

19. Grislis, "The Manner of Christ's Eucharistic Presence in the Early and Medieval Church," 7. Note the "medicine of immortality" theme.

20. Patrick Jacquemont, "Origen" in *The Eucharist of the Early Christians*, Willy Rordorf *et al*, trans. Matthew J. O'Connell (New York: Pueblo Publishing Co., 1978), 184.

21. Heron, *Table and Tradition*, 68.

22. Ibid., 68-69.

23. E. Glenn Hinson, "The Lord's Supper in Early Church History," *Review and Expositor* 66 (Winter 1969): 20-21.

24. Victor Saxer, "Tertullian" in *The Eucharist of the Early Christians*, Willy Rordorf *et al*, trans. Matthew J. O'Connell (New York: Pueblo Publishing Co., 1978), 143.

25. Stone, *A History of the Doctrine*, 35.

26. Grislis, "The Manner of Christ's Eucharistic Presence in the Early and Medieval Church," 6. Again, the theme of "medicine of immortality" is present.

27. Ibid.

28. William R. Crockett, *Eucharist: Symbol of Transformation* (New York: Pueblo Publishing Co., 1989), 79-88.

29. Heron, *Table and Tradition*, 62.

30. Wainwright, *Eucharist and Eschatology*, 62-63.

31. The author is indebted to Wainwright, *Eucharist and Eschatology*, 60-93.

32. Ibid., 68.

33. The evidence includes Pliny's Letter to Trajan, the *Didache*, and the writings of Justin Martyr and Tertullian. See Wainwright, *Eucharist and Eschatology*, 76.

34. Ibid., 79.

35. Ibid., 124-125.

36. David E. Aune, "The Presence of God in the Community: The Eucharist in its Early Christian Cultic Context," *Scottish Journal of Theology* 29, no. 5 (1976): 457-458.

37. Ibid., 454.

38. Heron, *Table and Tradition*, 40; Nicholas Lash, *His Presence in the World* (Dayton: Pflaum Press, 1968), 143; and Elert, *Eucharist and Church Fellowship*, 4-5, 35-36.

39. Elert, *Eucharist and Church Fellowship*, 37.

40. Schmemann, *Introduction to Liturgical Theology*, 73.

41. Dix, *Shape of the Liturgy*, 36-37.

42. David Bourke, "Introduction" in Saint Thomas Aquinas, "The Sacraments," in *Summa Theologiae*, vol. 56, trans. David Bourke (New York: Blackfriars; McGraw-Hill Book Co., 1975), xv.

43. Andre Hamman, comp., *The Mass' Ancient Liturgies and Patristic Texts*, trans. Thomas Halton (Staten Island: Alba House, 1967), 207.

44. Heron, *Table and Tradition*, 70.

45. Ibid., 71.

46. Mitchell, *Cult and Controversy*, 44.

47. Ibid., 45.

48. John F. Fahey, *The Eucharistic Teaching of Ratram of Corbie* (Mundeleim, IL: St. Mary of the Lake Seminary, 1951), 155.

49. Hamman, *The Mass*, 207.

50. Heron, *Table and Tradition*, 72.

51. Stanislaus J. Grabowski, *The Church: An Introduction to the Theology of St. Augustine* (St. Louis: B. Herder, 1957), 177.

52. Dugmore, *The Mass and the English Reformers*, 7-8.

53. Brilioth, *Eucharistic Faith*, 33.

54. Elert, *Eucharist And Church Fellowship*, 27-28.

55. Wainwright, *Eucharist and Eschatology*, 114.

56. Elert, *Eucharist And Church Fellowship*, 33.

57. Couratin, "Liturgy," 216.

58. Mitchell, *Cult and Controversy*, 34.

59. Ibid., 35.

60. Ibid., 39.

61. The following section is indebted to Mitchell, *Cult and Controversy*, 46-62.

62. Ibid., 50.

63. Ibid., 54.

64. Ibid., 197.

65. Ibid., 47.

66. Couratin, "Liturgy," 175.

67. These insights are indebted to William J. Bausch, *A New Look at the Sacraments* (Mystic: Twenty-Third Publications, 1984), 142-143; Geoffrey Wainwright, *Doxology: The Praise of God in Worship, Doctrine, and Life* (New York: Oxford University Press, 1980), 327; and William H. Willimon, *Word, Water, Wine and Bread* (Valley Forge: Judson Press, 1980), 44.

68. Voeoebus, "The Eucharist in the Ancient Church," 70-71 and Stone, *A History of the Doctrine*, 71. The motive of rulership over fellowship for understanding the eucharist can be dated from the fourth century in the East but it is later in the West (Elert, *Eucharist And Church Fellowship*, viii).

69. Voeoebus, "The Eucharist in the Ancient Church," 70-71.

70. Brilioth, *Eucharistic Faith*, 65.

71. Dix, *Shape of the Liturgy*, 319 and Couratin, "Liturgy," 172.

72. Schmemann, *Introduction to Liturgical Theology*, 98-99.

73. Ibid.

74. This section on monasticism is greatly influenced by Schmemann, *Introduction to Liturgical Theology*, 102-110.

75. Ibid., 109.

76. Voeoebus, "The Eucharist in the Ancient Church," 64.

77. Heron, *Table and Tradition*, 66.

78. Paul F. Palmer, *Sacraments and Worship* (New York: Longmans, Green and Co., 1957), 205.

79. Mitchell, *Cult and Controversy*, 55-56.

80. Palmer, *Sacraments and Worship*, 205.

81. Ibid., 207.

82. Ambrose *De Sacramentis* V, 3, 17 and Augustine *De trin.* III, 4, 10, PL 42, 874 in Wainwright, *Eucharist and Eschatology*, 101.

83. Lampe, "The Eucharist in the Thought of the Early Church," 53.

84. Stone, *A History of the Doctrine*, 99.

85. Ibid., 101.

86. Dix, *Shape of the Liturgy*, 198.

87. Palmer, *Sacraments and Worship*, 202.

88. Adolf von Harnack, *History of Dogma*, vol. 4, trans. Neil Buchanan (New York: Russell and Russell, 1958), 295.

89. Palmer, *Sacraments and Worship*, 206.

90. Guzie, *Jesus and the Eucharist*, 124.

91. Max Thurian and Geoffrey Wainwright, eds., *Baptism and Eucharist: Ecumenical Convergence in Celebration* (Geneva: World Council of Churches, 1983), 118.

92. The following section is influenced by Dix, *Shape of the Liturgy*, 257-265.

93. Schmemann, *Introduction to Liturgical Theology*, 140.

94. Wainwright, *Eucharist and Eschatology*, 125.

95. Stone, *History of the Doctrine*, 61.

96. Ibid., 89.

97. Ibid., 64.

98. Ibid.

99. Ibid.

100. Ibid., 71.

101. Ibid., 75-76.

102. Ibid., 78.

103. Harnack, *History of Dogma*, vol. 4, 297.

104. Ibid.

105. Stone, *History of the Doctrine*, 79.

106. Ibid., 81.

107. Ibid., 84.

108. Ibid., 194.

109. Ibid.

110. McDonnell, *John Calvin*, 46-47.

111. Stone, *History of the Doctrine*, 197.

112. Ibid., 199.

113. Ibid., 146.

114. William D. Maxwell, *An Outline of Christian Worship* (London: Oxford University Press, 1936), 34; Dix, *Shape of the Liturgy*, 548; and Stone, *History of the Doctrine*, 156.

115. Stone, 156-173 & 192-193.

CHAPTER THREE

THE CONCEPT OF SUBSTANTIAL PRESENCE

This chapter, detailing the formulations of Christ's eucharistic presence from the Carolingian Age to the dawn of the Reformation, begins with the coronation of Charlemagne as the first "Holy Roman Emperor" by Pope Leo III on Christmas Day in the year 800. By itself this event is neither responsible nor decisive for the dramatic shift in emphasis from a concept of ecclesial presence to a concept of substantial presence. The gradual erosion of the corporate nature of the eucharist and the increasing preoccupation with the eucharistic elements had already begun in the middle of the first millennium; these interpretive trends would continue.

Initiated by Charlemagne and directed by Alcuin, Abbot of Tours and chief adviser to the emperor, the "Carolingian Renaissance" provided a relatively stable religious milieu and, therefore, the possibility for focused attention on the eucharist. The emphasis on conformity is best reflected in Alcuin's monumental accomplishment, the development of a standard worship manual. Based on a copy of the *Gregorian sacramentary* secured from Pope Hadrian I, Alcuin's *Missale Romanum* unified the eucharistic and other rites by remodeling and supplementing the old Roman source. The completion of this standard missal constitutes the decisive moment for the synthesis of the Western liturgy and identifies the origin of the missals that would serve the whole West till the Reformation, and half of all Christendom to this day.

Without question, the heart and soul of the Western missal and medieval Christianity was the eucharist.[1] According to Jaroslav Pelikan:

> Except for certain heretics, there was general agreement that the proper celebration of the Eucharist and the proper understanding of it lay at the center of the Christian faith. Among all the actions of the church, the Mass was 'the supreme sacrament.'[2]

Beginning with the controversy of the ninth century and continuing through the fifteenth century, the eucharist would be interpreted almost exclusively from the viewpoint of real presence and the manner of its accomplishment. Although other explanations of Christ's eucharistic presence were permitted, this period witnessed the triumph of the doctrine of transubstantiation and the concept of substantial presence.

The affirmation of transubstantiation had a critical impact on our three requisite features of eucharistic presence as well as on the communal context. Because these three features were virtually eliminated during this period, we shall begin with an examination of their fate. The bulk of this chapter will detail, however, the triumph of the doctrine of transubstantiation and the emergence of the concept of substantial presence. Finally, we shall describe the devastating effects of this shift on the sense of corporate worship.

The Three Requisite Features

As in New Testament times, the sacred food of the eucharist "had achieved ritual independence from (the) community meal, so in the early Medieval period the eucharistic food began to gain cultic independence from the eucharistic liturgy."[3] Stimulated by theological controversies, the tendency to isolate and focus upon the elements, exclusive of the eucharistic action as a whole, resulted in the concentration of medieval eucharistic theology on real presence and medieval worship on adoration of the host. The connection of ritual and material elements was severed.

This preoccupation with the eucharistic elements was attested by texts for blessing sacred vessels and other church furnishings. These prayers for paten, chalice, and chrism focused more and more attention on the consecration of the bread and wine into the body and blood of Christ, and on the localized presence of Christ at the altar. Therefore, the vessel of reservation was often referred to as "a new sepulchre for the body of Christ." Furthermore, the liturgy for the consecration of churches included a provision for the sealing of a consecrated host within the crypt or saint's tomb over which the high altar was built.

These liturgical customs reflect a profound shift in the consciousness of the worshiping Christian. The metaphorical exchange of table for tomb was complete. Instead of being a table from which the Christian community was fed, the altar became a "sepulchre in which the relics of Christ and his saints (were) carefully enshrined."[4] Not surprisingly, the medieval period witnessed a gradual decline in lay reception of communion and a corresponding increase in clerical control of communion.

As attention shifted from the eucharistic action to the eucharistic elements, the danger of objectivism increased. Instead of participating in the liturgy, the people merely received the elements. Thus, the "legitimate ritual gestures" became overlaid with superstitious and magical intentions. Consequently, reverence for the sacred food gave rise to the notion of the eucharistic elements as cultic objects in themselves, independent of the eucharistic action. This objectification produced a literature of legendary material and miracle stories that tended to supplement and support orthodox eucharistic dogma.

The medieval preoccupation with the eucharistic elements had a disastrous effect on the dialectics of presence-absence and past-future. Ever since the Apostle Paul, the notion of Christ's simultaneous presence and absence in the eucharist had been central to the tradition. Although the risen Lord had ascended, he was, nonetheless, present to his people in the midst of his physical absence. The medieval domination of the issue of real presence precluded, however, any theological expression of Christ's absence. As a result, the tension between presence and absence was reduced. With few exceptions, medieval eucharistic theology failed to express a theological justification for the absence of Christ.

Medieval theology's silence about Christ's absence had a residual impact on the past-future dialectic. As long as there was an emphasis on Christ's absence, there could be a corresponding emphasis on the "yet to come" or eschatological dimension of the eucharist. But the parousia was rendered superfluous if Christ was really present in the eucharistic consecration. Consequently, medieval Western liturgy seldom referred to the second coming of Christ. Wherever the eschatological perspective was mentioned, it was "only in a rather fossilized way and call(ed) forth no developed exposition."[5]

In the eucharistic prayers the *anamnesis* no longer included the futuristic parousia but concentrated exclusively on Christ's passion. Thus, the eucharist proclaimed the Lord's death to the exclusion of "till he comes."

It was necessary to begin our study of this period with the three requisite features because the medieval preoccupation with the eucharistic elements undermined these polarities. By virtually eliminating the absence dimension from the presence-absence dialectic and the future dimension from the past-future dialectic, medieval eucharistic theology collapsed the dialectics and appropriated their remaining attributes in service of a substantial concept of Christ's eucharistic presence.

The Triumph of Transubstantiation and Substantial Presence

Our examination of the Middle Ages will concentrate on the theological controversies that contributed to the isolation of the eucharistic elements from the liturgy, and to the triumph of transubstantiation. As a result, the ecclesial concept of Christ's eucharistic presence faded from sacramental theology and was replaced by the substantial concept of Christ's eucharistic presence.

In direct contrast to the early centuries, the period from the ninth to the fifteenth century was replete with eucharistic controversies. The major loci of the faith were defined. Theological attention was now directed to the eucharist in general, and to the mode of Christ's eucharistic presence in particular.

Although a cursory reading of the Middle Ages may suggest a progressive march toward the doctrine of transubstantiation, there were, at minimum, three acceptable and operative theories of Christ's eucharistic presence. As late as the thirteenth century Peter of Capua posited three positions, none of which was considered an article of faith.

The first "opinion," as he called it, when the substance of the bread and wine remained together with the body and blood of Christ, was "consubstantiation."

Some say that there is not any mutation here; rather, while the substance of bread and the substance of wine remain, when the words of consecration are spoken, the flesh and blood of Christ begin to be present beneath the same appearances, though at first only the substance of bread and wine are present. And wherever one reads something about change, it is understood as follows: where first there was only bread and wine, there also begins to be the flesh and blood of Christ.[6]

The second position, where the original substance of bread and wine were annihilated and replaced by the body and blood of Christ, was labeled "annihilation" or "succession" theory. Peter of Capua described it:

Others say that the substance of bread and wine are totally annihilated and while the appearances remain the same, there begins to be present only the flesh and blood of Christ; and it is in this fashion that they explain this change.[7]

Transubstantiation, the most prominent theory and Peter's preference, explained the conversion by positing that the substance of bread and wine were changed into Christ's body and blood while the accidents of bread and wine remained.

We say (and this is what the commentators assert) that the very substance of the bread is changed into the true flesh of Christ, which the Virgin bore, and the substance of wine into the true blood; and that while the original appearances remain, the flesh and blood of Christ begin to be present.[8]

Throughout the Middle Ages these three theories of Christ's real presence in the eucharist received support. However, the bitter disputes which began in the ninth century resulted in the church eventually selecting at the Fourth Lateran Council of 1215 transubstantiation as the official explanation of the conversion of the eucharistic elements into Christ's eucharistic body and blood. Although Thomas' refined and celebrated version was soon to follow, advocates of all three positions could still be found through the fifteenth century.

We now turn to a historical and theological account of the eucharistic controversies, and to the triumph of transubstantiation and the concept of substantial presence.

Radbertus and Ratramnus

The watershed event in eucharistic theology occurred in the year 831 with the publication of Paschasius Radbertus' treatise, *De Corpore et Sanguine Domini*

(*On the Body and Blood of the Lord*). Written for his monks at the Benedictine monastery of Corbie, the abbot's book represents the first systematic treatment of the doctrine of the eucharist independent of its liturgical context and the first document that directly focuses on the elements of bread and wine.

The metaphorical shift from table to tomb was complete. Uprooted from its original meal context, the starting point for eucharistic theology shifted from the ritual action to the sacred objects on the altar. Blending Augustinian sacramentalism with Ambrosian realism, Radbertus was hailed by the tradition as the *theologus eucharisticus*[9] and "the Origen of the Catholic doctrine of the Lord's Supper."[10]

Reflecting the Carolingian theological milieu, Radbertus was concerned with four questions:

> 1) What is the relation between the eucharistic body of Christ and the historical body of Jesus who lived, died, rose and ascended to the Father?
> 2) How can one explain the 'real presence' of Christ in the eucharist—especially since the sacrament is often celebrated in many different places at the same time?
> 3) What is the difference in the bread and wine before and after the consecration?
> 4) What is the relation between the sacramental signs (bread, wine) and the realities which those signs signify (Christ's true body and blood)?[11]

Influenced by Ambrosian legacy, Radbertus insisted upon the "utter realism of Christ's presence" and, therefore, employed emphatic language.

> Let not any one then be disturbed concerning this body and blood of Christ, that in the mystery there is real flesh and real blood, so long as He who created has so willed; ... and, because He has willed, though the figure of bread and wine remain, yet these are altogether a figure, and after consecration we must believe that there is nothing else than the flesh and blood of Christ. ... And that I may speak more wonderfully, this certainly is no other flesh than that which was born of Mary and suffered on the cross and rose from the tomb.[12]

Following Ambrose, Radbertus confirmed the identity between Christ's eucharistic body and Christ's historical body.

This strict equation often compelled a carnal interpretation. Citing hagiographical legends of "bleeding hosts," he wrote:

No one who reads the lives and deeds of saints can remain unaware
that often these mystical sacraments of the body and blood have been
revealed under the visible form of a lamb or the actual color of flesh
and blood. . . . when the gifts are broken or the host is offered, a
lamb appears in the hands (of the priest) and blood flows in the
chalice as at a sacrifice.[13]

The citation of miracle stories that bordered on "cannibalism" not only
underscored Radbertus' commitment to eucharistic realism, but it also revealed
his failure to take seriously the function of sacramental signs.[14] Although
he acknowledged the distinction between the image (*figura*) and truth (*veritas*)
in the sacrament, he seemed uncomfortable and unwilling to concede theological
validity to the language of signs.

He (Christ) left us this sacrament—visible figure and image of his
flesh and blood—so that our mind and our flesh could be more richly
nourished through them, and so that we could grasp things invisible
and spiritual through faith. What is externally perceived in this
sacrament is an image or sign; but what is received internally is truth,
and no mere shadow. . . .[15]

Radbertus' lengthy treatment of the relationship between sign (*figura*: bread
and wine) and things signified (*veritas*: the body and blood of Christ) is significant
for at least two reasons. First, it represents one of the earliest attempts to work
out this exact relation. Like Augustine, he viewed the connection between image
and truth as a real one which was, however, perceptible only to those of faith.
Anticipating the conclusions of the scholastic period, he believed that the external
signs act as a trigger which transports the believer into the invisible and spiritual
realm of sacramental truth.

Second, Radbertus' discussion nullifies the "butcher-shop" language of the
miracle stories. Although a revised edition of his treatise, that appeared in 844,
contained a new and blatantly crude story,[16] his more sophisticated theological
sections preserved Augustine's teaching on the spiritual character of Christ's
presence in the eucharist.

These mysteries are not carnal, though they are flesh and blood, but
are rightly understood as spiritual. . . . It is foolish . . . to speculate
about . . . the mixture of this food with other food in the process
of digestion. When spiritual food and drink are taken, and through
them the Holy Ghost works in man, so that anything still carnal in
us is made spiritual and man becomes spiritual, where can such

mixture come at all? . . . Wrong is the thought of those who have carnal ideas about this mystery.[17]

Because Radbertus resolutely avoided any literalistic language of "tearing" the flesh or "crushing" the bones, his penchant for realistic language and crude illustrations does not condemn him as an "ultra-realist." His treatises contain elements of realism as well as refined sacramental observations.

In response to his own questions, we can unequivocally state that Radbertus affirmed an identity between the eucharistic and historical bodies of Christ. Equally clear, the real presence of Christ in the eucharist was assured by God's omnipotent power which was invoked by the recital of the Words of Institution. Via the consecration, God created or multiplied the natural body of Christ. Utilizing the language of a later era, Radbertus inferred that the bread and wine were "annihilated" although their appearances remained. This "notion that at every Eucharist there is a new creation of the body of Christ"[18] represents Radbertus' most notable contribution to the tradition.

Extrapolating from real presence, Radbertus insisted on a difference in the bread and wine before and after consecration. Before the recitation of the Words of Institution, the elements were plain bread and wine. After consecration, the appearances of bread and wine remained, since "God knows that human nature cannot bear to eat raw flesh." Yet, the elements became masks that veiled the sacramental truth of Christ's flesh and blood on the altar.

Radbertus also acknowledged a distinction between the sign and the thing signified in the sacrament. Although the sign was not always taken seriously, its role was indispensable if the believer was to grasp the spiritual truth signified by the sign.

Regardless of how bold Radbertus' realism may appear, it was not conceived in metaphysical terms and was not the doctrine of transubstantiation. Yet, his occasional crass realism led to highly materialistic interpretations.

Although the tradition may debate the status of Paschasius Radbertus as either the innovator who broke from the Augustinian heritage[19] or the reconciler of two eucharistic traditions (real and figurative),[20] it, nevertheless, incorporated his insights. Consequently, the shift from ritual action to sacred objects was complete. The starting point for eucharistic theology for the duration of the Middle Ages would be the real presence of Christ as located in the eucharistic elements, and the central eucharistic questions would be how Christ is present in the eucharist and what the relationship is between the outward signs of bread and wine, and the inward reality of the body and blood of Christ.

Paschasius Radbertus' noble effort to combine Ambrosian realism and Augustinian sacramentalism, destined to triumph over alternative theological positions, was not exempt from opposition. Many of his contemporaries were disturbed by a realism that too often verged on crass materialism. One of those who found Radbertus' treatise excessively realistic was Emperor Charles the Bald.

In an effort to locate a less offensive assertion of Christ's real presence in the eucharist, the emperor commissioned Ratramnus, also a monk of Corbie, to write a treatise on the same subject. The crown's request was divided by Ratramnus into two separate questions. The first question concerned "whether there is present in the consecrated elements something which faith alone can recognise, something secret and veiled in mystery."[21] The second question concerned "whether that something is the very body of Christ which was born of Mary, suffered, died, was buried, rose, ascended into heaven and sits at the right hand of the Father."[22]

As these two queries illustrate, the center of the impending debate was not real presence. Both theologians—Paschasius Radbertus, the teacher, and Ratramnus, the student—affirmed Christ's eucharistic presence. Radbertus' second question elicited agreement from all parties. Responses to Radbertus' first and third questions (Ratramnus' second and first questions respectively) elicited, however, strong disagreement.

In reply to his first question concerning the perceptible difference between the bread and wine before and after consecration, Ratramnus wholeheartedly endorsed a change that was hidden except to the eyes of faith.

> That bread which through the ministry of the priest is made the body of Christ appears one thing externally to the human senses, but proclaims itself another to the minds of the faithful. Externally, the form of the bread which it previously was is presented, its colour is seen, its flavour tasted. But internally something far and away more precious, more excellent, is intimated.[23]

Although undetected by sensory perception, the bread and wine were made into the body and blood of Christ.

> Let it not be thought that in the mystery of the Sacrament the body and blood of the Lord Himself are not taken by the faithful, for faith receives what it believes, not what the eye sees.[24]

Yet, the spiritual presence of Christ was not to be equated with a subjective or figurative presence. On the contrary, Ratramnus affirmed a sacramental and real presence under the veil of bread and wine.

> If there is nothing changed then there is nothing here other than what was here before. But there is something else, because the bread has become the Body and the wine the Blood of Christ.[25]

The reality of the mystery was confirmed. The degree of its perceptibility was dependent, however, upon faith.

Although Ratramnus agreed that the elements were changed into the body and blood of Christ, he refused to identify Christ's eucharistic body as Christ's historical body. Consequently, Ratramnus' second question elicited the fundamental difference between himself and Paschasius Radbertus.

Ratramnus' insistence that eucharistic realism did not require the identity of Christ's two bodies was grounded in his theology of a sacrament (Radbertus' fourth question on sign and the thing signified). To affirm such an identity would, for Ratramnus, destroy the very heart of a sacrament, viz., its mystery.

> For if that mystery is celebrated under no figure at all, it is no longer properly called a mystery. Since that cannot be called a mystery in which there is nothing hidden, nothing covered with some sort of veil. But that bread which is made the body of Christ through the ministry of the priest manifests itself externally to the senses as one thing, and yet internally it demands recognition from the minds of the faithful as something different.[26]

Presupposing Augustine's sacramental theology and, therefore, the Platonic concept of participation, Ratramnus affirmed real presence but denied an identity between the two bodies. Without compromising the integrity of sacramental signs or the necessity of faith for perceiving them, Ratramnus averred a real presence that permitted the elements to be more than mirages that concealed raw flesh and dripping blood.

Anticipating the language of later medieval scholasticism, Ratramnus advocated a real and substantial presence of Christ in the eucharist.

> The body and blood of Christ which the faithful receive in church are images (signs), according to their visible appearance; but according to their invisible substance—that is, according to the power of the divine Word—the body and blood of Christ truly exist. As visible creatures (of bread and wine) they nourish the body; as the greater power of substance, they feed and sanctify the minds of the faithful.[27]

Like Paschasius Radbertus, Ratramnus distinguished between image (*figura*) or sacrament (*mysterium, sacramentum*), and truth (*veritas*). Unlike Radbertus, Ratramnus regarded this distinction as essential to the proper understanding of a sacrament. In his own defense, Ratramnus quoted the theology of Ambrose, a realist, and provided his own commentary.

It was true flesh that was crucified and buried; and this (the eucharist)
is truly the sacrament of that flesh. For the Lord Jesus himself cried,
'This is my body.' (St. Ambrose).

How carefully, how prudently this distinction is made! Concerning
the flesh that was crucified and buried—that is, insofar as Christ
himself was crucified and buried—(Ambrose) said: This is the true
flesh of Christ. But concerning that which is consumed in the
sacrament, he said: This is truly the sacrament of that flesh.
(Ambrose) thus distinguished between the sacrament of flesh and
the truth of flesh. In the truth of flesh taken from the Virgin,
(Ambrose) says Christ was crucified and buried. But the mystery
now celebrated by the church he would call the sacrament of that
true flesh which was crucified.[28]

Thus, the historical body of Christ was neither re-created nor multiplied
in the sacrament. When the gathered community celebrated the sacrament
of the eucharist, it affirmed the true "mystery" of the flesh of Christ. That mystery
cannot be diminished by identifying Christ's eucharistic body with the physical
re-creation of the natural body of Christ.

In summary, Ratramnus, like Radbertus, affirmed Christ's real presence.
Unlike his teacher, Ratramnus disavowed the identification of Christ's eucharistic
body and Christ's historical body. This distinction was required by the prior
and fundamental distinction between the sign and the thing signified. Ratramnus'
theology of a sacrament precluded the collapsing of a sign into the thing signified
and, therefore, the identification of the two bodies. The integrity of the
sacramental sign prevented the identity but it did not preclude Christ's real
presence. To the faithful, Christ was spiritually and sacramentally present.

Although some scholars have depicted this controversy as an open conflict
between Ambrosian and Augustinian traditions, it seems more accurate to label
this debate a domestic quarrel. Both Paschasius Radbertus and Ratramnus
were monks of the monastery of Corbie and disciples of Augustine. But they
borrowed selectively. Radbertus emphasized the realistic teachings of Augustine,
while Ratramnus emphasized the spiritual teachings. This tendency was
particularly evident in their respective discussions on the nature of a sacrament.
Radbertus stressed the reality side almost to the exclusion of the symbol side,
while Ratramnus stressed the symbol side almost to the exclusion of the reality
side. Regrettably, the tradition has imitated this controversy and posed the
sacramental question in terms of symbol *or* reality instead of symbol *and* reality.

Ratramnus' assertion that Christ's eucharistic presence did not require the
identification of the eucharistic and historical bodies was neither formally
condemned nor unique to him.[29] Although Radbertus' treatise was destined

to win ecclesiological acceptance, Ratramnus' rebuttal was not condemned until the Synod of Vercelli in 1050. In 1559 the treatise was placed on the Index, but it was removed in 1900.

Berengar and Lanfranc

By the eleventh century Radbertus' assertions on real presence and the identification of the two bodies, without much emphasis on the spiritual character of eucharistic presence, were generally accepted in the West. Consequently, the issues which were to divide Berengar of Tours and his orthodox opponents, most notably Lanfranc, mirrored the ninth century controversy. The key issue was the Augustinian concept of the sacrament as sign.

As in the previous debate, it is an oversimplification to depict this controversy as a conflict between Ambrosian realism (Lanfranc) and Augustinian symbolism (Berengar). Rather, the debate revolved around the question of emphasis. Fearing the dangers of an exaggerated realism, that would identify the invisible body with the visible sign and thereby eliminate the constitutive bipolar structure of a sacrament, Berengar stressed the symbol side. Fearing the dangers of a bare symbolism, that would deny all reality to the sacrament and obviate the means of our real union with Christ, Lanfranc stressed the reality side.

The debate lines were drawn. The fledgling controversy of the ninth century would reach a new level of maturity in its eleventh century replay.

Initial rumblings of the controversy occurred in 1048. Adelman of Liège, subsequent Bishop of Brixen, who had been a student of Fulbert with Berengar at Chartres, had heard that Berengar did not believe that the real body and real blood of Christ were offered on the holy altar. In a letter, Adelman requested Berengar to deny the accusation that he merely believed the body and blood were "a kind of figure and likeness." Within a year Hugh, Bishop of Langres and also a fellow pupil with Berengar, wrote to him on the same subject.

Two years later Berengar responded to these inquiries in a short letter addressed to Lanfranc, then Prior of Bec and subsequent Archbishop of Canterbury. Succinctly, Berengar affirmed "the opinions of John the Scot about the Sacrament of the altar" and rejected the opinions of Radbertus. This letter was eventually read at a council held in Rome under Pope Leo IX in 1050 and was responsible for the sentence of excommunication passed on Berengar *in absentia*. The controversy began.

At a Roman synod in 1059, during the pontificate of Nicholas II, Berengar recanted, burned his own writings, and assented to the following confession of faith:

> I, Berengarius, . . . acknowledging the true and apostolic faith, anathematize every heresy, especially that one for which heretofore

I have been infamous: which [heresy] attempted to prove that the
bread and wine which are placed on the altar remain merely a
sacrament after consecration—and not the true body and blood of
our Lord Jesus Christ; and further, that [the body and blood] are
touched and broken by the hands of the priests and crushed by the
teeth of the faithful in a sacramental manner only—and not physically
(*sensualiter*). I assent to the Holy Roman Church and the Apostolic
See, and I confess with mouth and heart that . . . the bread and wine
which are placed on the altar are not merely a sacrament after
consecration, but are rather the true body and blood of our Lord
Jesus Christ—and that these are truly, physically and not merely
sacramentally, touched and broken by the hands of the priests and
crushed by the teeth of the faithful.[30]

This confession is shocking for at least two reasons. First, its condemnation
of Berengar's symbolic teachings illustrates the extent to which the category
of sign had been rendered invalid for interpreting sacramental reality. Second,
its explicit materialistic language, particularly the use of the word *sensualiter*,
illustrates the extent to which real presence had become identified with sensory
presence. The preservation of orthodoxy and the protection of eucharistic real
presence were thought to require the affirmation of physical presence. Thus,
the categories for interpreting the sacred "had become absorbed into the objects
representing the sacred."[31]

In an effort to clarify his position and reply to Lanfranc and other critics,
Berengar wrote his treatise "On the Holy Supper." Although he unequivocally
affirmed the real presence by declaring that "after consecration the bread and
wine are really the body and blood of Christ,"[32] he was equally emphatic
that the bread and wine were "not destroyed but abide" and that the body and
blood of Christ were "not carnally" placed before the believer.

Not surprisingly, Berengar was summoned back to Rome by Pope Gregory
VII and forced to subscribe, in 1079, after much resistance and evasion, to the
following statement:

I, Berengarius, believe with my heart and confess with my mouth
that the bread and wine which are placed upon the altar are by the
mystery of the sacred prayer and the words of our Redeemer
substantially changed into the true and real and life-giving flesh and
blood of Jesus Christ our Lord, and that after the consecration there
is the true body of Christ which was born of the Virgin and which
hung on the cross as a sacrifice for the salvation of the world and
which sits at the right hand of the Father, and the true blood of Christ

which flowed from his side, not just by the sign and virtue of the
sacrament but in its real nature and true substance. . . .[33]

Most noteworthy in this confession is the absence of the grossly carnal expressions of twenty years earlier.

Having provided a historical outline of the controversy, we now turn to an examination of the theological positions of the chief rivals, Berengar and Lanfranc.[34]

Although Berengar affirmed the real presence of Christ's body and blood in the eucharist, he insisted that Christ's eucharistic presence and the change in the bread and wine constituted two separate issues. Like Ratramnus, he opposed this merger on both philosophical and theological grounds.

Philosophically, the change of one material reality (bread) into another material reality (Christ's body) violated the principles of nature. If physical objects replaced another physical object, their appearances must reflect that exchange. However, the bread and wine retained their external features. Berengar concluded that a change of properties, i.e., physical reality, was impossible. Furthermore, scripture supported him.

> . . . whoever affirms that the body of Christ, in whole or in part, is touched by the hands of the priest at the altar, or broken, or crushed, by the teeth—except insofar as this pertains to the *sacrament* (the sacramental signs themselves)—speaks against the truth and against the dignity of the teaching of Christ.[35]

Theologically, a change was likewise prohibited. "The body of Christ, having conquered death, (was) no longer subject to suffering and mortality; the risen and glorified Lord cannot therefore be injured by a priest's hands or a Christian's teeth."[36] Affirmation of a physical change in the eucharist would, therefore, challenge the truth of the resurrection.

Thus, the language of change for Berengar was not compatible with the doctrine of real presence. Change can be used to refer only to the way in which the bread and wine become sacramental signs to the faithful after consecration.

The separation of the doctrine of real presence from the issue of change permitted Berengar to launch a negative attack on the concept of substantial conversion and to fortify the theology of the eucharist as a sacrament. Although these two agenda overlap, we shall examine them separately.

Like his defense for the belief in the separation of real presence and change, Berengar justified his rejection of the idea of substantial conversion on both theological and philosophical grounds. Utilizing Augustine's theology of the ascension, Berengar concluded that Christ's substantial presence on the altar would require either a denial of Christ's enthronement at the right hand of God or a "doubled" body of Christ present in heaven and on earth. The former was contrary to faith and the latter was contrary to reason.[37]

Berengar supplemented his appeal to the ascension by positing an eschatological justification for his denial of substantial presence. The appearance of Christ's body upon the altar would anticipate the eschaton. Since the parousia resided in the future, Christ cannot be substantially present in the present.

By introducing for the first time the concepts of *materia, forma, subjectum*, and *id, quod in subjecto est (accidens)*, Berengar posed the problem of change in metaphysical terms.[38] Although these categories lacked the precision of Aristotelianism, they forced the tradition to develop a theory that finally became the doctrine of transubstantiation and they compelled Berengar to insist upon the survival of the substance of bread and wine after consecration. It was absurd, he argued against both Radbertus and Lanfranc, to assert a change in substance without a corresponding change in appearance. Since color, smell, and taste cannot be separated from their substances; Christ's body and blood cannot be affirmed as present as long as the senses detect bread and wine.[39]

Consecration did, however, have an effect. Although it cannot violate the laws of nature, it can provide the abiding bread and wine with a religious value. Berengar permitted, therefore, a conversion of value or efficacy, but not a conversion of substance.

In short, Berengar rejected substantial conversion on the theological grounds that it would undermine the doctrine of Christ's ascension and his second coming, and on the philosophical grounds that it would undermine the inseparable connection between a substance and its appearance. Bread cannot cease to exist by the replacement of its substance, and Christ's body cannot begin to exist by the generation of its substance.[40]

Like the tradition before him, Berengar appealed to Augustine's sacramental theology and particularly his distinction between sacrament (*sacramentum*) and reality (*res*) to refute the realistic interpretation of the eucharist. By quoting Augustine's definition of *signum* (sign), Berengar located the key relationship to the sacrament.

> 'A sign is something beyond the outward appearance which the senses perceive; by doing one thing it brings something else to mind.' He did not say 'to hand, to the mouth, to the teeth, to the stomach,' but 'to mind.'[41]

To Augustine, thought Berengar, the visible sign pointed to something invisible and the proper relation between sacrament and reality can be perceived only by human intelligence or thought. This foundational structure of a sacrament precluded the eucharist from undergoing a material change. The bread and wine are physical signs which upon consecration act as sacraments that signal the invisible yet spiritual reality of Christ's body and blood. Both sides of this polar structure are essential. To impose a natural change upon the elements of bread and wine collapsed the *signum* into the *res* and vitiated the sacrament.

Berengar's sacramental theology enabled him to affirm the real presence of Christ in the eucharist and to renounce materialistic terminology. Furthermore, it reintroduced, for a short while, the doctrine of the ascension and its stress on Christ's absence, along with the doctrine of the second coming and its stress on Christ's future return. Although his protest hardly restrained the crude realistic language of his contemporaries, it forced successive generations to formulate a sounder philosophical theory. In particular, his criticism of substantial conversion anticipated later criticism of transubstantiation. That is, how can an accident remain without its substance, as in the case with the bread and wine after consecration, and, conversely, how can a substance be generated without its accidents, as in the case of the body and blood of Christ?

In spite of these monumental achievements, Berengar's fate was sealed. His overemphasis on the spiritual side of the sacrament made him susceptible to the charge of denying the reality of real presence and advocating bare symbolism. Although he claimed a conversion of value or efficacy, it remained at the level of an interior psychological event.[42] Consequently, the church authorities could not locate a reality referent within his spiritualistic categories and, therefore, condemned him as a heretic.

Without question the prevailing eucharistic theologies of the eleventh century were indebted to Paschasius Radbertus and, therefore, biased against Berengar.[43] Hence, many theologians championed the cause of orthodoxy against the heretical views of Berengar.[44] Of the three great anti-Berengarian theologians,[45] Lanfranc of Bec offers the most representative position.

Although it was not until 1063 that Lanfranc became fully involved in the dispute, he quickly established himself as the main defender of the church. In his treatise "On the Body and Blood of the Lord," he not only berated Berengar for misquoting Ambrose but he also appropriated this same patristic witness to affirm that "God's infinite power can and does in the eucharist cause," at the moment of consecration, the bread and wine to become the body and blood of the Lord.[46] Thus, Lanfranc utilized the insights of Ambrose both to counteract Berengar's use of Augustine and to negate Berengar's philosophy of nature, which labeled as impossible any change of material reality from one thing into another.

Lanfranc confirmed a substantial conversion, effected by the onmipotent power of God, that distinguished between outward appearances (bread and wine) and hidden truth (body and blood).

We believe that through the ministry of the priest, the earthly substances on the Lord's table are sanctified by divine power in a

manner that is unspeakable, incomprehensible, marvelous; and that
(these substances) are changed into the essence of the Lord's body,
even though the appearances of earthly elements remain. . . .[47]

Recognizing that a specific essence cannot be in two things simultaneously,
Lanfranc posited a theory of change that generated "a new principle of being,
which is communicated to the recipient under the covering of the qualities of
bread and wine, which remain objectively in the sacrament, not merely subjectively
to the perception of the recipient."[48] Consequently, he overcame the traditional
theory that declared the creation of a new principle of action under the elements
and, thereby, became the first theologian to define the sacramental process as
one of transubstantiation.[49]

Yet, his theory of change was not the mature doctrine of transubstantiation.
Without the full complement of the metaphysical theory of substance and accident,
his criticisms of Berengarian symbolism involved contradictory claims of "super-
substantial" and material change.

Lanfranc attempted to resolve his own antinomy, and thereby overcome
the Berengarian system, by separating the internal essence of Christ's body and
blood from the external appearance of bread and wine, which retained their
color, taste, and smell. In this way Lanfranc affirmed a change in the total reality
of Christ's body and blood, and the continued sensory perception of bread and
wine after consecration.

At the heart of the eleventh century controversy over substantial presence,
and the immediate opposition between Berengar and Lanfranc, stood the validity
of the eucharist as a sacrament. Relying exclusively on Augustine's sacramental
theology, Berengar believed that the sacrament was destroyed if the bread and
wine were substantially changed. Relying primarily on Ambrose's sacramental
theology, Lanfranc believed that the sacrament was destroyed if the bread and
wine were not substantially changed.

> (Ambrose) attests, indeed, that what existed according to its visible
> appearances (bread and wine) is now changed in its interior essence
> into those things (body and blood) which, before, were not.[50]

To Berengar the integrity of the sacrament required that the *res* of Christ's
body and blood remain independent of the *signum* and, therefore, be located
in heaven. To Lanfranc the sacrament required that the signs be changed into
that reality. Consequently, for him the sacrament simultaneously signified the
res and was the *res* itself.[51] For Berengar this belief turned the sacramental
signs into "mere shells empty of their hidden (but real) content."[52]

In short, Berengar's interpretation of Augustine prevented him from equating
the sacrament and the reality, although their relatedness was essential. Lanfranc's

interpretation of both Augustine and Ambrose compelled him to equate the sacrament and the reality, although their outward appearances and hidden truth remained distinct.

This latter distinction was critical for Lanfranc's sacramental theology because it enabled him both to affirm the identity of the eucharistic and historical bodies of Christ, and to deny the literal eating of Christ. Christians partake of the true flesh and blood of Christ in the eucharist but they receive the flesh and blood under the appearances of bread and wine. In the sacrament of the eucharist, the outward appearances of bread and wine contain the hidden truth of Christ's flesh and blood, and Christ's body which is in heaven (Berengar's point) can be broken by the priest and eaten by believers in the flesh.

This ingenious set of distinctions rested upon a prior distinction between partial and total reality. To Lanfranc, the outward appearances of bread and wine constituted a partial reality, while the hidden truth of Christ's flesh and blood constituted a total reality. Similarly, the flesh and blood of Christ in the eucharist constituted a partial reality, while the body of Christ now glorified in heaven constituted a total reality.[53]

> ... the Lord's body itself none the less existing in heaven at the right hand of the Father, immortal, unviolated, whole, unbroken, unhurt, so that it can be truly said that we receive that very body which was taken from the Virgin, and yet that it is not the same: —the same indeed so far as concerns the essence and peculiarity and power of the real nature, but not the same as regards the species of bread and the species of wine and the other things mentioned above.[54]

Lanfranc's amazing network of distinctions allowed him "to overcome the apparent opposition between sacramentalism and realism, between appearances and truth, between a body that is glorified in heaven and flesh that is eaten on earth."[55]

In summary, the eleventh century controversy between Berengar and his orthodox opponents inaugurated a new era in sacramental theology. By challenging the crudely realistic notion of substantial conversion, Berengar forced Western eucharistic theology to reformulate its interpretation of the transformation of bread and wine into Christ's body and blood. Although he was unable to reverse the tide toward substantial presence, his insistence upon the importance of the doctrines of the ascension and eschatology proved to be invaluable reminders to the tradition.

Lanfranc and his colleagues answered Berengar's challenge by forging a mediating position between the two Carolingian positions of Paschasius Radbertus and Ratramnus. Christ's eucharistic and historical bodies were "essentially" the same but their appearances were different. Overcoming Berengar's objection, punctuated by the ascension, "that if the bread is changed into Christ's Body, then either the bread must be raised up to heaven or the Body must come down to earth";[56] Lanfranc proposed a distinction between partial and total realities that relied on a change in the bread and not in Christ. Thus, Christ's presence in the eucharist was real and substantial, though invisible and spiritual. Christ's total presence on earth at the altar did not, then, conflict with his enthronement in heaven since the presences were not "formally" identical.[57]

The formulations of Lanfranc and his associates, though early and inadequate expressions of substantial conversion and transubstantiation, provided sacramental theology with its initial efforts to affirm Christ's real presence without being excessively realistic.

Conclusion

Together, the ninth century eucharistic controversy between Paschasius Radbertus and Ratramnus, and the eleventh century eucharistic controversy between Berengar and Lanfranc, launched a new era in sacramental theology. For the first time the eucharist in general and the mode of Christ's eucharistic presence in particular were thematized. With the erosion of the concept of ecclesial presence, the assertion of Christ's real presence in the eucharist became tied to the elements of bread and wine. These two controversies served, then, to define the parameters of the Middle Ages' debate.

Succinctly, the disagreements revolved around the nature of a sacrament. How does the symbolic side relate to the reality side? Are the two sides closely connected or basically distinct? Ratramnus and Berengar emphasized the symbolic side, while Radbertus and Lanfranc emphasized the reality side. The former pair feared that too close an identity between the visible sign and the invisible reality would undermine the sign character of the sacrament, while the latter pair feared that too loose an identity would preclude the means for a real union with Christ through the sacrament. The former pair upheld the close connection between sign and reality by stressing the bipolar nature of a sacrament, while the latter pair maintained a basic distinction by stressing the substantial change and collapsing the *signum* into the *res*. Regrettably, the subsequent centuries accepted uncritically the terms of these two controversies and, therefore, posed the sacramental question in terms of either *signum* or *res* instead of both *signum* and *res*.

Age of the Systematists

The dawning of the twelfth century ushered in the first phase of the age of the systematists and concluded prior to the Fourth Lateran Council of 1215 and the time of Thomas Aquinas.

Although a short revival of Berengarianism occurred in this early period, for the most part the concept of substantial presence became further codified in eucharistic teachings. Peter Lombard, Bishop of Paris and author of the most influential scholastic work, the *Sentences*, continued the march toward a formal theory of transubstantiation by observing that the tradition from Lanfranc onward used

> the realistic distinction between the substance—the impalpable universal which was held to inhere in every particular included under it—and the accidents or sensible properties which came into existence when the pure Form clothed itself in matter. . . .[58]

He speculated that this change in the eucharistic elements could occur in four possible ways:

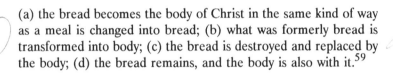

> (a) the bread becomes the body of Christ in the same kind of way as a meal is changed into bread; (b) what was formerly bread is transformed into body; (c) the bread is destroyed and replaced by the body; (d) the bread remains, and the body is also with it.[59]

He dismissed all but the second alternative. Bread was not altered digestively (a), and the extremes of annihilation (c) and consubstantiation (d) were rejected outright. Thus, bread and wine were changed substantially into the body and blood of Christ.

Hugh of St. Victor, Master of the School of St. Victor at Paris and preeminent theologian of scholasticism, addressed the subject of the eucharist in his works *The Sum of the Sentences* and *On the Sacraments*. In the latter he described a sacrament as a:

> physical or material element presented clearly to the senses, by similitude representing, by institution signifying, and by consecration containing an invisible and spiritual grace.[60]

Employing this definition, Hugh denounced both Berengarianism and annihilation, while endorsing the teaching that the substance of the bread and wine were converted into the substance of the body and blood of Christ.

Bernard of Clairvaux represented scholasticism's uncanny ability to mix seemingly contradictory positions. Following the prevailing eucharistic theology, he concurred that "the real substance of the flesh itself is undoubtedly present to us in the sacrament."[61] Yet, he also wanted to maintain Augustine's stress on the spiritual character of Christ's eucharistic presence. Consequently, he insisted upon the distinction between the visible and the invisible. This was evident in his sermon *In Coena Domini*.

> A sacred sign or a sacred mystery is called a sacrament. For many
> things exist only for their own sakes; but others are to be accounted
> because of other things, and these are called signs, and are (such).
> . . . take an example from everyday affairs—a ring is given simply
> as a ring, and it has no signification; it is given for the purpose of
> investing with a certain inheritance, and it becomes a sign so that
> he who receives it can now say: The ring is of no value at all in
> comparison, but the inheritance is what I was seeking. In this manner,
> therefore, drawing near to his passion the Lord took care to invest
> his own with his own grace, that invisible grace might be guaranteed
> by some visible sign. For this were all sacraments instituted. . . .
> that you may be secure, you have as an investiture the sacrament
> of the Lord's body and precious blood. . . .[62]

Thus, St. Bernard agreed that the sacrament of the eucharist was "given to us spiritually not carnally," yet substantially.

In the wake of Berengarianism, the twelfth century's endorsement of substantial change required further refinement in the theological language of eucharistic presence. Not only did the question of the exact moment of consecration need answering, but the doctrines of *ex opere operato* and concomitance emerged as supplements.

To counteract the subjectivism of Berengar's conversion of value or efficacy, medieval theology insisted "that grace is objectively *there*" in the eucharist independent of the celebrant and the recipient. Since God alone "creates grace," the eucharist, authorized by Christ, served as an instrument by which God dispensed grace. Thus, the sacrament was effective *ex opere operato*, through the performance of the objective rite, and was not effective *ex opere operantis*, through the agency of the dispenser. The objective reality of the eucharist was secured by the *episkope* of the church, qualified by ordination. Neither the personal qualities of the celebrant nor the personal faith of the recipient created grace. However, the chosen instruments, the priests and bishops of the church, were significant. The validity of the objective reality of God's grace was tied to the efficacious action of the Mass and to the priestly office.

The desire to affirm that communicants received the living and whole body of Christ in the eucharist began with the ninth century controversy over the relation between the historical and eucharistic bodies of Christ. By the eleventh century Lanfranc identified Christ's glorified body in heaven with Christ's flesh in the eucharist. In the twelfth century the comparison was narrowed to the relation between Christ's body and blood in each one of the eucharistic elements of bread and wine. This restrictive focus on the individual sacramental signs required a further distinction between concomitance and conversion. If concomitance assured the presence of the living and whole Christ, at what exact moment of consecration was Christ wholly present? How can eucharistic theology overcome the objection of Peter the Singer that a "separate consecration" theory precluded the presence of Christ since "a body cannot exist without blood"? A technical distinction between concomitance and conversion was needed.[63]

As described earlier, the fourth century witnessed a growing interest in "when" Christ became present in the eucharist. Speculation about "the moment of consecration" continued through the millennium. By the Middle Ages the traditional eucharistic prayer took on the character of a petition. That is, the prayer resembled a formula which was repeated at the table in order to effect something in the rite. This "something" was the moment when Christ's presence was felt especially real, and this moment was the recitation by the priest of the words, *Hoc est corpus meum* (This is my body).

By the mid-twelfth century, most theologians agreed that the bread and wine were changed into the body and blood of Christ, and that the change occurred via the words of Christ spoken by the priest in the eucharistic prayer. The unresolved question was the exact moment of consecration.[64]

V. L. Kennedy claims that "three schools of thought about the moment of consecration emerged between the years 1160 and 1208."

The "safe" school, represented by Peter of Troyes, adhered to a position that "was sufficiently ambiguous to be considered safe, and sufficiently exact to be considered acceptable." Peter's formula was: *Quando totum dictum est, totum factum est* (When everything has been said, everything has been done). Clearly it affirmed that the consecration was accomplished by reciting the words of Christ, but just as clearly it avoided deciding whether it occurred all at once or separately (for the bread, then for the cup).

Dissatisfied with Peter's formula, theologians like Stephen Langton and Simon of Tournai argued that each species was consecrated separately. This "separate consecration" school often had difficulty defending church practice that did not imitate exactly the actions as well as the words of Jesus.

The "single consecration" school was championed by Peter the Singer, who reasoned that:

> A true body cannot exist without blood; but there is no blood in this sacrament until the wine is consecrated; therefore, the bread is not truly consecrated until the entire formula for both species has been said by the priest.[65]

The preoccupation with the question of the moment of consecration underscores several related issues. First, can Christians commune under one species or do both bread and wine need to be present in order to receive Christ's body and blood? The theory of concomitance addressed this issue. Second, is the practice of intinction theologically justified? Third, should the consecrated bread and wine be shown to the people that they might be adored and if so, at what point in the liturgy? The practice of the elevation of the host became routine. Fourth, the attention focused on the consecration further illustrates the shift in the liturgy (etymologically the "work of the people") away from lay participation and toward a theophany or epiphany (Christ's mysterious presence and the elevation of the host) that inspires wonder and adoration.

Convened at Paris between 1205 and 1208, a synod rejected Peter the Singer's position of "single consecration" and approved the "separate consecration" school. Furthermore, the synod decreed that the host should be shown to the public only after the bread was consecrated.

First formulated by Anselm of Canterbury and adopted at the Council of Constance in 1415 to justify the withholding of the cup from the laity, the doctrine of concomitance stated that Christ's blood was concomitantly or consequently present upon the consecration of the bread. Peter the Singer's concern that a body cannot exist without blood was addressed. The transformation of bread into Christ's body necessarily required that blood also be present. Although the conversion of wine into Christ's blood by consecration was still affirmed, its equal status with the bread was severely undermined.

This compromise between the "single" and "separate" consecration theories permitted twelfth century theologians to declare that:

> Christ's blood is present under the species of bread through the mode of concomitance; hence it is perfectly acceptable for Christians to reverence and adore the host after the words 'This is my body,' for the host contains the whole Christ, body and blood, soul and divinity. Christ's blood is present under the species of wine through the mode of immediate, direct conversion; hence the mode by which Christ's blood is present in the consecrated wine differs from the mode by which it is present in the bread.[66]

This theological distinction between the utility of the bread and the wine had a decisive impact on the eucharistic liturgy. Not only did it justify the eventual withdrawal of the cup from the laity, but it also justified the reinterpretation of the elevation of bread. Instead of imitating Jesus' fourfold action of taking, blessing, breaking, and giving the bread; the elevation signaled the completed act of consecration.[67]

Because of the doctrine of concomitance and its corollary, the theory of permanence, the eucharist was further distinguished from the other sacraments since it "not only causes grace but permanently contains the Author of grace Himself."[68] These theological accolades were soon acted out in gestures of adoration. Most dramatic was the feast and procession of Corpus Christi which began in the thirteenth century.[69]

The Fourth Lateran Council and Thomas Aquinas

With the calling of the Fourth Lateran Council and the publishing of Thomas'
Summa Theologiae in the thirteenth century, the systematization of eucharistic
doctrine culminated in the wholesale adoption of the concept of substantial
presence.

Lothair Conti, elected Pope Innocent III in 1198 and convener of the Fourth
Lateran Council in 1215, represents the mainline teaching on the doctrine of
Christ's eucharistic presence. In his book *On the Holy Mystery of the Altar*, written
before he became pope, he argued that the sacrament was the "real body of
Christ" because at the consecration the substance of bread and wine were
"transubstantiated" into the body and blood of Christ although the appearances
remained. The eucharistic and historical bodies were the same, but the flesh
was not torn since it remained whole and unbroken.

Reflecting the influence of Lanfranc, he grounded his concept of substantial
presence and its spiritual nourishment in an Augustinian sacramental system.
In his letter *Cum Marthae circa* to John, Archbishop of Lyons, in 1202, this
dependence was clarified:

> (The eucharist) is called the 'mystery of faith' because what is believed
> is not what is seen, and what is seen is not what is believed. What
> is seen is the appearance of bread and wine; what is believed is the
> truth of the body and blood of Christ, and the power, unity and love.
> . . . We must distinguish between three different things in this
> sacrament: the visible form, the truth of the body, and the spiritual
> power. The form is that of bread and wine; the truth is that of flesh
> and blood; the power is that of unity and love. The first is sacrament
> and not reality (*sacramentum et non res*). The second is sacrament
> and reality (*sacramentum et res*). The third is reality and not
> sacrament (*res et non sacramentum*).[70]

In the first decree of the Fourth Lateran Council this substantialist conception,
with its twin goals of defending the realism of Christ's presence and the
sacramental mystery of that presence, received the official sanction of
the church.

> There is one true universal church of the faithful, outside which no
> one can be saved, in which Jesus Christ Himself is the priest and
> sacrifice, whose body and blood are truly contained in the sacrament
> of the altar beneath the species of bread and wine, the bread being
> transubstantiated into the body, and the wine into the blood, by divine

power, so that we receive for perfecting the mystery of unity from His very self, that which He received from us.[71]

This decree proved pivotal for the doctrine of transubstantiation for several reasons. Although the Fourth Lateran Council was not the only authority cited on behalf of the concept of substantial presence, it became the most crucial witness until the Council of Trent. Second, it elevated the doctrine of real presence to the same level as the doctrines of the Trinity and the dual nature Christology. According to Harnack, this development was "the most distinctive and boldest act of the Middle Ages."[72] Third, its actual definition of the substantial change and the retention of the accidents was sufficiently "guarded" to permit adherence by those who professed either carnal or spiritual interpretations. Because of this cautious language, the alternative positions of consubstantiation and annihilation, mentioned by Peter of Capua and considered erroneous by Innocent III, were not labeled heretical. Although they were vigorously criticized, Thomas Aquinas was the first to denounce them. Thus, the solidification of the doctrine of transubstantiation was not complete until the end of the thirteenth century.

The thirteenth century witnessed an extended use of the writings of Aristotle by both Franciscan and Dominican theologians.

Alexander of Hales, who entered the Franciscan Order in 1222 and died in Paris in 1245, was the first schoolman to employ the entire corpus of Aristotle. In his magnum opus _Summa Theologiae_, completed posthumously in 1252, he averred the accepted opinion that the eucharistic elements were converted by transubstantiation and were not annihilated. The accidents remained without a subject and Christ's presence was neither local nor circumscribed. Although Alexander used Aristotle to safeguard the spiritual interpretation of Christ's substantial presence, his tome was replete with realistic overtones.[73]

Bonaventura, General of the Franciscan Order and predecessor to Duns Scotus, was in remarkable accord with his contemporary Dominican rival, Thomas Aquinas, as stated in Bonaventura's book _On Preparation for Mass_:

> When the words of Christ are uttered, the material and visible bread . . . leaves its own place, that is, the visible species of the accidents, to perform the office of sacramental service; and as soon as it ceases to be there really exists under those accidents in a wonderful and ineffable way: —First, that most pure flesh and sacred body of Christ which, by the operation of the Holy Ghost, was the offspring of the womb of the glorious Virgin Mary, was hung on the cross, was laid in the tomb, was glorified in heaven. Secondly, since flesh does not live without blood, that precious blood which with happy result flowed on the cross for the salvation of the world is necessarily there. Thirdly,

since there cannot be true man without rational soul, the glorious soul of Christ, exceeding in grace all virtue and glory and power, in which are stored all the treasures of wisdom and of the knowledge of God, is there. Fourthly, because Christ is true God and true Man, it follows that God is there, glorious in His majesty. All these four at the same time, and each wholly at the same time, are perfectly contained under the species of bread and wine, not less in the cup than in the host, and not less in the host than in the cup.[74]

The use of Aristotelian philosophy to augment the concept of substantial presence was carried even further by the Dominicans' Albert the Great (Albertus Magnus) and his celebrated pupil, Thomas Aquinas.

Teacher in Paris and Cologne, Albert reflected the prevailing interpretation that via the consecration the whole substance of the bread and wine were transubstantiated into the whole substance of the body and blood of Christ. Although the substance of the bread and wine were not destroyed upon conversion (annihilation), neither did they remain "so as to co-exist together with the body of Christ" (consubstantiation).[75] Like his contemporaries, he concurred with Berengar's confession of 1059 since Christ's circumscribed presence by place is in heaven and his "supernatural" presence by grace is in the eucharist.[76]

Thomas Aquinas, born at Roccasecca in the Kingdom of Nayles in 1225, member of the Dominican Order, teacher in Paris and Rome, represents the zenith of scholasticism. Basically a clarifier and not an innovator, Thomas affirmed the dominant theme that "the real body of Christ and his blood" are in the sacrament of the eucharist. Thus, he sided with the dominant trends of the tradition in rejecting a literal, carnal eating of Christ, on the one hand, and an imagined, figurative representation of Christ, on the other hand. Somehow the eucharistic body and blood of Christ are present in a different modality than a physical object. That "somehow," the doctrine of transubstantiation, is summarized in his *Summa Theologiae* Part 3, questions 75-77.

From the beginning of question 75, article 1, Thomas assured his readers of his assent to Christ's real presence in the eucharist.

We could never know by our senses that the real body of Christ and his blood are in this sacrament, but only by our faith which is based on the authority of God. . . . this sacrament . . . really contains Christ himself . . . *the fulfilment of all the other sacraments.* . . . he has not left us without his bodily presence in this our pilgrimage, but he joins us to himself in this sacrament in the reality of his body and blood.[77]

The uniqueness of the eucharist as a sacrament was that "we have . . . got Christ himself really."[78] In the other sacraments, the substance of the material sign remained, but not in the eucharist. Thus, the importance of the eucharist resided in Thomas' understanding of a sacrament.

Inheritor of Augustinian sacramental theology, Thomas believed that the sacrament as a sign conveyed something else to the mind besides the species which it impressed on the senses. Hence, the sacrament consisted of more than the relation between the object signified and the person who received the sign. Deeper than this subjective level, the sacrament, by the will of the one who instituted it, guaranteed the presence and efficacy of the reality which it symbolized. Consequently, all sacraments were instrumental causes of grace which depended on neither the faith of the recipient nor the intention of the celebrant.[79]

Echoing Augustine, Thomas summarized his understanding of the relation between the *signum* and the *res* in question 60, article 4:

> Now it is conatural to man to arrive at a knowledge of intelligible realities through sensible ones, and a sign is something through which a person arrives at knowledge of some further thing beyond itself. Moreover the sacred realities signified by the sacraments are certain spiritual and intelligible goods by which man is sanctified. And the consequence of this fact is that the function of the sacrament as signifying is implemented by means of some sensible realities. . . . it is because of this that sensible realities are needed for the sacraments.[80]

The uniqueness of the eucharist and the efficacy of its reality, the eucharistic presence of Christ, were effected by the priest's uttering the Words of Institution.[81] By these words, the substance of the bread and wine were changed into the substance of Christ's body and blood.

> And this actually happens by divine power in this sacrament. The complete substance of the bread is converted into the complete substance of Christ's body, and the complete substance of the wine into the complete substance of Christ's blood. Hence this change is not a formal change, but a substantial one. It does not belong to the natural kinds of change, and it can be called by a name proper to itself—'transubstantiation.'[82]

The manner by which Christ's eucharistic presence was conceptualized, transubstantiation, presupposed the distinctions between material, substance, and accident. Following Aristotle and the Greeks, Thomas believed that earth, air, fire, and water were the four constitutive materials or "physical stuff" which composed, in varying combinations, all material things. Underlying the sense appearance of physical things was that which provided the definable essence of a thing. This objective reality, which was neither a purely imaginary construct (like a unicorn) nor an account of the surface characteristics of a thing, was the substance. The visible qualities of a physical thing—its color, shape, taste, smell, and so forth—were constituted by accidents which inhered in the substance. Thus, the particular combination of material, substance, and accidents made up any particular object.[83]

Employing this language, Thomas clarified with immense precision the already approved doctrine of transubstantiation. Substantial conversion was the only logical explanation for a change that guaranteed real presence.

> ... it remains that there is no other way in which the body of Christ can begin to be in this sacrament except through the substance of the bread being changed into it.[84]

Consequently, this language now permitted the substance of the bread not to remain, while the accidents of the bread to remain without their substance.

> Now, what is changed into something else is no longer there after the change. The reality of Christ's body in this sacrament demands, then, that the substance of the bread be no longer there after the consecration.[85]

> It is obvious to our senses that, after the consecration, all the accidents of the bread and wine remain. Divine providence very wisely arranged for this. First of all, men have not the custom of eating human flesh and drinking human blood; indeed, the thought revolts them. And so the flesh and blood of Christ are given to us to be taken under the appearances of things in common human use, namely bread and wine.[86]

The substance of bread and wine were, therefore, changed into the substance of Christ's body and blood without a physical change. Although this substantial transformation was perceptible only to those of faith, the accidents remained visible to all.

Yet, a dilemma persisted. How can a substance and its accidents be divorced from one another? Thomas concluded that the ordinary laws governing the relationship between substance and accidents were "suspended in the eucharist by the same divine power that brings about the transformation of the bread and wine."[87] He surmised:

> We are left to conclude that the accidents in this sacrament do not inhere in any subject. God's power is able to bring this about. Seeing

that all effects depend more on the first cause than on secondary causes, God, who is the first cause of both substance and accident, by using his infinite power, is able to conserve an accident in being, even when the substance which hitherto as its immediate cause was keeping it in existence has disappeared.[88]

Thus, the doctrine of transubstantiation superseded the alternatives of annihilation and consubstantiation. Annihilation was both impossible and heretical since substantial change was the only means of assuring Christ's eucharistic presence while retaining the form of the sacrament.[89] Consubstantiation[90] was both impossible and heretical since "it would involve the local motion of the body of Christ to many different places simultaneously."[91]

Through the sophisticated category of substance, Thomas affirmed the mode of Christ's eucharistic presence as real, and rejected Christ's eucharistic presence as local, "as if in a place" (*sicut in loco*).[92] To the sensual eye Christ's body and blood were absent, but to the faithful eye Christ was present. "Locally and quantitatively, Jesus (was) absent; 'substantially' he (was) present."[93]

Like the apostle Paul but unlike his contemporaries, Thomas built the presence-absence dialectic into his eucharistic theology. Consequently, Thomas retained both the future dimension, since there existed an absent one who was "yet to come," and the ecclesial dimension, since there existed a present one who offered communion with himself.

> (The eucharist) has a third significance with regard to the future. It prefigures that enjoyment of God which will be ours in heaven. That is, why it is called 'viaticum,' because it keeps us on the way to heaven.[94]

Commenting on the text of I Corinthians 10:17, Thomas noted:

> This text shows clearly that the Eucharist is the sacrament of the Church's unity. But a sacrament bears the likeness of that of which it is a sacrament. Therefore, the Eucharist itself should be one.[95]

> The Church is the gathering together of all the different baptized faithful, in the same way *bread is made of different grains of wheat and wine flows together from different grapes*, as the Gloss on I Corinthians 10, 17 puts it.[96]

Supported by common sense observation, Thomas renounced the physical presence of Christ, since that would imply a "measurable" presence. Yet, he affirmed the real presence of Christ wherever the eucharist was celebrated.

> The body of Christ is not in this sacrament in the way a body is in place. The dimensions of a body in place correspond with the dimensions of the place that contains it. Christ's body is here in a special way that is proper to this sacrament. For this reason we say that the body of Christ is on different altars, not as in different places, but as in the sacrament. In saying this we do not mean that Christ is only symbolically there, although it is true that every sacrament is a sign, but we understand that Christ's body is there, as we have said, in a way that is proper to this sacrament.[97]

By recognizing three different modes of presence, Thomas clearly abstained from conceiving Christ's eucharistic presence as either according to the flesh or in an angelic sense. In the first mode, physical or historical presence, "the boundaries of the body coincide with the boundary of the space that it fills."[98] This local or circumscriptive sense of presence was clearly inappropriate since it precluded Christ from being at more than one place at a single time. In the second mode, glorified or definitive presence, the body set a boundary but did not fill it. Thus, an angel may be in a house without filling it. This angelic sense of presence was clearly inappropriate since it would preclude the visible sign of the sacrament. In the third mode, sacramental presence, Thomas found the presence proper to the eucharist.[99]

Because the sacramental presence of Christ was not there before the consecration, it must be "brought in" either by local motion or "by something already there being changed into it." The former was rejected by Thomas since, at minimum, it would nullify Christ's ascension into heaven.

> Now it is clear that the body of Christ does not begin to exist in this sacrament by being brought in locally. First, because it would thereby cease to be in heaven, since anything that is locally moved begins to be somewhere only by leaving where it was.[100]

Thomas concluded:

> . . . that there is no other way in which the body of Christ can begin to be in this sacrament except through the substance of the bread changed into it.[101]

Thus, the doctrine of transubstantiation became the most appropriate way to explain the mode and reality of Christ's eucharistic presence. The body of Christ was not present via the mode of dimension since Christ was present in heaven. Rather, Christ was present in the eucharist according to the mode of substance. Devoid of all sensible elements and accessible only to those of faith, the reality of Christ's eucharistic presence was metaphysical and not empirical—the substance of Christ himself. Hence, transubstantiation explained how a complete conversion took place, while the elements were not noticeably changed. This was the great asset of the doctrine of transubstantiation.

Criticisms of Transubstantiation

Thomas Aquinas' eloquent and precise definition of the doctrine of transubstantiation assured the medieval church that the decree of the Fourth Lateran Council would remain the official position throughout the fourteenth and fifteenth centuries. Rival theories, particularly consubstantiation, met with swift and sometimes brutal suppression.[102] Yet, free thinkers such as Duns Scotus, William of Occam, and John Wyclif did not hesitate to propound the rational shortcomings of the doctrine of transubstantiation and thereby prepared the way for alternative Reformation positions.

Johannes Duns Scotus, architect of Franciscan theology and forerunner of Luther, supported the doctrine of transubstantiation more on the basis of church authority than rational plausibility. Faced with the difficulties of the scholastic explanation and the absence of scriptural mandate, Scotus deemed consubstantiation more reasonable than transubstantiation. He posed the dilemma in the form of a question:

> Since the true Principle of each and every thing is the divine Power
> alone, in what way is consubstantiation, which permits the substance
> of the bread and that of the body to coexist, a less valid possibility
> than transubstantiation which effects the conversion of the first into
> the second or even annihilation which suppresses the substance of
> the bread? Miracle for miracle, which is preferable?[103]

Although consubstantiation may be more favorable on philosophical grounds, Scotus, reflecting the judgment of the era, interpreted the pronouncement of the Fourth Lateran Council as a dogmatic affirmation of the doctrine of transubstantiation over against all other alternatives. Thus, Scotus taught what he called *transubstantiatio adductiva* (distinct from Thomas' *transubstantia productiva*) wherein the "substance of the body of Christ is added to the substance of the bread."[104] To avoid charges of consubstantiation and to reconcile this position with official doctrine, he assumed that the substance of the bread was annihilated. Luther would later echo Scotus' observation that the dogma of transubstantiation has no support other than the authority of the church and that the doctrine of the real presence is altogether independent from it.

Another Franciscan, William of Occam (or Ockham), came to a similar conclusion. As a nominalist,[105] who radically criticized the prevailing realism of his day and who is cited as the innovator of the *via moderna* (as opposed to the *via antiqua* of Thomas and Scotus), Occam "denied the real distinction between substance and quantity and therefore denied that there was a quantitative presence of Christ as distinct from his substantial presence."[106] Consequently, Christ's eucharistic presence was primarily spiritual. Furthermore, this rigorously independent thinker maintained that the notion of substantial change could not be defended by Scripture:

> Although it is expressly set forth in the canonical scriptures that the body of Christ is to be offered to the faithful under the species of bread, yet that the substance of bread is really converted or transubstantiated into the body of Christ is not found expressed in the canon of the Bible.[107]

Although Occam adhered to the dictates of Rome, he seemed especially attracted to the alternative position of consubstantiation. Not only was it "very reasonable apart from a decision of the Church to the contrary," but it also seemed to avoid "all the difficulties that result from the separation of accidents from their subject" while being neither "contrary to anything in the canon of the Bible" nor "repugnant to reason."[108] On the positive side, Occam appealed to the omnipotence of God:

> For a Christian ought not to say that God might not through his absolute power be able to make some substance to coexist with something corporeal, so that the whole may coexist with that whole body and with each part of it. . . .[109]

Like Scotus, Occam judged the doctrine of consubstantiation more defensible than transubstantiation in all ways except one—the authority of the church.

In addition, Occam contributed significantly to the concept of ubiquity which Luther would later appropriate. Throughout the Middle Ages the interest in Christ's omnipresence increased as the doctrine of the real presence of Christ in the eucharist gained currency and expression in the theory of transubstantiation. In particular, the unresolved question became: how can the body be in heaven and simultaneously on earth?

Both Guitmund of Aversa and Alger of Cluny, adversaries of Berengar, assumed a sort of "ubiquity." Theologically grounded in Christ's omnipotence, Alger reasoned that Christ can be bodily omnipresent. "In heaven and on earth he can be corporeally present everywhere, in whatsoever way it may please him—contrary to the nature of flesh—always the same and entire."[110]

Both Peter Lombard and Thomas Aquinas, following John of Damascus, distinguished between Christ as *totus* and *totum*, i.e., Christ being omnipresent in the former case in virtue of the unity of his person, but not in the latter as the conception of both natures. The Christological justification was: "Deity follows humanity everywhere, but not vice versa." Consequently, Lombard and Thomas rejected the omnipresence of the physical body but affirmed a sacramental omnipresence. Peter Lombard taught that the exalted body of Christ was in one place while his sacramental body was multipresent. Thomas Aquinas, as we have seen, espoused a threefold scheme of presence and invoked a sacramental presence for Christ's eucharistic presence.

Yet, the difficult problem of explaining how the circumscribed celestial body of Christ, with its attributes of quantity and dimension, could replace the bread in the host without lapsing into self-contradiction remained. For example, Thomas argued that the portion present in the host was conceived as at once quantitative and non-quantitative.

Occam advanced the concept of ubiquity by postulating that the body of Christ was not quantitatively in the sacrament of the altar and by suggesting the possibility that the body of Christ was ubiquitous ("repletive existence").

As a nominalist, Occam believed that quantity had no independent existence. Consequently, the quantity of a thing may be increased or decreased without altering the thing itself. "Definitive existence" pertained only to non-quantitative things. Thus, the body of Christ existed in the Lord's Supper but "the body of Christ (was) not quantitatively (*quantum*) in the sacrament of the altar."[111]

Therefore, Occam promoted three modes of bodily presence of a thing. The first mode, "circumscriptive presence," referred to the way in which any physical body is present in the world, viz., the way Christ's body was present during his earthly life. Occam called the second mode of presence *esse diffinitive*. Although the word *diffinitive* was a late form of what Thomas called "definitive" and was interchangeable in medieval Latin, there existed a difference in the understanding. For Thomas, "definitive" presence meant that "the thing present in a certain place does not fill the place." Accordingly, "the body of Christ could be in the host, but in an illocal way be present in each part of the host."[112] For Occam, *diffinitive* presence meant that the presence was no longer bound to a certain space. Christ's glorified body was at one place in heaven in extended form and quantitative but it was also present everywhere as a whole in the host.

But this illocal, incomprehensible, spiritual presence was not limited to the host. Consequently, a third mode of presence, *esse repletive*, which referred to divine omnipresence and was ascribed only to God, was sometimes applied to Christ. "The body of Christ is present to everyone, is present to himself immediately, and consequently that form of bread, i.e., the host, has nothing to do with (*nihil facit*) the presence of the body."[113]

Occam's suggestion, though applied infrequently, that the body of Christ can possibly be everywhere (*ubique*) just as God is everywhere, constitutes his major contribution to the theological discussion of the mode of Christ's eucharistic presence and a major idea appropriated by Luther.

Over against Scotus and Occam, John Wyclif advanced a realist critique of the theories of annihilation and transubstantiation. He objected to annihilation, as proposed by Scotus, because it reduced Christ in the eucharist to a phantom and unreality.[114] He opposed Occam's tepid endorsement of transubstantiation and timid acceptance of church authority with a robust defense of scriptural authority. Around 1381 Wyclif began his attack with a series of published statements on the eucharist. The propositions that related to the doctrine of Christ's eucharistic presence are as follows:

> The consecrated host which we see on the altar is neither Christ nor any part of Him but an effectual sign.

> Transubstantiation, identification, and imparation . . . are not to be established from scripture.

> It is contrary to the opinions of saints to assert that there is accident without subject in a real host.

> The Sacrament of the Eucharist is in its nature bread and wine, containing, by virtue of the sacramental words, the real body and blood of Christ in every part of it.

> The Sacrament of the Eucharist is in figure the body and blood of Christ, into which the bread and wine are transubstantiated, of which some being remains after consecration, although as the faithful believe, laid asleep.

> The existence of accidents without subject is not tenable.[115]

These objections were soon followed by the declaration known as the *Confession*. In it Wyclif declared that the problem was not the primary doctrine of real presence but rather the secondary explanation.

> I have often confessed, and do still confess, that the bread in the Sacrament, or consecrated host, which the faithful perceive in the hands of the priest, is really and actually the very same body of Christ and the same substance as was taken from the Virgin and as suffered on the cross and lay dead in the tomb for the holy three days, and rose on the third day, and after forty days ascended into heaven, and sitteth on the right hand of God the Father. The proof of this

is, that Christ, who cannot lie, so declares. Nevertheless, I do not
dare to say that this bread is the body of Christ essentially or
substantially or corporally or identically.... For we believe that there
is a threefold way in which the body of Christ is in the consecrated
host, namely, virtual, spiritual, and sacramental. Virtual, whereby
throughout His whole rule He benefits in the good things of nature
and grace. The spiritual way is that whereby the body of Christ is
in the Eucharist and in the saints by means of grace. And the third
way, the sacramental, is that whereby the body of Christ is in the
consecrated host after a unique manner.... But, besides these three
ways of being, there are three other ways more actual and more real,
which the body of Christ fitly has in heaven, namely substantially,
corporally, and by dimensions. And men of gross ideas understand
no other way of the being of a natural substance besides these. But
they are not at all fit to grasp the mystery of the Eucharist and the
subtlety of Scripture.[116]

As a thorough Augustinian who must emphasize, on the one hand, the
ascension and the locus of Christ's body in heaven, and who must distinguish,
on the other hand, between the sign and the thing signified, Wyclif offered a
more rational scholastic interpretation of Christ's eucharistic presence. Outwardly,
the consecrated host cannot be identified as flesh of Christ since Christ resides
in his corporeal state in heaven. Inwardly, the consecrated elements are symbols
of the body and blood of Christ since Christ resides in his sacramental state
in the eucharist. Through an elaborate scheme of "modes of being" Wyclif
overcame the position of eucharistic materialism and secured eucharistic
presence.[117]

Reluctant to define any further how Christ's body was present, Wyclif, when
pressed, fell back upon consubstantiation. The eucharist was the miraculous
renewal of the doctrine of incarnation with its two substances in one person.

The truth and faith of the Church is that as Christ is at once God and
man, so the Sacrament is at once the body of Christ and bread—bread
and wine naturally, the body and blood sacramentally.[118]

Due in part to the influence of Wyclif's beliefs upon the Bohemian Reformers,
John Hus and Jerome of Prague, who were put to death at the stake,[119] Wyclif's
writings were condemned in 1413 by a synod in Rome and he himself was
posthumously condemned a heretic by the Council of Constance in 1415.
Parenthetically, Calvin and Zwingli were also indebted to Wyclif for his emphasis
upon the ascension, his abhorrence of excessive objectivism, his rejection of
transubstantiation, and his referral to Augustine as the great patristic authority.[120]

Our brief excursion into the eucharistic theologies of Scotus, Occam, and Wyclif should not deter us from acknowledging the triumph of the concept of substantial presence in the medieval period. Although the most representative and influential scholars avoided a wholly mechanical and carnal doctrine of real presence, and articulated the spiritual character of Christ's eucharistic presence, the substantial language of transubstantiation was often mistaken for materialism. Gabriel Biel, the last of the schoolmen, who died in 1495, illustrates this tendency.

> Not only are these four constituents aforesaid present in the Holy Eucharist—viz., Body, Blood, Soul, and Godhead—but also their properties, accidents and perfections of nature and glory. . . . Wherefore [the consecrated elements] contain four endowments of the body of glory; a fixed harmony of the parts, the primary and secondary qualities, and the due complexion of the working parts and organs. . . . Nor do they only contain all things which make for the perfection of the body and limbs, but also everything which belongs to the adornment and beauty of a body; as hair, nails, beard, and all else pertaining to the comeliness of that glorious Body which Christ resumed at His wondrous and glorious resurrection, wherein also He sitteth at the right hand of the Father and is presented to the sight of the Saints. . . . To this we must add the operations and qualities of His senses, both external and internal. For, if any of these perfections were lacking to Christ as [He is] in the sacrament, then His being in the sacrament would tend to the great imperfection of Christ's Soul and Body; for, as existing there, He would lose some perfection which would inexist for Him in heaven; and this would seem absurd. For thus it would be less delectable to Christ, (as to the Body and Soul,) to be in the Eucharist than to be in heaven, if, as being there, He lacked any bodily or spiritual delectation.[121]

As the Middle Ages drew to a close the real presence of Christ in the eucharist was affirmed with intense conviction and was confessed as an authentic miracle. With virtual unanimity the doctrine of transubstantiation triumphed over alternative formulations and received full ecclesiastical endorsement as the theological interpretation of the doctrine of real presence. It secured the mode of Christ's eucharistic presence against the two unaccepted extremes of excessive objectivism and bare symbolism.

> (1) The eucharistic presence of Christ is not to be thought of as a primitivistic devouring of the flesh of the divine-human Christ; (2) the eucharistic presence is not to be defined by the use of such vague categories as 'symbolic' or 'spiritual presence' which can lead to the evaporation of both religious meaning and devotion.[122]

Through the category of substance, the authentic real presence of Christ in the eucharist was affirmed for the faithful and protected from the heretics.

This monumental achievement of scholasticism is sharply criticized today. Unlike the Reformation's criticisms, the current problems are metaphysical in nature and three in number.[123]

The first problem involves the requirement of two distinct miracles to sustain the theological doctrine of transubstantiation. Not only does the conversion of the substance of the bread and the wine into the body and blood of Christ require a miracle, but a second miracle is required to explain how the accidents of the bread and wine, the sacramental *species*, still remain in being after their original substance has been transformed. Thomas acknowledges this difficulty and relies on the miraculous omnipotence of God to secure the doctrine. The first criticism does not, therefore, question the power of God. More fundamental to this doctrine, it questions the multiple miracles this doctrine demands.

The second problem relates to the category of substance and its Aristotelian framework. Since we no longer think in this philosopical paradigm, it is increasingly difficult to maintain that the idea of a substance is in fact something "real." The question of the reality referent of substance is not peculiar, however, to our age. It has vexed philosophy from the time of Plato and Aristotle, and it erupted anew in the Middle Ages in the controversy between nominalism and realism.

The suspicion cast on the category of substance is heightened even more by the insistence of the doctrine of transubstantiation that the miracle of transformation requires that substance and accidents inhere in a being independently. Not only is a miracle demanded, as the first problem pinpointed, but, more important, it requires that the categories of substance and accident remain intelligible outside of their philosophical framework. The second problem asks, therefore, whether the categories can retain their meaning when their application within the doctrine of transubstantiation contradicts the presupposition within Aristotelian metaphysics that a substance and its accidents inhere together. In short, category confusion leads to epistemological incoherence.

The third current problem concerns the almost exclusive concentration of Christ's eucharistic presence with the link between bread and wine, and flesh and blood. According to the theory of transubstantiation Christ is not, technically speaking, present under the eucharistic elements. Under the bread and wine is the substance of Christ's body and blood. In order to guarantee the whole reality of Christ himself in the eucharist, Thomas and others must introduce the additional doctrine of concomitance. Similar to the first problem, transubstantiation must be supplemented.

Pope Innocent III in his letter *Cum Marthae circa*, from which we have already quoted, expressed this same concern in a different manner.

> A careful distinction must be made between three distinct things
> which are in this sacrament, namely the visible form, the truth of
> the body, and the spiritual power. The form is of bread and wine,
> the truth of flesh and blood, the power of unity and love. The first
> is 'sacrament and not reality.' The second is 'sacrament and reality.'
> The third is 'reality and not sacrament.' But the first is sacrament of
> both realities. The second is sacrament of the one reality, and the reality
> of the other. The third is the reality of both sacraments.[124]

For Pope Innocent III and Thomas Aquinas, the central reality of the eucharist
requires more than the form of bread and wine, and the truth of flesh and blood.
The exclusive connection, which the doctrine of transubstantiation claims between
the eucharistic elements of bread and wine, and the eucharistic presence of
Christ's body and blood, is not sufficient. Our third problem warns us against
such a narrow focus.

Conclusion

During the Middle Ages, the concept of substantial presence dominated
the theological formulations of Christ's eucharistic presence and disastrous effects
ensued. Emphasis on analogical language and the ritual act was supplanted
by realistic language and a preoccupation with the elements. Beginning with
the Paschasius Radbertus and Ratramnus controversy of the ninth century, the
eucharistic dialectics of presence-absence and past-future were gradually but
steadily undermined. The center of contention for eucharistic theology shifted
to the manner of Christ's presence under the elements and to the manner of
Christ's passion in the past. With few exceptions, neither the ascension, which
theologically justified the absence of Christ, nor the parousia, which theologically
justified the future return of Christ, was incorporated into sacramental theology.

The inevitable consequence of depriving the eucharist of its futuristic
orientation would surface in the Roman Catholic-Reformation eucharistic
controversy. Envisioned by both groups as wholly residing within history and
time, the redeeming activity of Christ, into which the eucharist enters, was tied
to the passion. Consequently, the church, through the celebration of the eucharist,
usually entered into this past action by one of two routes: "either purely *mentally*
by remembering and imagining it; or else, if the entering into it is to have any
objective reality outside the mind, by way of some sort of *repetition* or iteration
of the redeeming act of Christ."[125] In general, the Roman Catholic Church
chose the latter alternative and adopted the belief that in the eucharist a new
accessing of the merits of the one sacrifice of Calvary occurred. (Catholic doctrine
affirmed repeated Masses but denied repeated sacrifices.) The Reformers usually

chose the former alternative and believed that the external rite became an
acted memorial whose elements conveyed a figurative meaning. In contrast
to the eucharistic action of the priest, the Reformation focused on the
individual's own mental remembrance of the passion. The eucharistic
controversies of the sixteenth century were, therefore, extensions of the Middle
Ages' formulations.

The Communal Context

Composed of committed believers who, often at personal risk, assembled
on the day of the resurrection, the church of the first centuries constituted
an *ecclesia*, and not merely an aggregate of individuals. Shaped by their
corporate liturgical action, these people of God were identified as the body
of Christ at the celebration of the eucharist.

Theoretically, the consciousness of being the one community of the risen
Lord remained intact after Christianity became the state religion. Practically,
the corporate consciousness began to erode soon after the Roman Empire
embraced the church in the fourth century. Gradually yet steadily, the
participatory character of corporate worship dwindled and the laity became
spectators. This fundamental shift in liturgy reached its zenith in the
Middle Ages.

Like the previous centuries, the Middle Ages paid homage to the communal
character of eucharistic worship. During the Carolingian Age, Bishop
Theodulph decreed that worship should remain public and communal:

> A priest should never celebrate Mass alone; for just as it cannot be
> celebrated without the priest's greeting, so it cannot be celebrated
> without the people's response. Most certainly, therefore, Mass ought
> never to be celebrated by one individual alone. For there must be
> others who stand about with the priest; others whom he may greet;
> others who may respond to him.[126]

Though Ratramnus' eucharistic theology was judged peripheral, he never
wavered concerning the ecclesial significance of the eucharist.

> St. Augustine teaches us that just as the bread placed on the altar
> signifies the body of Christ, so also it (signifies) the body of the people
> who receive it. . . . For what is placed on the Lord's Table contains
> not only the sacramental (*mysterium*) of Christ, but also the sacrament
> of the body of the faithful people.[127]

The ecclesial character of the eucharist was prominent in the writings of Thomas Aquinas, too. Echoes of Augustine can be heard in Thomas' offertory prayer of the Roman missal for the feast of Corpus Christi:

> O Lord, we beseech Thee, be pleased to grant unto Thy church the gifts of unity and peace, which by these offered gifts are mystically signified: through Jesus Christ our Lord. . . .[128]

Despite these assertions, the Middle Ages did not reverse the trend toward decreasing the role of the laity and increasing the role of the clergy. With respect to the communal context, the ninth century constitutes a watershed in the history of the relation between the worshiping community and the eucharistic celebration.

It was during the ninth century "that lay persons began to be denied direct access to the eucharistic cup."[129] Although this change can be traced to the eighth century practice of using a reed or straw in administering the chalice, the intense focus on Christ's eucharistic body and blood under the elements, as a result of the Radbertus-Ratramnus controversy, may have spurred the need to prevent any profanation of the elements. For practical reasons the withdrawal of the cup made sense. Bread was obviously cheaper and more available than wine. And by the late twelfth century this custom was provided the theological rationale of concomitance. Since Christ's blood was concomitantly present in the consecrated host, the reception of the cup was unnecessary. The whole Christ, body and blood, was received under the single species of bread.

Alterations in the reception of the bread also occurred during this period. Not only was the type of bread used in communion changed to unleavened bread but due to the increased reverence for the elements the pure white wafer was also introduced to minimize crumbs.[130] In addition, the custom of anointing the priest's hands and of locating the power of consecration in the office of the priest alone, encouraged the change from communion in the hand to communion in the mouth for the laity.

These changes in the mode of reception and in the withdrawal of the cup from the people contributed greatly to the further distancing of the worshipers from the action on the altar.

However, the most devastating blow to communal worship was linguistic. With the dissolution of Latin as a *lingua franca*, already evident by the sixth century, the church was faced with a difficult dilemma: should it retain uniformity by the continued use of the single liturgical language of Latin or should it ensure participation by the introduction of vernacular tongues? By opting for the former, the church effectively eliminated the people's access to both participation and power. Without direct knowledge of the special language of worship, the laity's level of participation was reduced to visual images (elevation of the host) and communal gestures (Corpus Christi procession). Without actual possession of the special formulas of consecration, the laity was disenfranchised from liturgical and political power.[131]

This widening separation of the people from the eucharistic liturgy was especially evident in the loss of liturgical participation. Now that linguistic access was denied, the laity's role in corporate worship steadily diminished. The loss of the Litany of the Deacon probably involved the loss of the prayer for the unity of the church.[132] Decline in lay communion, though partially restored in the twelfth and thirteenth centuries, was accompanied by the loss of the laity's ability to bring the bread and wine at the offertory.[133] The presentation of the eucharistic elements for the preparation of the table was replaced by the presentation of money and other gifts.[134]

Passivity also applied to music. The congregational chants and hymnic texts were gradually taken over from the people by the choir of clerics and finally by the church choirs.[135] What were once corporate expressions of unity were now reduced to stimuli for religious devotion. Not surprisingly, the decline in lay participation was accompanied by an increase in texts for private prayers within the eucharistic celebration.[136]

During the Carolingian Age devotional prayers within the liturgical action also appeared for the clergy. In Martene's *De Antiquis Ecclesiae Ritibus*, an old Sarum manuscript, the following prayer is offered at the eucharist:

> (here the priest bows and speaks to the host;)
> 'I adore you; I glorify you; with all the intensity of my heart I praise you. And I pray that you will not leave your servants, but that you will forgive our sins. . . .'

The text of this prayer continues:

> '*Before he receives, let him humbly say to the body*: Hail forever, most holy flesh of Christ, before all else and above all else the highest sweetness! . . .
> *Then, with great devotion, let him say to the blood*:
> Hail forever, heavenly drink, before all else and above all else the highest sweetness!'[137]

Besides the obvious eucharistic realism of this prayer, the text underscores the intimate encounter between a solitary individual (the priest) and the "flesh and blood" of Christ. Ratramnus' insistence that the eucharist involve the Augustinian concept of the sacrament of the faithful people has disappeared. In lieu of a corporate experience, the eucharist has become a one-on-one experience.

These prayers inaugurated a new perception of the priest. Equipped with the proper language and empowered by the proper ordination, the priest began to achieve "sacramental and liturgical independence" from the laity. Only the priest could consecrate the elements. Only the priest could touch the flesh of Christ. Only the priest could address the body and blood. "The appearance of private prayers in the liturgy thus reflected not only a shift of emphasis in eucharistic piety, but also a shift of understanding about the relation of priest and people to the sacramental action."[138]

Access to the ritual language and to the holy power of consecration elevated the priest to the status of "sacred person." This was best typified by the locational change of the priest from his position behind the table facing the congregation to a position in front of the table with his back to the congregation.

Although this shift in location may have been necessitated by the custom of placing the relics of the saints on top of and behind the altar, thereby displacing the priest, it vividly illustrates the complete distortion of the eucharistic celebration. No longer the paternal figure at the head of the family, the leader of the priestly people who all participate in the communal eucharistic action, the priest is now endowed with supernatural powers and is the mediator between the almighty God and the disenfranchised people.[139]

By practical necessity as well as liturgical intention these changes of the Middle Ages effected a radical transformation in the communal character of the eucharist. For the church of the early centuries the *eucharistia*, the prayer of thanksgiving from the congregation, gave its name to the whole communal activity of invoking and celebrating the presence of the risen Lord among God's people. For the church of the Middle Ages the whole action had been transferred to the celebrant. The assembly of the faithful ceased to be *ecclesia orans* and became instead a gathering of individuals intent on their own private devotion. Corporate worship continued as a sort of *ecclesia representativa* where the sacred officers of the church performed the elaborate rites on behalf of the laity.[140]

Remarkably, the decline in both lay communion and participation did not diminish the centrality of the eucharist. On the contrary, the awe inspiring mystery of communion was intensified. What could not be comprehended could be adored all the more! Hence, the new climax of the eucharist was the elevation of the consecrated host.

Without access to the eucharist through sound or touch, the eye provided the only means of participation. As a result, worshipers would frequently dash from church to church in hopes of glimpsing the sacred host and body of Christ. Many congregants would not enter the church until the bell signaled the completed consecration.[141] The custom of parading the host, which evolved into the feast of Corpus Christi, was intended to encourage popular participation in the eucharist. Likewise the practice of genuflecting and kneeling before the blessed sacrament was a means of adoring as well as participating in the worship experience.[142]

In conclusion, the *eucharistia* of the early centuries became an *epiphania* in the Middle Ages.[143] The communal character of worship was replaced by a "devotional explosion." With the disappearance of the offertory and fraction, and the decline in lay communion, the consecration and subsequent elevation of the blessed host achieved an exalted status. As mediators between God and humanity, the empowered priests performed the entire eucharistic liturgy on behalf of the disenfranchised laity. Denied visible and audible access to the eucharist, except at the moment of elevation, the medieval worshiper was detached from the external rite and, therefore, turned inward. Public worship became in effect private devotion. While the number of Masses increased dramatically (to as many as fifty a week in an average parish), the reception of communion by lay people decreased significantly (from about three times a year at the beginning of the Carolingian period to about once a year after the thirteenth century).[144]

Throughout the Middle Ages, the theologians with their controversies and the laity with their adoration were preoccupied with the eucharistic presence of Christ. Regrettably, most lost sight of one of the primary purposes for which Christ was present. The sacrament of the unity of God's people, which imprints ecclesial identity, had been transformed into a mechanism to promote individual salvation. The connection between the Christological and the ecclesiological meanings of the "body of Christ" was severed. Now the term "body of Christ" was associated exclusively with the eucharistic presence of Christ under the elements of bread and wine. The communal character of the eucharist was lost.

Conclusion

The Middle Ages, from the ninth century controversy between Paschasius Radbertus and Ratramnus, through the eleventh century controversy between Berengar and Lanfranc, to the thirteenth century theology of Thomas Aquinas, evidenced the gradual movement toward, and the eventual triumph of, the doctrine of transubstantiation and the concept of substantial presence. Both practical and theoretical factors converged.

Practically, the disenfranchisement of the laity and the prominence of the clergy contributed to the virtual loss of the communal character of worship. Denied the cup and the vernacular, the laity were reduced to mere spectators of a ritual drama that culminated in the visible elevation of the host. The actions of the liturgy, which were once symbolic vehicles by which the mysteries of Christ's eucharistic presence were made known, now served as simple reminders that elicited wonder and adoration. The visible overwhelmed the invisible.

Theoretically, Aristotelian philosophy and sacramental theology contributed to the triumph of transubstantiation and substantial presence. Perfected in the eucharistic theology of Thomas Aquinas, the doctrines of consecration and concomitance merged with the subtleties of Aristotelian metaphysics to formulate a plausible and eloquent explanation of how matter could be changed into the holy through an exercise of divine power. Furthermore, the bipolar nature of a sacrament, which preserved the dialectic balance between the symbol and the reality sides, collapsed into the reality side. Even when theologians avowed both sides, they rarely established a clear connection.

Obsessed with the eucharistic elements and Christ's real presence at the Mass to the exclusion of the eucharistic action as a whole, the theology of the Middle Ages insisted upon a substantial change. The connection of ritual and material elements was irreparably split.

The domination of real presence muted, if not silenced, any articulation of Christ's absence via the ascension and Christ's second coming via the parousia. Consequently, the requisite presence-absence and past-future polarities were severed by the period's preoccupation with making Christ's past sacrifice available to the present.

In short, the doctrine of transubstantiation, with its emphasis on the concept of substantial presence, had triumphed as the theological interpretation of the doctrine of real presence, and was, therefore, passed on to the sixteenth century.

Notes

1. David N. Power in *The Eucharistic Mystery*, chapter 8, chronicles how the eucharist was at "the center of a cultural vision of church and society."

2. Grislis, "Manner of Christ's Eucharistic Presence in the Early and Medieval Church," 9.

3. Mitchell, *Cult and Controversy*, 67.

4. Ibid., 109.

5. Wainwright, *Eucharist and Eschatology*, 47.

6. James F. McCue, "The Doctrine of Transubstantiation from Berengar Through Trent: The Point At Issue," *Harvard Theological Review* 61 (July 1968): 390, ft. 4.

7. Ibid.

8. Ibid.

9. Dugmore, *The Mass and the English Reformers*, 25.

10. Harnack, *History of Dogma*, vol. 5, 312.

11. Mitchell, *Cult and Controversy*, 74-75.

12. Stone, *A History of the Doctrine*, 218.

13. Mitchell, *Cult and Controversy*, 75-76.

14. The following discussion is dependent upon Mitchell, *Cult and Controversy*, 76-78.

15. Ibid., 77.

16. The story is recounted in Mitchell, *Cult and Controversy*, 78-79.

17. Stone, *A History of the Doctrine*, 217.

18. Dugmore, *The Mass and the English Reformers*, 26-27.

19. Allen J. MacDonald, *Berengar and the Reform of Sacramental Doctrine* (Merrick, NY: Richmond Publishing Co., 1977), 236-238.

20. R. P. Redmond, "The Real Presence in the Early Middle Ages" *Clergy Review* 8 (1934): 454-455.

21. Heron, *Table and Tradition*, 93.

22. Ibid.

23. Ibid.

24. Stone, *A History of the Doctrine*, 232.

25. Fahey, *The Eucharistic Teaching of Ratramn*, 82-83.

26. Mitchell, *Cult and Controversy*, 81-82.

27. Ibid., 83-84.

28. Ibid., 84.

29. Gottschalk and Rabanus Maurus, ninth century contemporaries, also protested against Radbertus' realistic teaching and professed a distinction between the two bodies. For additional information on both see Fahey, *The Eucharistic Teaching of Ratramn*, 106-107, 118, 164; on Rabanus Maurus see McDonnell, *John Calvin*, 49-50; MacDonald, *Berengar and the Reform*, 241; and Stone, *A History of the Doctrine*, 222-224.

30. Mitchell, *Cult and Controversy*, 137.

31. Guzie, *Jesus and the Eucharist*, 64.

32. Stone, *A History of the Doctrine*, 256.

33. Grislis, "Manner of Christ's Eucharistic Presence in the Early and Medieval Church," 9-10.

34. Although the eucharistic issues are crucial for our study, they do not necessarily reflect the full reason for Lanfranc's triumph and Berengar's defeat. Ebersolt, as reported by Sheedy, *The Eucharistic Controversy of the Eleventh Century*, 53, pinpoints Berengar's rejection of ecclesiastical authority as his fundamental flaw. The politics of eleventh century France must also be considered. Mitchell in *Cult and Controversy*, 140, contends that Berengar's eventual condemnation may be attributed to the "declining power of his chief political patron."

35. Mitchell, *Cult and Controversy*, 141.

36. Ibid.

37. The following discussion is influenced by McDonnell, *John Calvin*, 53-54 and Crockett, *Eucharist*, 110.

38. McDonnell, *Calvin*, 54.

39. MacDonald, *Berengar and the Reform*, 304-305.

40. Sheedy, *The Eucharistic Controversy of the Eleventh Century*, 69.

41. Mitchell, *Cult and Controversy*, 142.

42. Ibid., 145. Quite remarkably, Berengar's position anticipates the twentieth century concept of transignification.

43. See Stone, *A History of the Doctrine*, on St. Anselm of Canterbury, 261-263; on Odo of Cambrai, 263-266; and on Hildebert of Tours, 275-278.

44. Important treatises against Berengar include: Durand, Abbot of Troarn, "On the Body and Blood of the Lord" (Stone, *A History of the Doctrine*, 250-251); and Witmund of Aversa, "On the Reality of the Body and Blood of Christ in the Eucharist" (Ibid., 252-253).

45. The three great anti-Berengarian writers and their works are: Lanfranc of Bec, "De Corpore et Sanguine Domini adversus Berengarium Turonensem"; Guitmund of Aversa, "De Corporis et Sanguinis Christi veritate in Eucharistia"; and Alger of Liège or Alger of Cluny, "De Sacramentis Corporis et Sanguinis Domini." Their unifiying theme was the acceptance of the doctrine of substantial conversion and, therefore, a real but not carnal presence of Christ at the eucharist.

46. Mitchell, *Cult and Controversy*, 146.

47. Ibid., 146-147.

48. MacDonald, *Berengar and the Reform*, 296.

49. Ibid., 296 and Sheedy, *The Eucharistic Controversy of the Eleventh Century*, 81. We do not know precisely who was the first person to use the term "transubstantiation" or exactly what the theologian meant by it. Hermann Sasse, *This is My Body*, 41, nominates Stephen of Autun, before 1139, as a likely candidate. Reinhold Seeberg, *Text-Book of the History of Doctrines*, vol 2, trans. Charles E. Hay (Grand Rapids: Baker Book House, 1952), 77, believes that the term is first found in the sermons of Hildebert of Lavardin in 1134. William Crockett, *Eucharist*, 118, and David Power, *The Eucharistic Mystery*, 245, agree that the term *transubstantiatio* was first used by Roland Bandinelli, later Pope Alexander III, in his *Sentences*, written in the 1140's.

50. Mitchell, *Cult and Controversy*, 147.

51. Sheedy, *The Eucharistic Controversy of the Eleventh Century*, 112.

52. Mitchell, *Cult and Controversy*, 147.

53. Ibid., 148-149.

54. Stone, *A History of the Doctrine*, 249.

55. Mitchell, *Cult and Controversy*, 149.

56. Sheedy, *The Eucharistic Controversy of the Eleventh Century*, 89.

57. Ibid., 88-90 and Mitchell, *Cult and Controversy*, 150.

58. Stone, *A History of the Doctrine*, 304.

59. Heron, *Table and Tradition*, 95.

60. Kenneth Scott Latourette, *A History of Christianity* (New York: Harper and Brothers, 1953), 505.

61. Dugmore, *The Mass and the English Reformers*, 42.

62. Ibid., 40-41.

63. Mitchell, *Cult and Controversy*, 157-160.

64. This section is indebted to Mitchell, *Cult and Controversy*, 151-157.

65. Ibid., 153.

66. Ibid., 158.

67. Ibid., 159.

68. Wilhelm Niesel, *The Gospel and the Churches*, trans. David Lewis (Philadelphia: Westminster Press, 1962), 106.

69. Mitchell provides the socioeconomic as well as religious background of the celebration, *Cult and Controversy*, 172-176.

70. Provided by Eugene TeSelle, Professor of Theology, The Divinity School, Vanderbilt University, Nashville, Tennessee.

71. MacDonald, *Berengar and the Reform*, 404.

72. Ibid.

73. Stone, *History of the Doctrine*, 314-317.

74. Ibid., 337.

75. Ibid., 320.

76. Ibid., 321.

77. Thomas Aquinas, Saint, "The Eucharistic Presence" in *Summa Theologiae*, vol. 58, trans. William Barden (New York: Blackfriars; McGraw-Hill Book Co., 1965), 3, 75, 1.

78. Ibid., 3, 75, 2.

79. Although Thomas uses the term *ex opere operato* in his earlier writings, it does not appear in the *Summa*. See Edward C. F. A. Schillebeeckx, *Christ the Sacrament of the Encounter with God*, trans. Paul Barrett (New York: Sheed and Ward, 1963), 82-89.

80. Thomas, *Summa* 3, 60, 4.

81. Thomas, *Summa* 3, 76, 1 and 3, 78, 1 & 4.

82. Ibid., 3, 75, 4.

83. Heron, *Table and Tradition*, 95-96.

84. Thomas, *Summa* 3, 75, 2.

85. Ibid.

86. Ibid., 3, 75, 5.

87. Arthur C. McGiffert, *A History of Christian Thought*, vol. 2, *The West from Tertullian to Erasmus* (New York: Charles Scribner's Sons, 1933), 323.

88. Thomas, *Summa* 3, 77, 1.

89. See Thomas, *Summa* 3, 75, 3.

90. Thomas' condemnation of consubstantiation, though present in the *Summa* ("The Eucharistic Presence," 3, 75, 3), is best stated in his early work, *Commentum in IV libros Sententiarum* in McCue, "The Doctrine of Transubstantiation," 401, ft. 33.

91. Ibid., 401.

92. Thomas, *Summa* 3, 76, 6.

93. McCue, "The Doctrine of Transubstantiation," 401.

94. Thomas, *Summa* 3, 73, 4.

95. Ibid., 3, 73, 2.

96. Ibid., 3, 74, 1.

97. Ibid., 3, 75, 1 & 3.

98. Sasse, *This is My Body*, 39.

99. See the following for further elaboration: Grislis, "Manner of Christ's Eucharistic Presence in the Early and Medieval Church," 11; Sasse, *This is My Body*, 39; and Max Thurian, "The Real Presence," in *Christianity Divided: Protestant and Roman Catholic Theological Issues*, ed. Daniel J. Callahan, Heiko A. Oberman, Daniel J. O'Hanlon (New York: Sheed and Ward, 1961), 199-200.

100. Thomas, *Summa* 3, 75, 2.

101. Ibid.

102. See Stone, *A History of the Doctrine*, 373-375, for narratives on three people's fate.

103. Thurian, *Mystery of the Eucharist*, 60-61.

104. Sasse, *This is My Body*, 44.

105. Although Occam's philosophical position may more accurately be called "conceptualism," the traditional name is usually retained.

106. McDonnell, *John Calvin*, 200.

107. Grislis, "Manner of Christ's Eucharistic Presence in the Early and Medieval Church," 13.

108. Stone, *A History of the Doctrine*, 364.

109. Grislis, "Manner of Christ's Eucharistic Presence in the Early and Medieval Church," 13.

110. Seeberg, *Text-Book*, vol 2, 77.

111. Ibid., 204.

112. Sasse, *This is My Body*, 157.

113. Seeberg, *Text-Book*, vol 2, 205.

114. McDonnell, *John Calvin*, 55-56.

115. Stone, *A History of the Doctrine*, 365.

116. Ibid., 365-366.

117. Stone, *A History of the Doctrine*, 368; McDonnell, *John Calvin*, 56; and Dugmore, *The Mass and the English Reformers*, 54-55.

118. Herbert B. Workman, *John Wyclif* (Oxford: Clarendon Press, 1926), 38.

119. The eucharistic teachings of John Hus and Jerome of Prague are not clear. According to Stone, Hus "explicitly denied having taught that the material bread remains after consecration" and "acknowledges" the doctrine of transubstantiation "though deprecating close inquiries as to the manner of the change. . ." (Stone, *A History of the Doctrine*, 370). Although Jerome was charged by the Council of Constance with denying the doctrine of transubstantiation, it is uncertain what he believed.

120. McDonnell, *John Calvin*, 56 and Sasse, *This is My Body*, 47-48. Sasse cites both Berengar and Wyclif as a *Zwinglius ante Zwinglium*.

121. G. G. Coulton, *Five Centuries of Religion*, vol. 1 (London: Cambridge University Press, 1923), 105.

122. Grislis, "Manner of Christ's Eucharistic Presence in the Early and Medieval Church," 14.

123. This section relies on the insights of Heron, *Table and Tradition*, 98-100.

124. Ibid., 99-100.

125. Dix, *Shape of the Liturgy*, 623.

126. Mitchell, *Cult and Controversy*, 104.

127. Ibid., 83.

128. Dix, *Shape of the Liturgy*, 248.

129. Mitchell, *Cult and Controversy*, 92.

130. Jungmann, *The Mass of the Roman Rite*, 84.

131. Mitchell, *Cult and Controversy*, 87-89, 73, 118-119.

132. Brilioth, *Eucharistic Faith*, 80.

133. Dix, *Shape of the Liturgy*, 598.

134. Couratin, "Liturgy," 224.

135. Jungmann, *The Mass of the Roman Rite*, 238.

136. Mitchell, *Cult and Controversy*, 68.

137. Ibid., 106.

138. Ibid., 107. Also see Dix, *Shape of the Liturgy*, 524-525.

139. Dix, 591 and Couratin, "Liturgy," 225.

140. Dix, *Shape of the Liturgy*, 615 & 621 and Sasse, *This is My Body*, 50 & 53.

141. Jungmann, *The Mass of the Roman Rite*, 121 and Mitchell, *Cult and Controversy*, 178.

142. Jungmann, *The Mass of the Roman Rite*, 122-123 and Stone, *A History of the Doctrine*, 354.

143. Jungmann, *The Mass of the Roman Rite*, 117.

144. Tappert, "Meaning and Practice in the Middle Ages," 87.

CHAPTER FOUR

REFORMATION CONCEPTS OF PRESENCE

With the dawn of the sixteenth century, tears became visible in the sacred canopy of the Middle Ages. The great medieval union of the spiritual and the temporal realms slowly separated under the strain of significant change. Financially, the feudal economy shifted to a monetary system that embraced the spirit of profit and capitalism. Socially, a merchant class evolved and serfs were gradually emancipated from the land, sending waves of people into the cities. Politically, Europe witnessed the rise of centralized states and the decentralization of medieval political life. Intellectually, the *via antiqua* of Thomas Aquinas and the Dominicans was challenged by the *via moderna* of Pierre d'Ailly and Gabriel Biel. Furthermore, the rise of the Renaissance inaugurated a new confidence in human reason and a rebirth of interest in the classics and scholarship.

The impact of these monumental changes was felt keenly by the church. While the Renaissance encouraged intellectual daring, the institutional church recoiled at the rising tide of heresy. While Western Christendom sought unity, the church was desperately split. During the "Babylonian Captivity," the papacy was moved to Avignon, France. From 1378-1417, two popes, one in Rome and the other in Avignon, occupied the see of St. Peter. To make matters worse, the Council at Pisa in 1409 deposed both popes and in effect elected a rival third. It was not until 1414 at the Council of Constance, called by the Holy Roman Emperor, that all three contenders were summarily replaced by a new pope.

Yet, the need for papal reform was not resolved. Political and moral corruption continued to plague the reigns of Innocent VIII and Alexander VI. Although the exterior of the new basilica of St. Peter's flourished under the pontificates of Julius II and Leo X, the interior machinery of the institutional church was ignored. The times were ripe for reform.

One of the most visible and flagrant abuses of the church was the selling of indulgences. In order to finance continued construction of St. Peter's, Pope Julius II announced a plenary Jubilee Indulgence in 1503. In 1513, Pope Leo X revived the indulgence and by special arrangement with Albert of Hohenzollern introduced indulgences into designated North German ecclesiastical areas. The purchase of indulgences and the preaching of Johann Tetzel prompted Martin Luther to nail his ninety-five theses onto the Wittenberg Church door on All Saints' Day, 1517. This routine call for debate would evolve into the Protestant Reformation.

Worship at the beginning of the sixteenth century had not changed since the Fourth Lateran Council.

... the celebration of the Lord's Supper in the Western Church had become a dramatic spectacle, culminating not in communion but in the miracle of transubstantiation, and marked by adoration, not unmixed with superstition, at the elevation. Said inaudibly in an unknown tongue, and surrounded with ornate ceremonial and, if a sung mass, with elaborate musical accompaniment, the rite presented only meagre opportunity for popular participation.[1]

The medieval fascination with the doctrine of transubstantiation, whether intentional or not, narrowed the focus of the eucharist to two points: the sacredness of the elements and the individual communicant. These two themes, the doctrine of Christ's real presence in the eucharist as articulated by Thomas' theory of transubstantiation and the loss of the corporate worship experience, preoccupied the Reformers.

Examination of the Reformation concepts of presence will be the principal emphasis of this chapter and will center on Martin Luther, Ulrich Zwingli, John Calvin, and the Council of Trent. The concluding sections of this chapter will treat the three requisite features and the Reformers' well-intentioned but unsuccessful attempts to restore the notion of corporate worship.

Protestant Reformation Concepts of Eucharistic Presence

Reluctant Reformer but resolute champion of the grace of God and the means by which it is communicated, Martin Luther defended his theology of the Lord's Supper on two fronts. He opposed the Roman Catholic Church and he opposed the Enthusiasts and the Swiss. Against the former, Luther fought to preserve the genuine meaning of the sacrament as a gift of God in opposition to the doctrine of the sacrifice of the Mass and the connection of real presence with the doctrine of transubstantiation. Against the latter, Luther fought to preserve the real presence of the body and blood of Christ in the bread and wine in opposition to symbolic interpretations.

These two fronts represented, for Luther, expressions of the one great human heresy: the refusal to accept the external means of grace and the replacement of divine activity with human initiatives. Although the Roman Catholic Church endorsed the real presence of Christ in the eucharist, the work of the priest was placed along side the work of Christ, the High Priest. Although the Enthusiasts and the Swiss rejected the sacrificial character of the Lord's Supper, the feast of commemoration relied exclusively on the human act of remembrance. Both positions undermined, for Luther, the sacrament of the altar and, therefore, represented assaults on the gospel itself.

Since Luther's writings neatly divide along these two fronts, with the publications against Rome occurring between 1517 and 1524, and the publications against the Enthusiasts occurring after 1524, the format of this section will follow this division.[2] The first part will examine Luther's controversy with Rome and the second part will examine Luther's controversy with the Enthusiasts and the Swiss as represented by Ulrich Zwingli.

Luther Against Rome

Guided by the dual principles of preserving God's initiative in the divine-human relationship and of retaining the scriptural words of God in their simplest meaning, and undergirded by the conceptual framework of his day which was scholastic in general and Occamist in particular, Martin Luther not only relegated the doctrine of transubstantiation to an opinion but he also advanced the concept of copresence.

Luther first attacked the prevalent Roman Catholic understanding of the Mass in a sermon in April, 1520. Later in that same year he expanded his attack in the famous tract, *The Babylonian Captivity of the Church,* in which he protested against a threefold enslavement of the Lord's Supper: the practice of communion under one kind and the consequent withdrawal of the cup from the laity; the perception of the doctrine of transubstantiation as an article of faith; and the perception of the eucharist as a propitiatory sacrifice. Because our concern resides with real presence, our comments will be limited to the second "captivity."

Although Luther's critique of transubstantiation was restrained,[3] he emphatically affirmed the doctrine of real presence while concurrently denying any necessary connection between the doctrines of real presence and transubstantiation. Reflecting the Occamist perspective as found in the writings of Pierre d'Ailly, Cardinal of Cambrai, Luther discounted transubstantiation since it was philosophically unacceptable.

> Some time ago, when I was drinking in scholastic theology, the learned Cardinal of Cambrai gave me food for thought in his comments on the fourth book of the *Sentences*. He argues with great acumen that to hold that real bread and real wine, and not merely their accidents, are present on the altar, would be much more probable and require fewer superfluous miracles—if only the church had not decreed otherwise. When I learned later what church it was that had decreed this, namely the Thomistic—that is, the Aristotelian church—I grew bolder, and after floating in a sea of doubt, I at last found rest for my conscience in the above view, namely, that it is real bread and

real wine, in which Christ's real flesh and real blood are present in no other way and to no less a degree than the others assert them to be under their accidents.[4]

The philosophical explanation of transubstantiation was unacceptable to Luther because it tried futilely to explain the inexplicable by claiming that the accidents alone remained after consecration, and because it ignored the true faith which the church kept for more than twelve hundred years.

The philosophical untenability of the doctrine combined with scriptural prerequisites compelled Luther to reject the "monstrous idea" of transubstantiation as an article of faith and dogmatic definition of the church, and to view it as one opinion among several.

> I reached this conclusion because I saw that the opinions of the Thomists, whether approved by pope or by council, remain only opinions, and would not become articles of faith even if an angel from heaven were to decree otherwise (Gal. 1:8). For what is asserted without the Scriptures or proven revelation may be held as an opinion, but need not be believed. But this opinion of Thomas hangs so completely in the air without support of Scripture or reason that it seems to me he knows neither his philosophy nor his logic. . . . My only concern at present is to remove all scruples of conscience, so that no one may fear being called a heretic if he believes that real bread and real wine are present on the altar, and that every one may feel at liberty to ponder, hold, and believe either one view or the other without endangering his salvation.[5]

Appealing to the scriptural account of the Words of Institution, Luther moved beyond the doctrine of transubstantiation toward a theory of copresence.

> Why do we not put aside such curiosity and cling simply to the words of Christ, willing to remain in ignorance of what takes place here and content that the real body of Christ is present by virtue of the words?[6]

Building upon this scriptural basis, Luther offered a Christological analogy in lieu of a philosophical explanation. In the incarnation, which witnessed the divine dwelling in the complete and untransformed human nature of Jesus, no transformation of an earthly substance into a heavenly substance was required. Therefore, the sacrament should evidence none. For if a transformation did occur, a corresponding loss occurred. In the moment of conversion the bread and wine ceased to be what they were and became the body and blood of Christ.

The real presence of the "species" of bread and wine were destroyed. Luther wanted to know why the retention of the two natures of the incarnation should not be reflected in the sacrament.

> And why could not Christ include his body in the substance of the bread just as well as in the accidents? In red-hot iron, for instance, the two substances, fire and iron, are so mingled that every part is both iron and fire.[7]

> Thus, what is true in regard to Christ is also true in regard to the sacrament. In order for the divine nature to dwell in him bodily (Col. 2:9), it is not necessary for the human nature to be transubstantiated and the divine nature contained under the accidents of the human nature. Both natures are simply there in their entirety, and it is truly said: 'This man is God; this God is man.' . . . In like manner, it is not necessary in the sacrament that the bread and wine be transubstantiated and that Christ be contained under their accidents in order that the real body and real blood may be present. But both remain there at the same time, and it is truly said: 'This bread is my body; this wine is my blood,' and vice versa. Thus I will understand it for the time being to the honor of the holy words of God, . . . At the same time, I permit other men to follow the other opinion, . . . only let them not press us to accept their opinions as articles of faith (as I have said above).[8]

In short, Luther affirmed the intention of the doctrine of transubstantiation, viz., the real presence, but he summarily dismissed the doctrine as an article of faith. Because transubstantiation was philosophically inadequate and biblically untenable, it could stand only as a theological opinion—and the second choice for Luther! Throughout *The Babylonian Captivity* he espoused the virtues of a theory of copresence. Although he never explicitly used the term consubstantiation, his views resemble it.

Luther Against the Enthusiasts

Beginning in 1524, Luther shifted his focus from the Roman Catholic Mass to the left wing Enthusiasts. At this time, Ulrich Zwingli, Swiss humanist Reformer and eloquent Enthusiast representative,[9] advocated in a letter to Matthaus Alber of Reutlingen a purely symbolic interpretation of Christ's eucharistic presence.

Luther was incensed. Although the Roman Catholic Church's "monstrous" doctrine of transubstantiation was indefensible, it was at least tolerable, since it safeguarded the doctrine of Christ's real presence. The left wing Reformers, however, went too far. In forsaking the real presence, they abandoned the gospel. If the Words of Institution were not upheld in their simplest, i.e., literal, meaning then the cause of Christ was lost. Luther's attention naturally shifted to this new crisis.

Before we turn to Luther's defense of Christ's real presence in the eucharist, let us examine the Enthusiasts' position as represented by Zwingli.

Ulrich Zwingli

For Zwingli, the eucharistic doctrine held the key to the entire medieval system. As the source of much ignorance and superstition, the belief in the literal and corporeal presence of Christ's body and blood at the altar cast dark shadows across the gospel. Since Luther insisted on the real presence of Christ, Zwingli was compelled to indict him for retaining a residue of medieval superstition and thereby effecting only a halfway reformation.

Although Zwingli was better at serious criticism than constructive theology, he definitely affirmed Christ's presence in the eucharist. In *Auslegung des Christlichen Glaubens* (1531), the rich content of his doctrine was evident:

> We believe that Christ is truly present in the Lord's Supper; yea, we believe that there is no communion without such presence. This is the proof. 'Where two or three are gathered together in My name, there am I in the midst of them' (Matthew xviii. 20). How much more is He present, where the congregation is assembled to His honour? But that his body is literally eaten, is far from the truth, because He Himself says, 'I am no more in the world' (John xvii. 11), and the 'Flesh profiteth nothing' (John vi. 63). It is contrary to faith (I mean the holy and true faith, because faith embraces love, fear of God, and reverence, which abhor such carnal and gross eating. . . . We believe that the true body of Christ is eaten in the Communion, not in a gross and carnal manner, but in a sacramental and spiritual manner by the religious, believing, and pious heart. And this is in brief the substance of what we maintain in this controversy.[10]

Zwingli's defense of Christ's spiritual presence was grounded in two presuppositions. The first was a theological concern for faith and the sacrament, and the second was a philosophical extension of his humanist and nominalist training. Because Zwingli's doctrine of eucharistic presence is unintelligible apart from these premises, we shall examine them in turn.[11]

Theologically, Zwingli, like Luther, embraced the Reformation principles that faith was a gift from God and that God was not at the disposal of humanity. Prior to his debates with Luther, in a letter to his former teacher, Thomas Wyttenbach, Zwingli stressed the primary role of faith in the eucharist.

> Bread and wine are not transubstantiated, and profit nothing, if faith is not present. Faith is the essential thing in the Supper. Faith is the organ of appropriation. The Supper strengthens feeble faith, as the bread sustains the body.[12]

Years later in his *Fidei Ratio*, written for the Diet of Augsburg, Zwingli continued to underscore the priority of faith.

> I believe that in the Holy Eucharist, the true body of Christ is present by the contemplation of faith, i.e., that they who thank the Lord for the kindness bestowed on us in His son, acknowledge that He assumed true flesh; in it, truly suffered; truly washed away our sins in His own blood, and thus, everything done by Christ becomes present to them by the contemplation of faith.[13]

Initiated by God and created by the Holy Spirit, faith, for Zwingli, could not be reduced to knowledge, emotion, or imagination. Faith was a divine gift and the starting point for theology. Similar in intention to the Catholic doctrine of *ex opere operato*, Zwingli emphasized the role of the Holy Spirit in order to protect divine transcendence and sovereignty.

Uncharacteristic of a humanist, this "supernaturalist" element in Zwingli's theology made him fear the domination "of the sign over the signified, the external over the internal."[14] Consequently, Zwingli made a "sharp distinction between the sacramental signs and the reality signified by them."[15] Any form of sacramental mechanism or imperialism, as evident in the Roman Catholic Mass, was an anathema. "Faith," said Zwingli, "rests alone in God; faith can use corporal things but it can never be bound to them."[16] Consequently, the abuses in Roman Catholic sacramental theology and practice were protested by Zwingli because they placed God at humanity's disposal. When that occurs, the sacrament of the Lord's Supper cannot be a means of grace. God's grace and human salvation were not contingent upon the act of the celebrant. More important, Christ had already acted on our behalf and the eucharist was simply a public testimony to what had already been accomplished.[17]

As an act of thanksgiving for the gospel, the Lord's Supper reflected the gift of Christ which lay in the past. The sharing in the meal was "a pledge of something Christ *did* for us on the Cross, rather than a pledge of His abiding presence which does something for us *now*."[18] The community which gathers to give thanks, to remember, and to confess is the subject of the present sacramental action.[19]

Motivated by an absolute confidence in the divine to effect salvation and by a firm suspicion of the Roman Catholic and Lutheran tendency to collapse the *signum* into the *res*, Zwingli, on the one hand, discounted the value of an external sign and, on the other hand, concentrated almost exclusively upon it. Since faith alone was essential for salvation, sacraments were, ideally speaking, superfluous. Yet, humanity was fallen and required divine assistance. Sacraments were, therefore, necessary signs of past grace. However, a sharp distinction between the sign and the thing signified is mandated by the sovereign God. Zwingli insisted that a sign can be only a sign: "If (the sacraments) bestowed the thing or were the thing, they would be things and not a sacrament or sign."[20]

Regrettably, Zwingli's preoccupation with the Roman Catholic and Lutheran tendency to collapse the sign into the thing signified required Zwingli to isolate the two and thereby neglect any serious reflection on how signs participate in the reality signified. As a result, he held two divergent views on the role of signs.

Fearing the dominance of the material elements over the sign, as in transubstantiation and consubstantiation, Zwingli stressed the function of the sign as an external reminder of God's past act of redemption in Christ's death for us. Identifying the sacrament with the gospel and, therefore, as a means of grace, Luther, conversely, rebuked any denigration of the sacraments. For Zwingli, however, the sacrament of the altar was not a part of the gospel since only faith was essential for salvation. As an ordinance instituted by Christ, the eucharist was

> a remembrance of that deliverance by which he redeemed the whole world, that we might never forget that for our sakes he exposed his body to the ignominy of death, and not merely that we might not forget it in our hearts, but that we might publicly attest it with praise and thanksgiving. . . .[21]

Yet, Zwingli's stress on the sign had to avoid sacramental imperialism. Neither the sign nor the sacrament could possess a reality in themselves. Christ's eucharistic presence could not be connected with the elements. As a memorial, the sacrament was the sign of deliverance. The bread was a symbol and not the actual body of Christ. There could be no literal identity between the bread and wine, and the body and blood of Christ.

By denying an external connection, only an interior relationship remained. Christ was present by the interior act of remembrance and, therefore, independent of the external props. Hence, Christ's words, "This is my body," must be interpreted figuratively.

We now turn to the philosophical presuppositions of humanism and nominalism which informed this theological interpretation.

Under the indirect influence of John Wyclif and the direct influence of Dutch humanist Cornelius Hoen (Honius), Zwingli came to embrace the figurative interpretation of *Hoc est corpus meum*. From Hoen, Zwingli found the "pearl of great price"—the conviction that "is" should be taken in the sense of "signifies." This discovery became the fulcrum in Zwingli's doctrine of Christ's eucharistic presence which stood in opposition to the Lutheran stress on "is."

Zwingli's humanist training provided the foundation for both a negative and a positive reply to Luther. If the words of Christ were to be understood literally then Christ must be eaten literally and perceptibly, since Christ does not deceive. That is, if Christ spoke literally, than his words must be fulfilled literally. Yet that is absurd! Our inability to perceive or touch Christ can only mean that Christ did not speak literally. The flesh only profits believers because it is slain, not because it is eaten.[22] Thus, Berengar's confession is false and a figurative interpretation is true.

Furthermore, scriptural evidence on the relation of flesh and spirit supports this interpretation. Although the sixth chapter of the Gospel of John does not directly address the eucharist, it does illuminate the correct interpretation of the obscure phrase, "This is my body."

> It is true that Jesus does not speak there of the Supper directly, but His discourse contains a refutation of the literal interpretation of the Words of Institution. If John, chap. 6, does not give an explanation of these words, it at least indicates how *not* to understand them. It furnishes the correct point of view from which to examine them.[23]

Citing verse 63, Zwingli claimed that Christ's real presence was of no value since Christ's flesh would not profit us.

> 'The flesh profiteth nothing' (meaning the flesh as it is eaten, not as it is crucified) is quite enough to prove that Christ's words: 'This is my body,' cannot possibly refer to the literal, carnal flesh. For if the flesh profiteth nothing, then Christ did not give it.[24]

Consequently, any carnal interpretation was misguided since faith alone justifies.

> But Christ tells us that which profits when He says, 'The words which I speak unto you, they are spirit, and they are life.' What words? 'He who eats My flesh and drinks My blood, hath eternal life.' What flesh and what blood? Not the natural flesh or the natural blood, but the flesh and the blood which we know, are the pledges of our

salvation, because they died for us on the Cross. Faith alone justifies. It is then faith in Christ crucified, which Jesus understands by these words, 'words which are spirit and life.' In speaking of the manducation of His body, Christ understands faith in His expiatory death. There can be no question, then, of a corporal manducation. . . .[25]

It was only one short step from the denial of bodily presence to the affirmation of symbolic presence. Since the word *est* cannot be taken literally, it must be taken metaphorically or figuratively. The Bible itself, argued Zwingli, used, and thus permitted, this interpretation when it employs figures of speech called in the Greek *tropos*. For example, the verses "the seed is the Word of God" and "the field is the world" are absurd if understood literally. They make sense only when the word "is" becomes "signifies."[26] Consequently, "This is my body" necessarily changes to "This signifies my body."

Not only were transubstantiation and consubstantiation logically false from a humanist point of view but they were also philosophically false from a nominalist point of view. Cyril C. Richardson in *Zwingli and Cranmer on the Eucharist* comments:

> Were the words, 'This is my body,' to be taken in any literal sense, what would be involved would be a change of *accidents*, not of substance, for what makes a thing a thing is not its participation in a 'substance' (in the sense of an Aristotelian form united with matter), but its 'peculiarities and special properties' (i.e. its Aristotelian 'accidents').[27]

In addition, the nominalist destruction of the foundational relation between universals in the mind and in things, which relegated universals to mere mental constructs, further encouraged Zwingli's separation of the material from the spiritual. Reinforced by both theology and philosophy, Zwingli would not permit faith to be directed at a physical object.

Zwingli's Christology and its impact on his understanding of Christ's eucharistic presence were clearly informed by nominalism. Unlike Luther's full embrace of the ancient doctrine of the *communicatio idiomatum*, Zwingli felt more comfortable with the Christological axiom *finitum non est capax infinit.*[28] This Nestorian tendency to underscore the separation of the two natures enabled Zwingli to refute both transubstantiation and consubstantiation.

In his treatise "On the Lord's Supper," Zwingli argued that the preservation of the gospel was dependent upon a clear distinction between what we apply to Christ's human nature and what we apply to Christ's divine nature.

> If without distinction we were to apply to his human nature everything that refers to the divine, and conversely, if without distinction we were to apply to the divine nature everything that refers to the human,

we should overthrow all Scripture and indeed the whole of our faith.
... the proper character of each nature must be left intact, and we
ought to refer to it only those things which are proper to it.[29]

And what is the proper nature to which the eucharist refers? Zwingli was convinced that the ascension held the key. Understood literally, it indicated that Christ in his human nature had departed this world and is seated at the right hand of God. Therefore, Christ cannot be present in his flesh and blood at the Lord's Supper.

But if Christ is now seated at the right hand of God, and will sit there until he comes at the last day, how can he be literally eaten in the sacrament? You say: He is God. He can be everywhere. But note with what circumspection you say this. First you say: He is God. You give it to be understood that it is the property of God to be everywhere. But it is not the property of the body. I will elucidate. ... Therefore we have conclusive proof that the two sayings: 'Again, I leave the world,' and: 'Me ye have not always,' both refer to the departure and absence of his human nature. But if he has gone away, if he has left the world, if he is no longer with us, then either the Creed is unfaithful to the words of Christ, which is impossible, or else the body and blood of Christ cannot be present in the sacrament. The flesh may fume, but the words of Christ stand firm: he sits at the right hand of the Father, he has left the world, he is no longer present with us. And if these words are true, it is impossible to maintain that his flesh and blood are present in the sacrament.[30]

Transubstantiation and consubstantiation were false, Zwingli declared, because they both violated the distinction of Christ's two natures by positing the human nature of Christ to be in two places at once. Ubiquity was false since Christ is circumscriptively present at the right hand of God.

In conclusion, Zwingli did not dispute Christ's presence in the eucharist. His theological and philosophical perspectives precluded only a substantial presence. Christ's spiritual presence was affirmed. The Lord's Supper functions as both a memorial celebration which reminds participants of the redemption brought by the past death of Christ and a public profession of faith in Christ in the presence of the gathered community of believers.

Luther Against Zwingli

From the beginning, Luther taught that the real presence of the body of Christ was necessary in the eucharist to ensure the forgiveness of sins and salvation.

To say that one takes and receives the forgiveness of sins in this
Sacrament is not speaking incorrectly; for where Christ is, the
forgiveness of sins is. Here are His body and blood according to
His Word. He, then, who receives, eats, and drinks these elements
and believes that the body of Christ was given for him and His blood
was shed for the remission of sins—should he not have the remission
of sins? This is a benefit; indeed, it is the greatest and best one.
We derive it from this testament.[31]

Because the meaning of the Lord's Supper and the promise of forgiveness were
inextricably bound to the Words of Institution which, in turn, were synonymous
with the meaning of the incarnation; the Enthusiasts, e.g., Carlstadt,[32]
Oecolampadius,[33] and Zwingli, who denied the real presence, threatened the gospel
itself. Writing in 1526, Luther went so far as to assert that the inventor of symbolic
theories must be the devil himself since it enabled him to

suck the egg dry and leave us the shell, that is, remove the body and
blood of Christ from the bread and wine, so that it remains no more
than mere bread, such as the baker bakes.[34]

Little wonder Luther was so incensed!

Appealing to the priority of faith over reason and a literal interpretation
of the Words of Institution, Luther developed a Christological justification which
appropriated the idea of "ubiquity" from Occam.

In an effort to expose Zwingli's false correlation of reason and revelation,
Luther claimed that God's wisdom was not only qualitatively superior to human
reason but that God's words uttered by Jesus cannot deceive or lie.[35] When
Christ said "Take, eat; this is my body," it was the solemn responsibility of all
Christians to believe and obey. For if the human mind was permitted to measure
and evaluate God's words at one point, no article of faith would remain. Even
the heart of the gospel, the confession that "man is God," sounded just as foolish
to reason as the declaration that "the bread is the body."

I for one cannot admit that such clear words present a (hermeneutical)
problem. I do not ask how Christ can be God and man, and how his
natures could be united. For God is able to act far beyond our imagination. To the Word of God one must yield. . . . I do not want to hear
what reason says. . . . God is above and beyond all mathematics.[36]

Thus, the clear and precise words of Christ at the table were the sacrament's
own interpretation. Can the Enthusiasts, asked Luther, find where "it is written
in scripture that 'body' means 'sign of the body?'"[37]

To Luther, the words and nothing but the words of Christ were the cause of Christ's real presence. No secondary cause was permissible since the reality of the real presence was independent of the inner attitude of the believer (the Enthusiast position) and the spiritual power of the priest (the Roman Catholic position). Only through the promises of God and the power of Christ's commanded word do we receive his real presence in faith.

> *But I am captured by the Word of God* and cannot find a way out. The words are there, and they are too strong for me. Human words cannot take them out of my soul. Yea, even if it should happen today that someone should prove with strong reasons that only bread and wine are there, it would not be necessary to attack me so furiously. For, according to my old Adam, I am, unfortunately, very much inclined to that view. However, the way Dr. Carlstadt talks wantonly about it does not tempt me at all. On the contrary, it only confirms me in my opinion.[38]

Therefore, the Enthusiasts' interpretation of the Lord's Supper as a meal of remembrance vitiated the sacrament as God's gift of grace. Because an explicit activism was required of the participant, the essential posture of receptivity that characterizes the divine-human relationship was reversed. Instead of Christ lowering himself to us, the worshipers must lift themselves up to Christ by their own powers of remembering the Christ event. Hence, a subtle yet pronounced form of works-righteousness pervaded their interpretation.

The refutation of the Enthusiasts' exegesis of the Words of Institution completed only half of Luther's task. He still had to address the formidable charge that the bodily presence of Christ could not be in more than one place at a time. In order to prove that the ubiquity of the body was conceivable, Luther developed both a Christological and a speculative rationale.

Against Zwingli's attempt to separate Christ's two natures, Luther clung to the "personal union" (*unio personalis*) between the two natures and the communication of properties (*communicatio idiomatum*) by which the human nature shared in all the attributes of the divine. Since the distinction between Christ's humanity and divinity would leave Christ in need of a savior, the elimination of one of the natures of Jesus Christ had the result of destroying the full reality of the inscrutable mystery of the incarnation. For Luther, then, Jesus Christ could only mean the union of the two natures.

> We merge the two distinct natures into one single person, and say: God is man and man is God. We in turn raise a hue and cry against them for separating the person of Christ as though there were two persons.[39]

Luther's insistence upon the inseparable two natures permitted the bold but nonetheless logical inference that Christ's human nature shared the divine attribute of omnipresence. This meant that Christ could be omnipresent in the same manner that God was omnipresent—nonlocally and without extension or dimension in space. Not unlike the role that the non-spatial *substantia* played for Thomas Aquinas and like the role that "repletive existence" played for Occam, Luther employed the concept of divine omnipresence. Different from any previous Christological inference,

> the practical identity of the human and the divine natures in the earthly life of Jesus is deliberately transferred to the state of exaltation.[40]

This notion of transference proved to be a profound contribution to eucharistic theology and provided the second line of proof for the ubiquity of Christ's bodily presence. Contrary to Zwingli's specification that the right hand of God was a literal place where Christ's circumscriptive body dwelt, Luther interpreted the right hand of God to signify the power of God in which Christ shares.

> The right hand of God is not a specific place in which a body must or may be, such as on a golden throne, but is the almighty power of God, which at one and the same time can be nowhere and yet must be everywhere.[41]

Ironically, Zwingli's mixture of literalism and transcendence was compatible in heaven but not in the eucharist, while Luther, at this point, was unencumbered by literalism.

Therefore, the doctrine of the ascension did not nullify real presence. If Zwingli's ascension argument hinged on the idea that the meaning of Christ's dwelling in heaven was that his physical body cannot be present both there and in the bread, since that would mean he would be in two places simultaneously, then Luther thought Zwingli had entrapped himself in his own web of faulty reason. Although Zwingli wanted to affirm Christ's real presence in the bread at the first Lord's Supper, his logic would not permit it. He could not have it both ways! Turning Zwingli against Zwingli, Luther proclaimed:

> If Christ's body can sit at the table and still be in the bread, then it can also be in heaven and anywhere else he wishes and still be in the bread.[42]

Although Luther had advanced a biblical and Christological rationale for Christ's ubiquity and, therefore, Christ's eucharistic presence, he had not

specifically explained the exact mode of Christ's real presence. And he was
reluctant to speculate:

> But how this takes place or how he is in the bread, we do not know
> and are not meant to know.[43]

Aware, however, that he must clarify his position vis-à-vis the Enthusiasts,
Luther cautiously ventured into the realm of philosophy to explain, but not ground,
his belief in Christ's real presence. Returning to the Occamist perspective which
informed his earlier theology, Luther posited three modes of being present in
a given place: locally or circumscriptively, definitively or uncircumscriptively,
and repletively.[44]

In the first mode, local space, one perceives the object or person as being
present in the sense that the subject occupies the exact amount of space that
corresponds to its measure and volume. This mode correlates with the everyday
way in which one views objects in space.

In the second mode, definitive space, one perceives the object or person
as being present not in the sense of occupying the exact amount of space
correlative to its size or volume, but in the sense of having the capacity to occupy
either more or less room. This is the "presence" of angels and spirits, and also
Christ's body when he came out of the grave and walked through the closed door.

Both of these modes of presence pertain to Christ. Before the resurrection
Christ's presence was local presence, and after the resurrection Christ's presence
is definitive presence. It is according to the latter presence, thought Luther,
that Christ "can be and is in the bread."

In the third mode, repletive presence, a viewer perceives the object or person
as being present in the sense that the object is "simultaneously present in all
places whole and entire, and fills all places, yet without being measured or
circumscribed by any place."[45] Incomprehensible to reason, yet accessible
to faith, this final mode is applicable only to God and Christ.

> . . . since he is a man who is supernaturally one person with God,
> and apart from this man there is no God, it must follow that according
> to the third supernatural mode, he is and can be wherever God is
> and that everything is full of Christ through and through, even
> according to his humanity—not according to the first, corporeal,
> circumscribed mode, but according to the supernatural,
> divine mode.[46]

At the most crucial point in Luther's defense of Christ's bodily presence
in the sacrament, it is significant that he relies upon a "philosophical opinion."

The inference is that though Christ's eucharistic presence is a genuine mystery which surpasses the grasp of human reason, it is not intrinsically absurd. Cogency as well as courage of faith characterizes the believer. Either "we must use our reason," observed Luther, "or else give way to the fanatics."[47]

The appropriation of this philosophical scheme enabled Luther to justify Christ's presence in the bread, on the one hand, and to avoid any need for a conversion or transubstantiation theory, on the other hand. Christ's body can be present in the bread in an uncircumscribed manner and the bread can be present in a circumscribed manner. Although Christ is bound up with the elements, he is not, however, limited by them. That is, Luther did not equate real presence with local presence. Christ's body is in heaven as well as in the sacrament, but its presence in the eucharist differs from that of a place. Eucharistic local presence is not the same as an enclosed space and, therefore, Christ remains free and unbound.[48]

This elaborate explanation allowed Luther to escape the charges of crude literalism and of being a flesh-eater. Although he agreed with the Berengarian confession of 1059, his materialistic language obscures a double intentionality.

First, Luther's reliance upon ubiquity negated any correlation of Christ's real presence with Christ's real flesh.

> In plain language, we do not say that Christ's body is present in the Supper in the same form in which he was given for us—who would say that?—but that it is the same body which was given for us, not in the same form or mode but in the same essence and nature.[49]

Furthermore, a carnal eating assumed that only a physical eating could be beneficial. A spiritual partaking was just as important.

> The object is not always spiritual but its use must be spiritual.[50]

> So God arranges that the mouth eats physically for the heart and the heart eats spiritually for the mouth, and thus both are satisfied and saved by one and the same food.[51]

Second, Luther adhered to a bodily participation since the Word became flesh and there is no God apart from the Christ who embodies the two natures. Embodiment is, then, the essential and indispensable key to the incarnation. To say that Christ was in the body meant that he was near and comprehensible to humanity. God intentionally limits God's omnipresence for our benefit. Therefore, the incomprehensible and omnipresent God, who draws near to humanity through the humanity of Jesus Christ, also draws near to us at the Lord's Table through the incomprehensible and uncircumscribed humanity of Jesus Christ.

. . . that God in his essence is present everywhere, in and through the whole creation in all its parts and in all places, and so the world is full of God and he fills it all, yet he is not limited or circumscribed by it, but is at the same time beyond and above the whole creation? All this is an infinitely incomprehensible thing, yet these are articles of our faith, clearly and powerfully attested in the Scriptures. In comparison with this it is a trivial matter that Christ's body and blood are at the same time in heaven and in the Supper.[52]

Conclusion

Our examination of Luther's and Zwingli's interpretations of Christ's eucharistic presence reveals great diversity in Reformation thought. Although they shared an abhorrence for the Roman Catholic doctrine of transubstantiation and they sought to express their mutual affirmation of Christ's presence in the eucharist, their profound differences soon overshadowed their similarities.

Believing that the sacrament was synonymous with the gospel and, thus, a means of grace, and supported by the biblical testimony of Christ that "This is my body," by the Christological doctrine of the *communicatio idiomatum*, and by the philosophical explanation for the ubiquity of bodily presence, Luther insisted that the exalted Christ was truly, really, and invisibly present at the Lord's Table.

Believing that the sacrament was a memorial celebration of God's past act of redemption in Christ, and supported by the preeminence of faith, by the sharp distinction between the sacramental sign and the reality signified, by the figurative interpretation of "This is my body," and by the literal meaning of the ascension, Zwingli insisted that Christ's eucharistic presence was spiritual.

The best illustration of the overall eucharistic agreements as well as the fundamental difference between the Zwinglians and the Lutherans is found in Article 15 of the Marburg Conference of 1529. This last article, which addressed the Lord's Supper, cited their agreements as the reception of the eucharist in both kinds, the rejection of the Mass as a "work," the conception of the eucharist as "the sacrament of the true body and blood of Jesus Christ," and the emphasis on the "spiritual partaking of the same."[53]

However, Article 15 also acknowledged the inability of the two major opponents to agree on real presence.

And although, however, we have not reached an accord at this time as to whether the true body and blood of Christ are physically in the bread and wine, yet each party should show Christian love to the other, so far as the conscience of each can bear it, and both industriously beg Almighty God to confirm to us the right understanding through his Holy Spirit. Amen.[54]

Usually overlooked, both Reformers had serious defects in their respective positions. For Luther, the doctrine of ubiquity said both too much and too little. "Too much, in that it 'proves' the presence of Christ's human nature *everywhere*, not merely in the consecrated elements; too little, in that the *special* and *particular* connexion and presence in and with the eucharistic bread and wine does not follow from it."[55] The unique sacramental presence of Christ was compromised.

Yet, Luther's biblical literalism demanded that the localization of Christ's eucharistic presence be related to the elements. Although he may have escaped the problem of identifying Christ's eucharistic presence with a local presence, he did not avoid the medieval formulation of the problem. Christ's real presence was limited to the elements and thereby precluded other possibilities.

For Zwingli, his strong sense of God's transcendence, combined with his humanistic and nominalistic training, not only prevented *any* relation between Christ's presence and the elements, but also prevented any true sacramental encounter.[56] Instead of occupying a place of prominence, the eucharist was a memorial of Christ's past action. The meal was reduced to a sign bereft of its *res*.

Not surprisingly, these deficiencies in the eucharistic thoughts of Luther and Zwingli led the second generation Reformer, John Calvin, to posit an alternative.

John Calvin

Lawyer and humanist by training, John Calvin authored the great systematic theology of the Reformation, the *Institutes of the Christian Religion*. Though harassed by the Lutheran Joachim Westphal, for the most part Calvin was spared the excessive rhetoric of the earlier polemics on the eucharist. This may be attributed, in part, to Calvin's limited knowledge of the great controversy between Luther[57] and Zwingli.[58] Regardless, his eucharistic writings were more influenced by his contemporary, Martin Bucer,[59] and by the preeminent Western theologian, Augustine of Hippo.[60]

Although scholars have been quick to characterize Calvin's doctrine of the Lord's Supper as a *via media* between Luther and Zwingli, it may be more accurate to say that his role as a mediator results more from his position in the center than from an intentional desire to compromise. Therefore, we would be more faithful to Calvin if we were to begin with his chief theological concerns.

"For Calvin," Kilian McDonnell claims, "theology is not the clarification of a principle but rather the clarification of a mystery which is set forth in a dialogic form, where each pole of the mystery speaks an imperative, which is spoken back by the other pole of the mystery, but in terms of its own absolute."[61] The two voices of the conversation "form the *foci* of an *ellipse*," with each clarifying and refining the other, eventually yielding a unity.

This bipolar methodology is evident in the very first sentence of the *Institutes*.[62] It also structures his entire system. The dual foci of the sovereignty of God and union with Christ constitute the chief theological concerns of Calvin. The centrality of God's sovereignty informs Calvin's critique of Roman Catholic eucharistic practice while the centrality of union with Christ informs his Christological and pneumatological views of the eucharist.

As Calvin surveyed the eucharistic practices of Roman Catholicism in particular and reflected on the proper relationship of the absolute sovereignty of God to secondary causes in general, he was preeminently concerned with protecting God's unconditional freedom. Not surprisingly, he charged Roman Catholicism with reversing the proper order and, therefore, condemned its eucharistic practices as idolatrous.

Calvin cited the divinization of the church and the sacraments as the underlying defect of the Roman religious experience. This corruption resulted, thought Calvin, from an overemphasis on the centrality of union with Christ to the neglect of God's sovereignty. Consequently, the Roman identity between Christ and the church resulted in the divinization of the church. Like other Reformers, Calvin concluded that there was too much church and too little Christ in Roman Catholicism of his day.[63] In short, the bipolar methodology was undermined.

This process of divinization was manifest in both the usurpation of the office of Christ by the priests, who offer the sacramental sacrifice, and the belief that there is no salvation outside the sacraments.

> Hence, any man is deceived who thinks anything more is conferred upon him through the sacraments than what is offered by God's Word and received by him in true faith. From this something else follows: assurance of salvation does not depend upon participation in the sacraments, as if justification consisted in it.[64]

Sacramental imperialism must be opposed since it failed to distinguish "between the sign, which man dispenses, and the grace, which God dispenses."[65] God instituted these signs and, therefore, the sacraments cannot act as autonomous agents. The *signum* and the *res* are never equivalent. It was this identity of the sign and the reality signified that compelled Calvin to label transubstantiation a greater enemy than the sacrifice of the Mass.

Succinctly, Calvin leveled four charges against transubstantiation. First, by elevating the sign to the reality signified, the doctrine of transubstantiation objectivized the divine person and thereby committed blasphemy.

But, whatever words they introduce to disguise it, this is the purpose of them all: through consecration, what was previously bread is made Christ, so that thereupon Christ lies hidden under the appearance of bread. . . . They are little concerned about true faith by which alone we attain fellowship with Christ and cleave to him. Provided they have a physical presence of him, which they have fabricated apart from God's Word, they think that they have presence enough. Briefly, then, we see how through this ingenious subtlety bread came to be taken for God.[66]

It is blasphemy to declare literally of an ephemeral and corruptible element that it is Christ.[67]

Conversely, the transubstantiation of the bread into Christ destroyed the materiality of the bread and the significative function of the sacrament.

The nature of the Sacrament is therefore canceled, unless, in the mode of signifying, the earthly sign corresponds to the heavenly thing. And the truth of this mystery accordingly perishes for us unless true bread represents the true body of Christ. Again I repeat: since the Supper is nothing but a visible witnessing of that promise contained in the sixth chapter of John, namely, that Christ is the bread of life come down from heaven (John 6:51), visible bread must serve as an intermediary to rcprcscnt that spiritual bread—unless we are willing to lose all the benefit which God, to sustain our weakness, confers upon us.[68]

Second, transubstantiation confused the distinction between the presence of Christ in the sacrament and the local presence in the bread.

But greatly mistaken are those who conceive no presence of flesh in the Supper unless it lies in the bread. For thus they leave nothing to the secret working of the Spirit, which unites Christ himself to us. To them Christ does not seem present unless he comes down to us. As though, if he should lift us to himself, we should not just as much enjoy his presence! The question is therefore only of the manner, for they place Christ in the bread, while we do not think it lawful for us to drag him from heaven.[69]

By studying the medieval concept of transubstantiation, Calvin not only avoided the problem of identifying Christ's eucharistic presence with the elements, but he also discovered a new meaning of substance. Instead of associating substance with dimensional space, Calvin related it to power. T. M. Lindsay explains:

The substance of a body consists in its power, active and passive, and the presence of the substance of anything consists in the immediate application of that power. When Luther and Zwingli had spoken of the substance of the body of Christ, they had always in their mind the thought of something extended in space; and the one affirmed while the other denied that this body of Christ, this something extended in space, could be and was present in the Sacrament of the Supper. Calvin's conception of substance enabled him to say that wherever anything *acts*, there it is. He denied the crude 'substantial' presence which Luther insisted upon, and in this he sided with Zwingli. But he affirmed a real, because active presence, and in this, he sided with Luther.[70]

Third, Calvin believed that transubstantiation opposed scriptural evidence.

Therefore, to relieve ourselves of the undeserved obloquy that they lay upon us, it will be most appropriate to begin with the interpretation of (Christ's) words. . . .

The defenders of transubstantiation would have the pronoun 'this' refer to form of bread, because the consecration is effected by the whole content of the utterance, and there is no substance that can be pointed to. Yet if they must be so scrupulous about words, because Christ testified that what he handed to his disciples was his body, obviously this fiction of theirs is utterly foreign to the proper meaning—that what was bread is now body. What Christ took into his hands and gave to the apostles he declares to be his body; but he had taken bread—who, therefore, cannot understand that bread is still shown? And, accordingly, that there is nothing more absurd than to transfer to the form what is predicated of the bread?

Others, in interpreting the particle *est* as meaning 'to be transubstantiated,' take refuge in a more forced and violently distorted gloss. There is therefore no reason why they should pretend to be moved by reverence for words. For it is something unheard of in all nations and languages that the word *est* should be taken to mean 'to be converted into something else.'[71]

Fourth, transubstantiation was contrary to the faith of the ancient church.

But it is wonderful how they fell to such a point of ignorance, even of folly, that, despising not only Scripture but even the consensus of the ancient church, they unveiled that monster.

Indeed, I admit that some of the old writers used the term 'conversion' sometimes, not because they intended to wipe out the substance in the outward sign, but to teach that the bread dedicated to the mystery is far different from common bread, and is now something else. But they all everywhere clearly proclaim that the Sacred Supper consists of two parts, the earthly and the heavenly; and they interpret the earthly part to be indisputably bread and wine.

Surely, whatever our opponents may prate, it is plain that to confirm this doctrine they lack the support of antiquity, which they often dare oppose to God's clear Word. For transubstantiation was devised not so long ago; indeed, not only was it unknown to those better ages when the purer doctrine of religion still flourished, but even when that purity already was somewhat corrupted. There is no one of the ancient writers who does not admit in clear words that the sacred symbols of the Supper are bread and wine, even though, as has been said, they sometimes distinguish them with various titles to enhance the dignity of the mystery.[72]

Grounded in the conviction that "God himself is the sole and proper witness of himself,"[73] Calvin rejected any and all efforts of the church to divinize itself and its sacraments. Furthermore, the doctrine of the ascension assured us that Christ can be found only in heaven and that the *Sursum corda* was the proper manner of adoration. According to the latter, wrote Calvin, "we ought rather to have adored him spiritually in heavenly glory than to have devised some dangerous kind of adoration, replete with a carnal and crass conception of God."[74] What Calvin deemed the ritual Pelagianism of Catholicism, as particularly practiced in the eucharist, must yield to the sovereign God who alone can redeem us.[75]

Most scholars agree that the theme of union with Christ constitutes one of the centralities of Calvin's theology. That Christ became flesh for our redemption and that we, in turn, should be engrafted into his body comprises the heart of the gospel message.

Therefore, that joining together of Head and members, that indwelling of Christ in our hearts—in short, that mystical union—are accorded by us the highest degree of importance, so that Christ, having been made ours, makes us sharers with him in the gifts with which he has been endowed. We do not, therefore, contemplate him outside ourselves from afar in order that his righteousness may be imputed to us but because we put on Christ and are engrafted into his body—in short, because he deigns to make us one with him. For this reason, we glory that we have fellowship of righteousness with him.[76]

Since our union with Christ has its roots in election, and faith, which results from the work of the Holy Spirit, depends on election, the precise relationship of faith to union with Christ is crucial. Although Calvin made it clear that faith was not the same as union with Christ, it was the mode of union and, consequently, they occurred in one and the same act.[77]

This understanding has ramifications for both the content and the function of the eucharist. Because Christ comes to us, seeks us, and elects us by the Word, the union, for which the eucharist is a pledge, *already* exists. For Calvin, "there is no specific eucharistic gift, no object, person, effect, or grace given in the Eucharist which is not given in faith outside of the Eucharist."[78] The eucharist is not, then, the cause of our union with Christ.

Yet, the eucharist, with no unique content, has a specific function. It interprets "more precisely and more concretely that union we have with Christ, a union not just with the Godhead of Christ, but rather a union with him who took our flesh, a flesh that is now the instrument of eternal life."[79] Calvin explained:

> From this also these things follow: that his flesh is truly food, and his blood truly drink . . . and by these foods believers are nourished unto eternal life. It is therefore a special comfort for the godly that they now find life in their own flesh. For thus not only do they reach it by an easy approach, but they have it spontaneously presented and laid out before them. Let them but open the bosom of their heart to embrace its presence, and they will obtain it.[80]

Calvin countered what he perceived as the Roman divinization of ecclesiasticism and sacramentalism by constructing his theology of the church upon the foundation of union with Christ and upon the secondary supports of Christology and pneumatology. This last and interior norm assured that the sovereign God initiated the call to community. Neither the enjoyment of fellowship nor even the perceived need for repentance accounts for the church. Rather, Christ, as the Son of God, gathers his members into his body through the work of the Holy Spirit.

> But all the elect are so united in Christ (Eph. 1:22-23) that as they are dependent on one Head, they also grow together into one body, being joined and knit together (Eph. 4:16) as are the limbs of a body (Rom. 12:5; I Cor. 10:17; 12:12, 27). They are made truly one since they live together in one faith, hope, and love, and in the same Spirit of God.[81]

This inwardness, which reached its zenith in union with Christ and relied upon the agency of Christ and the Holy Spirit, was repeated in Calvin's eucharistic doctrine. Most important, the eucharist was possible only in view of a preceding and present union with Christ. Because grafting into Christ was at the same time a grafting into the body of the church, the two were inseparable.[82] The eucharist constituted a visible expression and pledge of our union with Christ through faith. Consequently, Calvin abhored the private character of the Roman Mass and insisted upon its ecclesial character.

Christology and pneumatology played significant roles in Calvin's eucharistic theology because they counteracted sacramental imperialism and efforts to compromise God's sovereignty. By insisting, on the one hand, that justification rested solely on Christ,[83] Calvin located the meaning of the eucharist in the promises that stand behind the sacrament.

> It is not, therefore, the chief function of the Sacrament simply and without higher consciousness to extend to us the body of Christ. Rather, it is to seal and confirm that promise by which he testifies that his flesh is food indeed and his blood is drink, which feed us unto eternal life.[84]

Since the sacrament added nothing to the promises, Calvin was freed from focusing exclusively on the body and blood of Christ.

By insisting, on the other hand, that the Holy Spirit effected this union, Calvin guarded against sacramental immanence. Neither God's transcendence nor union with Christ can dominate the other. The *opposita* between the two foci of distance and union was maintained.[85]

We now turn to a fuller treatment of how Christology and pneumatology informed Calvin's doctrine of Christ's eucharistic presence.

By redefining the concept of substance, Calvin not only avoided the medieval entrapment of restricting the mode of Christ's eucharistic presence to the elements, but he also interpreted the meaning of the eucharist as a Christological concern. This broader Christological context reshaped the issue of real presence.

> But we must establish such a presence of Christ in the Supper as may neither fasten him to the element of bread, nor enclose him in bread, nor circumscribe him in any way (all which things, it is clear, detract from his heavenly glory); finally, such as may not take from him his own stature, or parcel him out to many places at once, or invest him with boundless magnitude to be spread through heaven and earth. For these things are plainly in conflict with a nature truly human. Let us never (I say) allow these two limitations to be taken away from us: (1) Let nothing be withdrawn from Christ's heavenly

glory—as happens when he is brought under the corruptible elements of this world, or bound to any earthly creatures. (2) Let nothing inappropriate to human nature be ascribed to his body, as happens when it is said either to be infinite or to be put in a number of places at once.[86]

Calvin reformulated the mode of Christ's eucharistic presence in order to preserve the integrity of Christ's humanity. Consequently, Calvin's disagreements with both the Roman Catholic and the Lutheran positions rested on soteriological grounds. To deny the risen corporeality of Jesus, as the doctrines of transubstantiation and ubiquity did, vitiated for Calvin the hope of the resurrection of the body. In addition, these explanations reeked of a Marcionism which turned the Mediator into some kind of intermediate freak.[87] Both doctrines must be rejected since they endangered the integrity of Christ's humanity and thereby endangered our salvation.

Contrary to Luther's Christological emphasis on the unity of the person of Christ and the communication of properties, Calvin stressed the immutability and incommunicability of Christ's divinity.[88] The exchange of the properties applied only to the office of Christ as the Mediator and not to the ontological union of the two natures.[89] Calvin's stress on the dialectics of the divine and the human natures rather than on their union suggests a Nestorian tendency within an orthodox framework.[90]

Because of his Christological presuppositions, the doctrine of Christ's real presence in the eucharist was never an issue. In a letter to Bullinger, Calvin wrote:

> Although the flesh of Christ is in heaven. . . . I see no absurdity in saying that we truly and in all reality receive the flesh and blood of Christ, and that he is thus substantially our food so long as it is admitted that Christ comes down to us not only by means of external symbols but also by the secret workings of his Spirit, so that we through faith may rise up to him.[91]

He was equally adamant in the *Institutes*.

> But when these absurdities have been set aside, I freely accept whatever can be made to express the true and substantial partaking of the body and blood of the Lord, which is shown to believers under the sacred symbols of the Supper—and so to express it that they may be understood not to receive it solely by imagination or understanding of mind, but to enjoy the thing itself as nourishment of eternal life.[92]

Since the concept of Christ's real presence lay at the heart of Calvin's theological system and eucharistic thoughts, the next logical question concerned the manner of that presence. For Calvin, Christ was present in a threefold way. Christ was present to the believer through faith, through the agency of the Holy Spirit, and through the Word. All three vehicles of Christ's presence were necessary and inseparable in order to ensure the mystery of faith and the sovereignty of God.[93]

How then do the sacraments fit into this threefold structure? Borrowing from Augustine, Calvin described a sacrament as a "visible word."[94] With identical content as the proclamation, sacraments present a pictorial manifestation of the Word. It was, therefore, an egregious error to attribute any unique status or power to a sacrament. Like the preached Word, a sacrament conveyed the promises of faith.

> Hence, any man is deceived who thinks anything more is conferred upon him through the sacraments than what is offered by God's Word and received by him in true faith.[95]

Conveying no more nor no less than the Word, the sacrament of the eucharist constituted a vehicle of Christ's self-communication, of Christ's real presence.[96] Thus, the eucharist not only instructed by means of graphic symbols but it also functioned as a means of grace since the thing signified was communicated.

As Calvin surveyed the eucharistic controversy, the critical issue was not real presence but the mode of that presence. And he distinguished himself from the materialistic interpretation of the Catholics and Lutherans, and the bare symbolic interpretation of the Enthusiasts and Zwingli, by relying on a doctrine of sacramental signs borrowed from Augustine.

Reflecting his Christological presupposition of "distinction without division," Calvin differentiated but did not separate the *signum* from the *res*. Where the sign is, there also is the reality. Since Christ is the content of that reality—the "substance" of the sacraments—the sign acts as a vehicle for the manifestation of Christ's presence to his people. In short, "the sign cannot be or become the reality, but it is not the symbol of an absent reality either."[97]

Against the materialistic interpretation, which equated the sign and the reality signified, Calvin charged that the real presence had been denied since the proper dialectic tension between the sign and the thing signified had been destroyed. By elevating the sign to the reality, the Romans and Lutherans reduced the sign, i.e., the bread, to its shadow or its accident. Hence, the sacrament was incapable of effecting its reality. The destruction of the sign, and consequently its significative function, resulted in a corresponding destruction of the reality of the sacrament.[98]

Against the bare symbolic interpretation, which separated absolutely the sign and the reality signified, Calvin charged that the real presence had again been denied since the proper dialectic tension between the sign and the thing signified had been destroyed in the opposite manner. By overemphasizing the mnemonic role of the sign, the Zwinglians relied on personal faith for Christ's eucharistic presence. Hence, the sacrament was never granted its significative function and consequently emptied of its content.[99]

The integrity of the sacrament can be preserved only when sacraments are understood both to "cause and communicate (*apporter et communiquer*) what they signify."[100] Calvin wrote:

> And the godly ought by all means to keep this rule: whenever they see symbols appointed by the Lord, to think and be persuaded that the truth of the thing signified is surely present there. For why should the Lord put in your hand the symbol of his body, except to assure you of a true participation in it? But if it is true that a visible sign is given us to seal the gift of a thing invisible, when we have received the symbol of the body, let us no less surely trust that the body itself is also given to us.[101]

Calvin's interpretation, which affirmed that the benefits of Christ were given as well as signified, resembled at this foundational level Luther's doctrine more than Zwingli's.

Yet, Calvin sided with Zwingli against any notion of local presence. Attested by the doctrine of the ascension, Christ's body was contained in heaven.

> For as we do not doubt that Christ's body is limited by the general characteristics common to all human bodies, and is contained in heaven (where it was once for all received) until Christ return in judgment [Acts 3:21], so we deem it utterly unlawful to draw it back under these corruptible elements or to imagine it to be present everywhere.[102]

Therefore, any physical descent of the body of Christ would require that Christ be without measure or be in different places. Either way, Christ was reduced to a phantom and our salvation jeopardized.

Calvin's soteriological rejection of local presence hinged upon his two overarching theological presuppositions. On the one hand, any descent of Christ's physical body violated the sovereignty of God, since it placed the body of Christ at the disposal of humanity. On the other hand, any descent of Christ's physical body violated the union with Christ, since it implied a docetic view of his humanity.[103]

Like Zwingli, Calvin interpreted the debated phrase, the "right hand of God," as an injunction against local presence. Unlike Zwingli, Calvin was not content with the results of his negative critique. A bare symbolism could not effect union with Christ. In spite of the spatial separation between Christ in heaven and believers on earth, a real union must be possible. It was one of Calvin's greatest contributions to eucharistic theology that he believed that the circumscription of the glorified body of Christ in heaven did not exclude real union.[104]

Motivated both by his repulsion by the Roman and Lutheran doctrines in which the elements contained and gave the body of Christ and by his insistence upon the union between Christ and believers, Calvin introduced a new direction into Western Protestant sacramental theology. Instead of following the Western tradition of focusing on the Words of Institution, Calvin reappropriated the insights of the patristic and Eastern traditions by retrieving their emphasis on the *epiclesis* of the Spirit.[105]   Correcting Luther's Christomonism, which ascribed to the human nature of Christ the attribute of omnipresence (which properly belongs only to God), Calvin's eucharistic theology sought a broader trinitarian base. The *Institutes* clearly stated this intent.

> We must now examine this question. How do we receive those benefits which the Father bestowed on his only-begotten Son(?) . . . Therefore, to share with us what he has received from the Father, he had to become ours and to dwell within us. . . . reason itself teaches us to climb higher and to examine into the secret energy of the Spirit, by which we come to enjoy Christ and all his benefits. . . .

> . . . until our minds become intent upon the Spirit, Christ, so to speak, lies idle because we coldly contemplate him as outside ourselves. . . . But he unites himself to us by the Spirit alone. By the grace and power of the same Spirit we are made his members, to keep us under himself and in turn to possess him.[106]

In lieu of an extension of the humanity of Christ, Calvin proposed the "uniting and unifying activity and energy" of the Holy Spirit and thereby avoided what he deemed the false objectivism of Luther and the false subjectivism of Zwingli.[107]

Through the power of the Holy Spirit, the Christ, who has ascended into heaven, is made available on earth in the giving of the eucharistic elements. Functioning as two foci of an ellipse, the ascension of Christ and the coming of the Holy Spirit are antithetically yet dialectically related.[108] Calvin declared:

> Surely, the coming of the Spirit and the ascent of Christ are antithetical; consequently, Christ cannot dwell with us according to the flesh in the same way that he sends his Spirit.[109]

Dissatisfied with the spiritualizing of our communion with Christ, Calvin's linkage of the doctrine of the ascension with the work of the Holy Spirit secured a real, but, nonetheless, spiritual presence. The specific gift of the eucharist was the body of Christ.[110]

Therefore, Calvin utilized realistic terminology such as "truly," "really," "substantially," "essentially," and "bodily," although the philosophical notions that accompanied the Roman or Lutheran use of these terms were rejected. Christ's eucharistic presence was spiritual, since his presence was effected by the Holy Spirit.

Union with the body of Christ was achieved through the descent of the Holy Spirit and the ascent of our souls to heaven. Although Christ was spatially absent, the Spirit bridged the infinite separation and effected communion with the body and blood of Christ. This secret power (*virtus*) of the Spirit, though incomprehensible to human reason, accounted for Calvin's doctrine of "virtualism."

By reclaiming the *epiclesis*, Calvin affirmed sacramental realism while steering a middle course between the docetic and material tendencies of Luther and the subjective tendency of Zwingli. Yet, his pneumatology was not without problems. Although it is unfair to label Calvin's doctrine "the real presence of the Holy Spirit," it is not unfair to label Calvin's employment of the Holy Spirit as a kind of *deus ex machina*.[111] The personal concept of the Holy Spirit resembles an instrumental category or conduit that bridges the infinite gap between Christ and the communicant.[112]

Conclusion

Calvin's theological method, with its dual foci of the sovereignty of God and union with Christ, produced the most systematic and seminal Reformation statement on Christ's eucharistic presence. By accenting God's unconditional freedom and by affirming that the Lord's Supper is a gift, Calvin opposed both the works-righteousness and the imperialism of the Roman Mass as well as the "thankful recollection" of Zwingli's position. The former forgot that it is God who gives and we who receive, while the latter forgot that the Supper is the actual gift of Christ and not only a reminder.

By stressing our union with Christ and the secondary roles of Christology and pneumatology, Calvin declared that the gift is the whole Christ and that the gift is given by the Holy Spirit.

> When, therefore, we speak of the communion which believers have with Christ, we mean that they communicate with his flesh and blood not less than with his Spirit, so as to possess thus the whole Christ.[113]

Enclosed in neither the elements of bread and wine nor the believers' imagination, the Holy Spirit grants the "spiritual presence" of Christ.

> For us the manner is spiritual because the secret power of the Spirit
> is the bond of our union with Christ.[114]

Although Calvin's terminology and formulations resemble Zwingli more than
Luther, the heart of his eucharistic doctrine reflects Luther's dual concern for the
preservation of the sacrament as a gift and the protection of the real presence.
Yet, the content and mode of that presence were different. On the one hand, Luther,
like the Romans, believed that the substantive body and blood of Christ were brought
down from heaven and received with, in, and under the outward sign of bread and
wine. What is communicated to the Christian in the eucharist is a *res animata* (an
animated thing) and, therefore, we do not need to be raised up to heaven to find
Christ.[115] On the other hand, Calvin believed that the glorified body of Christ
remained in heaven and that the Holy Spirit raised the soul of the believer to heaven.
What is communicated to the Christian in the Lord's Supper is an *agens liberum*
(a freely-acting agent) that concerns the spiritual life and, therefore, can neither
be distributed with the eucharistic elements nor partaken by the mouth.[116] This
distinction between the substance of the body and blood of Christ, and the life-giving
power that proceeds from it, constitutes the fundamental difference between the
eucharistic views of Luther and Calvin.

Although Calvin agreed with Zwingli's rejection of Luther's "monstrous"
doctrine of ubiquity, he disagreed with Zwingli's declaration that the eucharist
is merely a sign of Christ's past redeeming act on behalf of humanity. For Calvin,
the sacrament consisted of a sign that conveyed a reality–the real presence of
Christ. Hence, Zwingli's reductions of the sacrament to an expression of faith
and of the bread to a "mere sign" destroyed the true nature of a sacrament.
If Zwingli had discovered the sacramental agency of the Holy Spirit, he might
have realized that the sacrament was a sign of God's promise and, therefore,
was given to awaken and strengthen faith.

Succinctly, Calvin believed that both Luther and Zwingli undermined real
presence. By concentrating exclusively on the reality of Christ's substantive
body and blood, Luther turned the eucharistic elements into shadows and thereby
thwarted their significative function. By concentrating exclusively on the mnemonic
role of the eucharistic signs, Zwingli divorced the sign from the thing signified
and thereby thwarted the reality of the sacrament. Both reduced the dialectic
tension in the sacrament between the sign and the reality signified and, therefore,
undermined the mystery of Christ's real presence.

The Catholic Reformation and the Council of Trent

Intended as the answering movement within the Roman Catholic Church
to the Protestant Reformation, the Catholic Reformation brought needed reform

and renewal within the Roman Catholic Church. In retrospect, however, antipathies prevailed. Forged in the fires of conflict, the official pronouncements of the Council of Trent, which was opened by Pope Paul III on December 13, 1545, and continued with extended interruptions till December 4, 1563, evidenced the marks of opposition. This was particularly true of the eucharistic teachings of Trent. Informed by the views of the medieval church, the eucharistic doctrine of Trent can be described as an apologetic against the varied Reformation eucharistic theologies and the "conclusion and climax of the medieval development."[117]

The eucharistic teachings of Trent revolved around two concerns. One pertained to the reality of Christ's presence while the other related to the mode of Christ's presence.

In positive terms, Trent affirmed the real presence of Christ by making the same distinction that Thomas Aquinas and others had earlier noted between the "natural" presence of Christ at the right hand of God and his real but sacramental presence upon the altar. The chapter, "On the Real Presence of our Lord Jesus Christ in the most holy Sacrament of the Eucharist," began:

> In the first place, this holy Synod teaches and openly and simply professes, that in the bountiful sacrament of the holy Eucharist after the consecration of the bread and wine, our Lord Jesus Christ, true God and true man, is truly, really, and substantially contained under the *species* of those things which the senses perceive. Nor is there any contradiction between these things, that the Saviour himself sits always at the right hand of the Father in heaven according to his natural mode of existence, and that he should nonetheless also be present sacramentally in his own substance in other places by that mode of existence which, although we can scarcely express it in words, we can conclude is possible for God, and ought most constantly to believe.[118]

In negative terms, Trent's affirmation of Christ's "true, real, and substantial" presence meant an absolute intolerance for alternative proposals.

> If any one shall deny that in the most holy Sacrament of the Eucharist is contained really and actually and substantially the body and blood together with the soul and Godhead of our Lord Jesus Christ, and therefore the whole Christ, but shall say that He is in it only as in a sign or a figure or in power, let him be anathema.[119]

Specifically, the Council of Trent and the subsequent *Catechism* rejected Zwingli's denial of real presence, Bucer's and Calvin's affirmation of spiritual presence and denial of substantial presence in the consecrated elements, and Luther's assertion that the bread and wine remain after consecration.[120]

Also important for the Roman doctrine of Christ's real presence was the declaration of concomitance. Trent declared:

> ... the body indeed under the form of bread and the blood under the form of wine, by the force of words; but the body itself under the species of wine and the blood under the species of bread and the soul under both, by the force of that natural connexion and concomitancy whereby the parts of Christ, our Lord, who hath now risen from the dead to die no more, are united together; and the divinity furthermore on account of the admirable hypostatic union whereof with His body and soul. Wherefore it is most true, that as much is contained under either species as under both.[121]

By affirming the whole Christ under each element, Trent justified the continued practice of withholding the cup from the laity and the continued rejection of the demands of John Hus, condemned at the Council of Constance (1415), and other Reformers who sought to reinstate the cup.

> If anyone says that, by the precept of God, or by necessity of salvation, all and each of the faithful of Christ ought to receive both species of the most holy sacrament of the Eucharist: let him be anathema.[122]

The second focus of Trent's eucharistic doctrine addressed the mode of Christ's presence. Relying on Thomas Aquinas' formulation of the theory of transubstantiation, the Council stated in positive terms:

> Since Christ our Redeemer declared that to be truly his body which he offered under the *species* of bread, this has always been believed in the church of God; and this holy Synod now affirms it afresh: through the consecration of the bread and wine there takes place a conversion of the whole substance of the bread into the substance of the body of Christ our Lord, and of the whole substance of the wine into the substance of his blood. This change is suitably and properly called transubstantiation by the holy catholic church.[123]

In negative terms, Trent rejected Luther's theory of copresence as well as other theories that asserted the substantial remains of bread and wine after consecration.

> If any one shall say that in the most holy Sacrament of the Eucharist the substance of the bread and wine remains together with the body

and blood of our Lord Jesus Christ, and shall deny that wonderful and unique conversion of the whole substance of the bread into the body and of the whole substance of the wine into the blood, the species of bread and wine only remaining, which conversion the Catholic Church most suitably calls transubstantiation, let him be anathema.[124]

Unequivocally, Trent affirmed the doctrine of Christ's real presence in the eucharist and the doctrine of transubstantiation. However, it is less certain whether the Council intended to identify the doctrines as two equivalent affirmations. That is, did Trent understand the doctrine of transubstantiation to be an essential dogma without which the certitude of real presence was denied? Obviously, the Council had little choice but to appropriate the contemporary philosophical framework that would secure its purpose. But did Trent intend to canonize this single formulation for subsequent centuries? For the most part, orthodox Roman Catholic theology until the Second Vatican Council has answered in the affirmative.

In conclusion, transubstantiation is the medieval answer to the specific question of how Christ is present under the elements of bread and wine. The doctrine of transubstantiation as expounded by Thomas Aquinas constitutes, therefore, the Roman Catholic theological explanation of the mode of Christ's real presence in the eucharist. The primary question, which we moderns must ask, is not whether this is an adequate formulation of the mystery of sacramental presence. Rather, the more fundamental question is whether this is the proper question! That is, should the mode of Christ's eucharistic presence be exclusively tied to the elements? It is our thesis that the medieval formulation of the problem is too restrictive because it precludes the communal context.

We now turn to the Protestant Reformation's treatment of our three requisite features and the rediscovery of the ecclesial component of eucharistic worship.

The Three Requisite Features

Connection of Ritual and Material Elements

A pivotal issue for the Reformers concerned the proper relationship between Christ's eucharistic presence and the consecrated elements. The Council of Trent, reflecting the medieval sacramental system, insisted that Christ's substantial presence was essentially connected to the consecrated elements. The Reformers were less certain that it was, and offered varied replies.

On one extreme, Luther, the most Catholic of the Reformers, followed the medieval sacramental tradition. Although he rejected the theory of transubstantiation as an essential doctrine, he, nevertheless, tied Christ's eucharistic presence to the consecrated elements. Any variance meant a denial of the real presence. Although his doctrine of ubiquity prohibited a corporeal interpretation, Luther's inability to escape the medieval formulation of the problem resulted in dogmatic interpretations in subsequent Lutheran theology—especially Westphal.

On the other extreme, Zwingli's adherence to the biblical admonition that "the flesh profit nothing" and to the literal interpretation of the ascension required a complete denial of the medieval statement of the problem. Since Christ's risen body resides in heaven and Christ's spiritual presence is available only through faith, the elements do not share in the divine. Furthermore, Zwingli's stress on the transcendence of God, and the corresponding division between the spiritual and the material, underscored the inability of a sensible instrument or channel to mediate divine presence. As a result, the substantial presence of Christ was irrelevant to Christian faith and the consecrated elements were unrelated to Christ's spiritual presence, except to act as external reminders.

Calvin adopted a middle position. Like Luther, Calvin believed that the communicant can participate in the substance of the body of Christ. Yet, his redefinition of substance as a power differed from both the Catholic and Lutheran interpretations. Like Zwingli, Calvin rejected the principle "that the consecrated elements bear an essential relation to this substance."[125] Any fixation upon the elements, he reasoned, diverted believers' minds from heaven and prevented their hearts from being lifted up.

Although the Protestant Reformers challenged the medieval formulation of the mode of Christ's eucharistic presence, they failed to advance a consensus replacement for it. Consequently, the dominant models for conveying Christ's eucharistic presence still relied on the consecrated elements.

Past-Future Dialectic

Neither the Protestant Reformation nor the Catholic Reformation challenged the medieval tendency to sever the past-future dialectic. Alasdair Heron laments:

> Consequently the decisive, once-for-all character of Jesus Christ himself was chiefly seen as the once-for-allness of a *past* event, from which the onward march of time carried us ever further away, rather than of *the event* in the past in which the mystery of *our future* is *already* broken open.[126]

Instead of asking how the past and the future correlated, the sixteenth century asked how the present related to this past redemptive event. Two predominant alternatives surfaced.[127] Either the past was made available to the present through the *mental* act of remembrance or, if the entrance into the past was to have any objective reality outside the mind, through the *repetition* of Christ's redeeming act.

Relying on the late medieval notion of a new accessing of the merits of Christ's sacrifice, the Roman Catholic Church chose the latter route. Unfortunately, in popular piety it was often difficult to escape the idea that the priest sacrificed Christ afresh at every Mass.

Denying the real sacrifice of the Mass, many Protestant Reformation theologians chose the former route. Consequently, the rite of the eucharist was valued as a memorial which acted as a visible reminder of what Christ had done in the past and as a visible stimulus to renew believers' allegiance and gratitude to the Lord in the present. More important, the eucharistic action was transferred for the Reformers from the priest to the individual. The real eucharistic action took place in the isolation of the communicant's mind. Thus, there was little need for the priest to act on behalf of the ecclesial body or for the consecrated elements, except to act as stimuli. Individual meditation eclipsed any need for corporate eucharistic action.

In short, "the practical restriction of the significance of the eucharist to the passion, as the historical element in the redeeming act, seen apart from its supra-historical elements in the resurrection, ascension and eternal priesthood"[128] forced these two incompatible alternatives upon the Roman Catholic and Reformation traditions. Neither party, with the exception of Calvin, could reappropriate the role of eschatology.

Because the loss of the eschatological dimension in medieval and Reformation eucharistic theologies may be attributed in part to the unavailability of early Christianity's eucharistic texts, Calvin's emphasis on the future is all the more significant. His eschatological instinct arose from his primary concern for the union of believers with Christ. Hence, both the ascension and the second coming played prominent roles in Calvin's sacramental theology.

Acting as a point of reference which points backward to the resurrection and forward to the parousia, the ascension occupied a central place in Calvin's theology.[129] By introducing a spatial element, the ascension nullified the corporeal presence of Christ under the elements, since Christ is in heaven. This denial of local presence recovered the eschatological emphasis and refocused this dimension onto a dual moment: a vertical and upward emphasis on the *Sursum corda* and a horizontal and forward emphasis upon the expectation of the parousia. Most important, the full mystery of our union with Christ is not complete until the vertical raising up of our hearts moves forward with Christ's history. The vertical movement of the *Sursum corda* offers the first fruits of our union with Christ but it can be fulfilled only in the consummation at the end of history. Thus, the tension between the spatial and eschatological dimensions is ultimately resolved by subsuming the spatial imperative under the eschatological imperative. Calvin expressed the tension in this way:

> Let us raise our hearts and minds on high where Jesus Christ is in
> the glory of his Father, and from which we look for him at our
> redemption.[130]

In conclusion, Calvin, unlike his Reformation colleagues, opened up the eucharist to a broader temporal framework. Eucharistic theology must encompass not only the past redemptive event, but it must also incorporate the Christ who stands before us and the Christ who breaks into our present. By stressing the active work of the risen Christ and by recapturing the eschatological dimension, Calvin moved beyond the prevailing twofold option of mental act or repetition.

Presence-Absence Dialectic

Preoccupied with the consecrated elements and the retrieval of the past redemptive act, the medieval sacramental system was enthralled with Christ's local presence to the virtual exclusion of Christ's absence. This legacy was continued in Catholic Reformation theology, but the Reformers offered varied alternatives.

Not surprisingly, Luther, who accepted the medieval formulation of the doctrine of Christ's real presence, was also preoccupied with Christ's eucharistic local presence. Although he acknowledged that Christ's body is in heaven as well as in the sacrament, Luther neglected the theme of Christ's absence.

Zwingli, however, rejected both the medieval formulation of the doctrine and Christ's local presence. Yet, his conception of the Lord's Supper as a memorial forced him to stress the present attitude of the gathered community—both individually and collectively. Individually, each communicant made present the past redemptive act of Christ via memory while, collectively, the church expressed its thanksgiving in the present for God's past acts in Christ. This notion of presence was, nevertheless, counterbalanced by Zwingli's stress on the ascension. Christ's body is literally in heaven and is, therefore, absent from the table. The reality of absence precluded any notion of local presence.

At this point, Calvin resembles Zwingli since his eucharistic theology was intended to safeguard the reality of the ascension and the true heavenly glory of Christ. The Holy Spirit assumed importance for Calvin because it substituted for Christ's presence and supplied "the defect of His absence." Thus, the eucharist conveyed both the presence of Christ and the absence of Christ.[131] Christ is present to the degree that the sacramental sign signifies the sacramental reality and Christ is absent to the degree that Christ's material body is in heaven. We have Christ, according to Calvin, in analogy to his incarnation.

> According to the presence of his majesty, we have Christ always;
> but according to the presence of the flesh, it is rightly said, 'You

will not always have me' (Matt. 26:11). For the church had him
according to the presence of the flesh for only a few days; now it
holds him by faith, but does not see him with the eyes.[132]

Unlike the other requisite features, the Reformers, with the exception of
Luther, acknowledged to some degree the presence-absence dialectic. Luther,
along with the Roman Catholic tradition, was too preoccupied with Christ's
local presence to incorporate Christ's absence into his eucharistic theology.

The Communal Context

Our examination in chapters three and four has shown that no aspect of
the Mass of the Middle Ages had been so neglected as the corporate nature
of worship. Governed by the doctrine of transubstantiation, the eucharistic
celebration focused exclusively on the consecrated elements. It was not that
the doctrine of the real presence under the elements said too much. On the
contrary, it said too little. Determined to protect the objectivity of the "Divine
operation" in the sacrament, the Roman Catholic formulation narrowed the
field of vision. Consequently, other modes of presence, particularly ecclesial
presence, were overlooked.[133]

As a result, the meal character of the eucharist was no longer discernible.
The congregational action shifted to the celebrant alone. In lieu of communal
participation at the table, only the priest partook and even then his back was
turned to the congregation. Furthermore, the metaphor of table was replaced
by the metaphor of tomb. Worshipers could barely hear or understand the
Latin words of the priest as they waited for the climactic moment of elevation.
Participation was reduced to visual contact. William D. Maxwell summarized
the loss of corporate worship in the Western rite in his previously quoted words:

> ... at the beginning of the sixteenth century, the celebration of the
> Lord's Supper in the Western Church had become a dramatic
> spectacle, culminating not in communion but in the miracle of
> transubstantiation, and marked by adoration, not unmixed with
> superstition, at the elevation. Said inaudibly in an unknown tongue,
> and surrounded with ornate ceremonial and, if a sung mass, with
> elaborate musical accompaniment, the rite presented only meager
> opportunity for popular participation.[134]

One of the truly positive and constructive Protestant contributions to Western
theology and liturgy was the rediscovery of the communal theme. This motif
was evident in both the Reformers' theologies and their eucharistic celebrations.

Regrettably, their emphasis on the corporate nature of worship receded and was never fully reappropriated by future generations.

Before 1520, Luther's writings on the eucharist were homiletic and non-controversial and, more important, contained positive statements on the meaning of the Lord's Supper as incorporation into the fellowship of the saints. In his sermon, *De digna praeparatione cordis pro suscipiendo sacramento eucharistiae*, he grounded this communal theme in the Augustinian distinction between *signum* and *res*.

> . . . therefore it is commonly called *Synaxis* or *Communio*, that is, fellowship; and the Latin *communicare* means to receive this fellowship, where we speak in German of 'going to the sacrament'; and the point is this: That Christ with all his saints is one spiritual body, just as the people in a city are a community and a body, and every citizen is related as a member to his neighbour and to the city. So are all saints members in Christ and in the church, which is a spiritual, eternal City of God; and when one is received into this City, he is said to be received into the fellowship of the saints, and incorporated into, made a member of, Christ's spiritual Body. . . . Thus to receive this sacrament in bread and wine is naught else than to receive a sign of this fellowship and incorporation with Christ and all his saints.[135]

His essay the "Blessed Sacrament" recovered the familiar imagery of the *Didache* to make the same point.

> To signify this fellowship, God has appointed such signs of this sacrament as in every way serve this purpose and by their very form stimulate and motivate us to this fellowship. For just as the bread is made out of many grains ground and mixed together, and out of the bodies of many grains there comes the body of one bread, in which each grain loses its form and body and takes upon itself the common body of the bread; and just as the drops of wine, in losing their own form, become the body of one common wine and drink—so it is and should be with us, if we use this sacrament properly. . . . we become one loaf, one bread, one body, one drink, and have all things in common. . . . That is real fellowship, and that is the true significance of this sacrament. In this way we are changed into one another and are made into a community by love.[136]

Shaped by *koinonia*, which is constituted by a *metalepsis*, a partaking of the body of Christ,[137] the fellowship character of the eucharist became a central feature of Luther's early theology. Communion, Luther insisted, should be a public act: "an act of confession before God, angels, and men, that we are Christians."[138] In short, Mass required communicants.

Luther's recovery of the communal context of the eucharist resulted in a corresponding decrease in the role of the priest and increase in the role of the laity. The "special status" of the priesthood was denied and the "priesthood of all believers" was affirmed. Luther admonished: "Whoever has been fished out of the font can pride himself that he has been ordained priest and bishop and pope!"[139] Although priestly vestments were retained, the celebrant faced the people. More important, the vernacular was used in the Mass and for hymns, while communion was received in both kinds.

Due in part to the eucharistic controversies against Rome and the Enthusiasts, these reforms, which were manifest in church practice, receded into the background of Luther's writings after 1520. In opposition to the Roman emphasis on the sacrifice, Luther stressed the gift given to the individual in communion. In opposition to the Enthusiasts' emphasis on the spiritual presence, Luther stressed the real presence under the elements. The latter had the effect of separating the spiritual body of Christ, which is the fellowship of the faithful, from the real body, which is given in the sacrament.[140]

These two shifts in emphases caused the focus of the eucharist to narrow almost exclusively to the individual and the elements. Consequently, the social dimension of the sacrament was obscured. Luther's promising recovery of the concept of corporate eucharistic worship, though never renounced, quickly disappeared from prominence and never secured full doctrinal formulation.

Contrary to Luther, Zwingli interpreted the Lord's Supper as an act of thanksgiving for the gospel and not as a concrete offer of the gospel. For Zwingli, the actual gift of Christ lay in the past and, therefore, the subject of the present sacramental action was the Christian community. The church gathered around the table in order that it might not forget the narrative of Christ's ignominious death by which the world was redeemed. This memorial feast served, then, a dual purpose: it bound the members together and it instilled them with a common identity.

Employing Pauline imagery, Zwingli, like Luther, stressed the communal nature of the eucharist:

> They who here eat and drink are one body, one bread; that is, all those who come together to proclaim Christ's death and eat the symbolical bread, declare themselves to be Christ's body, that is, members of his church; and as this church holds one faith and eats one symbolical bread, so it is one bread and one body.[141]

Thus, participation in this meal of fellowship engendered identity formation:

> He who partakes in this public giving of thanks declares in the
> presence of the whole church that he belongs to the number of those
> who trust in the death of Christ for us.[142]

Heiko Oberman goes so far as to label Zwingli's formulation an equivalent
of the doctrine of transubstantiation:

> ... not the medieval doctrine of transubstantiation of the elements,
> but the apostolic doctrine, mentioned in the *Didache* (*The Teaching
> of the Twelve Apostles*)—according to which the dispersed congregation
> is assembled and changed into the body of Christ.[143]

Unlike Luther, however, that which bound the members of the body together
was not the sacrament but their faith. Christ does not come to us in the
sacrament, since Christ is in heaven. The communicants bring Christ into the
sacrament by faith. In a letter to his teacher and friend, Thomas Wyttenbach,
Zwingli summarized this point:

> Think of it this way; you eat the Eucharist there where faith is.[144]

Because faith is the mode of Christ's presence and because there cannot
be two ways to salvation, the sacraments are not a means of grace. They provide
no unique function. Consequently, the subject of the eucharistic action is the
worshiping community.

Zwingli's preoccupation with communal worship found liturgical expression
in his *Action oder Bruch des Nachtmals*, one of the most remarkable documents
in the liturgical history of Protestantism. Because the purpose of worship is
to provide cultic expression in ritual form of theological thought, this liturgical
masterpiece thematized the eucharist as "a social meal in remembrance."[145]

Unfortunately, his liturgy separated the preaching service from the communion
service, and both were impoverished. The regular Sunday service "was abandoned
to the didactic tyranny of the spoken word" and lost its communal focus. The
communion service, uprooted from the life of the church through the ages, lost
its historical orientation by commemorating only one historical event. Hence,
the dimension of communion fellowship was restricted to the life of the present
congregation and was deprived access to the life of the universal church.[146]

In spite of Calvin's emphasis upon the Word and preaching, he continued
the Reformation's stress on the communal nature of worship.[147] While the
Word was spoken to individuals as well as to the congregation, "the Eucharist
was essentially and uniquely corporate worship."[148] The *Institutes*, borrowing
from the tradition, used the imagery of the bread to depict this communal
participation.

Now, since (the Lord) has only one body, of which he makes us all partakers, it is necessary that all of us also be made one body by such participation. The bread shown in the Sacrament represents this unity. As it is made of many grains so mixed together that one cannot be distinguished from another, so it is fitting that in the same way we should be joined and bound together by such great agreement of minds that no sort of disagreement or division may intrude. I prefer to explain it in Paul's words: 'The cup of blessing which we bless is a communicating of the blood of Christ; and the bread of blessing which we break is a participation in the body of Christ. . . . Therefore . . . we . . . are all one body, for we partake of one bread.'[149]

Like the other Reformers, Calvin's concern for communal participation meant a corresponding opposition to "liturgical clericalism." The Roman priests, Calvin observed, acted as if "the Supper had been turned over to them."[150] Instead of the eucharist being an act of the assembled community, it had become the domain of one person only.

Therefore, nothing more preposterous could happen in the Supper than for it to be turned into a silent action, as has happened under the pope's tyranny. For they wanted to have the whole force of the consecration depend upon the intention of the priest, as if it did not matter at all to the people, to whom the mystery ought most of all to have been explained.[151]

Calvin pinpointed two areas where clericalization of the eucharist had occurred: the private Masses and communion under one kind. In particular, the former inhibited communal worship since a public Mass can still be private if there is no communion of the people:

I call it a private mass (that no man may be mistaken) wherever there is no participation in the Lord's Supper among believers, even though a large multitude of men may otherwise be present.[152]

Thus, a private Mass defiled the sacrament and denied its true intention.

. . . I say that private masses are diametrically opposed to Christ's institution, and are for that reason an impious profaning of the Sacred Supper. For what has the Lord bidden us? Is it not to take and divide among us (Luke 22:17)? . . . When, therefore, one person receives it without sharing, what similarity is there? . . . Is this not openly to mock God, when one person privately seizes for himself what ought to have been done only among many? But because Christ's and Paul's words are clear enough, we may briefly conclude that wherever there is not this breaking of bread for the communion of believers, it is not the Lord's Supper, but a false and preposterous imitation of it.[153]

Private Masses not only oppose the unity which the eucharist effects but they also divide the worshiping community. Contrary to the sacrament's intention, private Masses are "a ritualized form of excommunication by means of which the community of believers is excluded from active participation in the eucharistic liturgy."[154] Like his earlier Reformation colleagues, Calvin also emphasized the essential corporate character of the eucharist.

One of the greatest gains of the Reformation was the recovery of the communal theme. Drawn from its Augustinian inheritance, the Reformers rediscovered the dual components of true eucharistic fellowship. Yngue Brilioth offers a brilliant summary:

> *Communio*—fellowship—has two sides: communion with the brethren and communion with God; and the eucharist is the expression and the seal of the unity of these two sides in communion with Christ. We cannot be members of Christ's body without being at the same time members one of another; and thus the unity of the brethren is lifted up into the mystery of union with God. This fellowship knows no limits narrower than the whole universal church of Christ; it begins with the circle round our own local altar, it extends to the fellowship of the whole church on earth, and it embraces not only the living but also those who are gone hence in the Lord. Thus it passes into Mystery—the Mystery of Christian fellowship; for these two aspects of the sacrament are inseparable, even though we are bound to study them separately. Finally, this fellowship is unreal if it does not find expression in life as well as in liturgy, and deepen and sanctify daily intercourse.[155]

The elimination of the communion of the people constituted one of the great losses of the medieval church. Its narrowed focus upon the consecrated elements created an imbalance in the worship service. By intention, the Reformers attempted to correct this liturgical dissonance. In practice, the corporate character of worship was restored by the introduction of congregational singing (except Zwingli), the common prayer made by both priest and people, the use of the native language, and the return to table fellowship. Although the actual styles varied (Calvin as well as French and German Reformed churches had people come forward in line to receive standing at the table, Scottish and Dutch Reformed churches served the people seated at long tables, Zwinglian and Anglican churches served the people in their places), the meal character of the eucharist was reinstated.

However, the celebration of communion was rare. Influenced by Zwingli's commemorative view of the eucharist and its demand for infrequent communion, as well as the medieval practice of annual communion, neither Luther's nor Calvin's desire for weekly communion could overcome lay resistance. Consequently, Protestants in general communed only three or four times a year.

Without question the practice of quarterly communion minimized the Reformation recovery of corporate fellowship. In essence, a vicious cycle existed. Although innovative liturgical practices encouraged communal participation, the infrequency of communion never permitted the actual experience of fellowship to inform the communicants. Therefore, the ability of the eucharist to draw believers out of their subjective worlds was never realized.

In addition, the overall theology of the Reformation tended to reinforce medieval individualism. Guided by the principles of "justification by grace through faith" and the "priesthood of all believers," and by the model of substitutionary atonement for sins, the Reformers were unable to construct a sacramental theology that could effectively counteract this milieu of individualism.

Furthermore, many Protestants believed that the eucharist provided nothing new to the worship service. If the eucharist is primarily an occasion by which the gathered community recalls its founder and heritage, then it essentially "duplicates the function of the normal *non*-eucharistic Protestant worship."[156] And because the eucharistic action within this framework is primarily mental, the bread and the wine become "Christ-ordained" stimuli which drive the individual away from the communal character of table fellowship and into the subjective self.

Despite the Reformers' emphasis on corporate fellowship, their theological perspectives reinforced the already entrenched emphasis on individualism. Protestant public worship became an opportunity for each individual within the ecclesial body to be "edified" and forgiven. Although the Reformers made admirable and well-intentioned efforts, the eucharist as a celebration of the whole assembly of God was never fully realized. The recovery of the corporate character of worship in general and of the eucharist in particular remained incomplete.

Conclusion

In spite of the Reformers' unanimous rejection of the Roman Catholic concept of substantial presence as expressed in the doctrine of transubstantiation, they were unable to agree on an alternative formulation of Christ's eucharistic presence.

Although Martin Luther affirmed the intention of the doctrine of transubstantiation to safeguard Christ's real presence in the eucharist, he renounced the doctrine as philosophically and biblically untenable. Believing that the sacrament of the altar was synonymous with the gospel and, thus, a means of grace, and supported by the biblical words of Christ that "This is my body," by the Christological doctrine of the *communicatio idiomatum*, and by the philosophical explanation for the ubiquity of bodily presence, Luther insisted that the exalted Christ was truly, really, and invisibly present at the Lord's Table.

Afraid of the dominance of the material elements over the sign function of the eucharist, Ulrich Zwingli rejected both the doctrines of transubstantiation and copresence. Believing that the sacrament was a memorial celebration of God's past act of redemption in Christ and a public confession of faith in Christ in the presence of the gathered community of believers, and supported by the preeminence of faith, by the sharp distinction between the sacramental sign and the reality signified, by the figurative interpretation of "This is my body," and by the literal meaning of the ascension, Zwingli insisted that Christ's eucharistic presence was spiritual.

Motivated by his repulsion by both the Roman and Lutheran doctrines, in which the elements contain and give the body of Christ, and Zwingli's declaration that the Lord's Supper is merely a sign of Christ's past act of redemption, John Calvin charted a middle course to secure Christ's eucharistic presence. He believed that both Luther and Zwingli undermined real presence. By concentrating exclusively on the reality of Christ's substantive body and blood, Luther turned the eucharistic elements into shadows and thereby thwarted their significative function. By concentrating exclusively on the mnemonic role of the eucharistic signs, Zwingli divorced the sign from the thing signified and thereby thwarted the reality of the sacrament. Both reduced the dialectic tension in the sacrament between the sign and the reality signified and, therefore, undermined the mystery of Christ's real presence.

Instead of following the Western tradition of focusing on the Words of Institution, Calvin reappropriated the insights of the patristic and Eastern traditions by retrieving their emphasis on the *epiclesis* of the Spirit. By linking the doctrine of the ascension with the work of the Holy Spirit, Calvin secured a real, but spiritual presence, that avoided the material tendency of Luther and the subjective tendency of Zwingli.

The Reformers' treatment of the three requisite features also evidenced diversity of thought.

Reflecting the medieval relationship between Christ's eucharistic presence and the consecrated elements, their respective positions on the connection of ritual and material elements are predictable. Luther, along with the Roman Catholic Church, tied the localization of Christ's presence to the elements, while Zwingli did not. Calvin adopted a middle position.

The inability of the Reformers to advance a consensus position meant that the dominant models for conveying Christ's eucharistic presence for the subsequent centuries would still rely on the consecrated elements. On the one extreme, the Roman Catholics and the Lutherans related the concept of substantial presence to the elements while, on the other extreme, the Zwinglians understood the elements as external reminders of Christ's past act of redemption.

With the exception of Calvin, Protestant and Roman Catholic theologians ignored the eschatological dimension of the past-future dialectic. Preoccupied with how the present relates to the past redemptive act of Christ, two alternatives emerged. The Roman Catholics made the past available to the present through repeated Masses, while the Protestants made the past available to the present through the mental act of remembrance. Calvin, however, advanced beyond both proposals by stressing the ascension and the parousia. Eucharistic theology included both the Christ who redeemed us in the past and the Christ who stands before us in the future.

Unlike the other requisite features, the Reformers, with the exception of Luther, acknowledged the presence-absence dialectic. The stress of Zwingli and Calvin on the ascension ensured that Christ's body is literally in heaven and, thus, absent from the table. However, the preoccupation of Luther and the Roman Catholic Church with Christ's local presence and the consecrated elements virtually excluded any mention of Christ's absence.

In conclusion, the Reformers unanimously opposed the Roman Catholic doctrine of transubstantiation, but they were unable to agree on an alternative formulation of Christ's eucharistic presence. Meanwhile, the Council of Trent reaffirmed for the Roman Catholic Church that transubstantiation was the answer to the specific question of how Christ is present under the elements. This declaration guaranteed that the legacy of the concept of substantial presence would continue. The Reformers could only pass on diversity and incompleteness. In particular, the promising recovery of the corporate character of worship, though championed by all three Reformers, never secured full doctrinal formulation. Consequently, the church in the next few centuries was destined to repeat these sixteenth century models of Christ's eucharistic presence.

Notes

1. Maxwell, *An Outline of Christian Worship*, 72.
2. The central writings against Rome include: *The Babylonian Captivity of the Church* (1520); *The Blessed Sacrament of the Holy And True Body of Christ* (1519); and *A Treatise on the New Testament, that is, the Holy Mass* (1520). *The Letter to the Christians At Strassburg in Opposition to the Fanatic Spirit* (1524) marks the transition to the second front. Works in the second period include: *Admonition Concerning the Sacrament of the Body and Blood of our Lord* (1530); *Against the Heavenly Prophets* (1525); *Brief Confession Concerning Christ's Supper*

(1528); *The Disputation Concerning the Passage: "The Word Was Made Flesh"* (1539); *The Sacrament of the Body and Blood of Christ* (1526); and *That These Words of Christ, "This is my Body"* (1527).

3. *"The second captivity of this sacrament* is less grievous as far as the conscience is concerned, yet the gravest of dangers threatens the man who would attack it, to say nothing of condemning it" (Martin Luther, *Babylonian Captivity of the Church, 1520* in *Selected Writings of Martin Luther*, vol. 1517-1520, ed. Theodore G. Tappert, trans. A. T. W. Steinhaeuser (Philadelphia: Fortress Press, 1967), 380).

4. Ibid., 380-381.

5. Ibid., 381-382.

6. Ibid., 385.

7. Ibid., 384.

8. Ibid., 387.

9. Along with Zwingli, Luther identified Carlstadt, Oecolampadius, Stenckefeld, Landtspergen, and Camoanus. See Martin Luther, *Brief Confession Concerning the Holy Sacrament, 1544* in *Luther's Works*, vol. 38, ed. Helmut T. Lehmann, trans. Martin E. Lehmann (Philadephia: Fortress Press, 1971), 296-298. Although Zwingli may not have perceived himself as an Enthusiast, Luther treated his opposition as a totality, i.e., all those who believed that the sacraments ceased to be means of grace and became mere signs.

10. Alexander Barclay, *The Protestant Doctrine of the Lord's Supper: A Study in the Eucharistic Teaching of Luther, Zwingli and Calvin* (Glasgow: Jackson, Wylie and Co., 1927), 103.

11. Alexander Barclay in *The Protestant Doctrine of the Lord's Supper*, 3, 87, 104, contends that Zwingli's doctrine of the Lord's Supper moves through three clearly defined stages. In the first phase (1521-1524), Zwingli combated the Mass as a "repeated and propitiatory sacrifice." In the second period (1524-1528), he opposed Luther's doctrine of the presence and was more negative in tone. In the third period (1528-1531), he was influenced by Bucer and more positive views surfaced. Our treatment of Zwingli will draw from the latter two periods.

12. Ibid., 46.

13. Ibid., 100-101.

14. McDonnell, *John Calvin*, 92-93.

15. Crockett, *Eucharist*, 135.

16. McDonnell, *John Calvin*, 93.

17. B. A. Gerrish, *The Old Protestantism and the New* (Chicago: The University of Chicago Press, 1982), 129.

18. Cyril C. Richardson, *Zwingli and Cranmer on the Eucharist* (Evanston: Seabury-Western Theological Seminary, 1949), 17.

19. Gerrish, *The Old Protestantism*, 129.

20. Ibid., 122.

21. Ulrich Zwingli, *On the Lord's Supper* in *Zwingli and Bullinger*, ed. and trans. G. W. Bromiley (Philadelphia: Westminster Press, 1953), 234.

22. Ibid., 191, 199, 201 & 209.

23. Barclay, *The Protestant Doctrine of the Lord's Supper*, 54.

24. Zwingli, *On the Lord's Supper*, 209.

25. Barclay, *The Protestant Doctrine of the Lord's Supper*, 54-55.

26. Zwingli, *On the Lord's Supper*, 223-225.

27. Richardson, *Zwingli and Cranmer*, 8-9.

28. McDonnell, *John Calvin*, 87.

29. Zwingli, *On the Lord's Supper*, 213.

30. Ibid., 214-215.

31. Ewald M. Plass, *What Luther Says: An Anthology*, vol. 2 (Saint Louis: Concordia Publishing House, 1959), 808, #2504.

32. Named for his birthplace, Carlstadt (c. 1480-1541), whose real name was Andreas Bodenstein, was a former associate and ally of Luther. Recognized as the most extreme of the Reformers, his views on the eucharist resembled Zwingli's. His suggestion that the "this" in *Hoc est corpus meum* meant that Jesus pointed to himself, rather than to the bread, was not taken seriously.

33. John Oecolampadius (1482-1531), cathedral preacher at Basle turned Reformer, interpreted the eucharist in the same manner as did Zwingli except that "my body" meant "the symbol (*figura*) of my Body" and not "signifies."

34. Grislis, "The Manner of Christ's Eucharistic Presence According to Martin Luther," 8.

35. On the one hand, Luther, trained in the philosophy and theology of the *via moderna*, contrasted reason and revelation and affirmed the God of the Bible over the God of the philosophers. And this God he found in the Bible "is God who is hidden (*Deus absconditus*) outside Christ and revealed (*Deus revelatus*) in Christ only. . . ." On the other hand, Zwingli, trained in the philosophy and theology of the *via antiqua*, correlated reason and revelation. Influenced by the Thomistic heritage, Zwingli believed that revelation would never contradict reason. The respective role of human reason in theology constitutes one of the deepest contrasts between Luther and Zwingli. See Sasse, *This is My Body*, 117-118 and Crockett, *Eucharist*, 140-141.

36. From the Marburg Colloquy, Sasse, *This is My Body*, 186.

37. Martin Luther, *That These Words of Christ, "This Is My Body," etc., Still Stands Firm Against the Fanatics, 1527* in *Luther's Works*, vol. 37, ed. Helmut T. Lehmann, trans. Robert H. Fischer (Philadelphia: Fortress Press, 1961), 33.

38. Sasse, *This is My Body*, 81.

39. Martin Luther, *Confession Concerning Christ's Supper, 1528* in *Luther's Works*, vol. 37, ed. Helmut T. Lehmann, trans. Robert H. Fischer (Philadelphia: Fortress Press, 1961), 212.

40. Barclay, *The Protestant Doctrine of the Lord's Supper*, 77.

41. Luther, *This Is My Body*, 57.

42. Luther, *Confession Concerning Christ's Supper*, 206.

43. Luther, *This Is My Body*, 29.

44. For elaboration on the three modes see Luther, *Confession Concerning Christ's Supper*, 215-218; Grislis, "The Manner of Christ's Eucharistic Presence According to Martin Luther," 12-13; and Barclay, *The Protestant Doctrine of the Lord's Supper*, 79-80.

45. Luther, *Confession Concerning Christ's Supper*, 216.

46. Ibid., 218.

47. Ibid., 224.

48. McDonnell, *John Calvin*, 63-64.

49. Luther, *Confession Concerning Christ's Supper*, 195.

50. Luther, *This Is My Body*, 89.

51. Heron, *Table and Tradition*, 118.

52. Luther, *This Is My Body*, 59.

53. Wiegand, "The History of the Doctrine of the Eucharist," 375.

54. Heron, *Table and Tradition*, 120.

55. Ibid., 118.

56. McDonnell, *John Calvin*, 94.

57. We know that Luther and Calvin never met. However, we cannot be as sure what works of Luther Calvin might have read in Latin. Kilian McDonnell in *John Calvin*, 60-61, believes that the following works of Luther were used by Calvin in composing the first edition of the *Institutes*: The *Prayerbook*, *Small Catechism*, *On the Freedom of the Christian Man*, *On the Babylonian Captivity of the Church*, the sermon "On the Blessed Sacrament of the True Body of Christ," and the sermon "On the Body and Blood of Christ Against the Fanatics." McDonnell also adds with less probability Luther's letter to Herwagen (1527) and Bucer's Latin translation of Luther's sermons.

58. Calvin definitely read and was greatly influenced by Zwingli's *Commentarius de vera et falsa religione*. See Sasse, *This is My Body*, 261.

59. A. Lang claims that Bucer was the spiritual father of Calvin since Calvin's doctrines of predestination and the sacraments were influenced by Bucer's *Commentary on the Gospels* and by personal association at Strasburg. See Sasse, *This is My Body*, 261.

60. Without question St. Augustine exercised the greatest influence on Calvin. There are 341 citations of Augustine in the last edition of the *Institutes*, 39 in the section on the sacraments in the first edition.

61. McDonnell, *John Calvin*, 158.

62. "Nearly all the wisdom we possess, that is to say, true and sound wisdom, consists of two parts: the knowledge of God and of ourselves. But, while joined by many bonds, which one precedes and brings forth the other is not easy to

discern" (John Calvin, *Institutes of the Christian Religion*, ed. John T. McNeill, trans. Ford Lewis Battles, The Library of Christian Classics, vols. xx & xxi (Philadelphia: The Westminster Press, 1960), I, 1, 1).

63. McDonnell, *John Calvin*, 109.
64. Calvin, *Institutes*, IV, 14, 14.
65. Ibid., IV, 14, 11. Although in this passage Calvin is specifically referring to preaching in relation to the sacraments, what he says of preaching is equally valid for his sacramental theology.
66. Ibid., IV, 17, 13.
67. Ibid., IV, 17, 20.
68. Ibid., IV, 17, 14.
69. Ibid., IV, 17, 31.
70. Barclay, *The Protestant Doctrine of the Lord's Supper*, 208.
71. Calvin, *Institutes*, IV, 17, 20.
72. Ibid., IV, 17, 14.
73. Ibid., I, 11, 1.
74. Ibid., IV, 17, 36.
75. McDonnell, *John Calvin*, 134.
76. Calvin, *Institutes*, III, 11, 10.
77. McDonnell, *John Calvin*, 177-178 and B. A. Gerrish, *Grace and Gratitude: The Eucharistic Theology of John Calvin* (Minneapolis: Fortress Press, 1993), 73.
78. Ibid., 179.
79. Ibid.
80. Calvin, *Institutes*, IV, 17, 8.
81. Ibid., IV, 1, 2.
82. Ibid., IV, 16, 9 & 22.
83. Ibid., IV, 14, 14.
84. Ibid., IV, 17, 4.
85. McDonnell, *John Calvin*, 191.
86. Calvin, *Institutes*, IV, 17, 19.
87. Ibid., IV, 17, 17 & 30.
88. McDonnell, *John Calvin*, 213.
89. Calvin, *Institutes*, II, 14, 2.
90. McDonnell, *John Calvin*, 219 and Thurian, "The Real Presence," 209-210.
91. Thurian, 214.
92. Calvin, *Institutes*, IV, 17, 19.
93. Gerrish, *The Old Protestantism*, 109-110.
94. Calvin, *Institutes*, IV, 14, 6.
95. Ibid., IV, 14, 14.
96. Ibid., IV, 14, 17.
97. Gerrish, *The Old Protestantism*, 111; see *Institutes*, IV, 17, 21.
98. McDonnell, *John Calvin*, 229-230 and Gerrish, *Grace and Gratitude*, 137.

99. Calvin, *Institutes*, IV, 17, 10 and Gerrish, *Grace and Gratitude*, 137.

100. Gerrish, *The Old Protestantism*, 122.

101. Calvin, *Institutes*, IV, 17, 10.

102. Ibid., IV, 17, 12.

103. McDonnell, *John Calvin*, 227.

104. Barclay, *The Protestant Doctrine of the Lord's Supper*, 116-118 and Gerrish, *Grace and Gratitude*, 175.

105. Heron, *Table and Tradition*, 128.

106. Calvin, *Institutes* III, 1, 1 & 3.

107. Heron, *Table and Tradition*, 129.

108. McDonnell, *John Calvin*, 260-261.

109. Calvin, *Institutes*, IV, 17, 26.

110. Ibid., IV, 17, 10.

111. McDonnell, *John Calvin*, 254 & 376.

112. Thurian, "The Real Presence," 213-214.

113. McDonnell, *John Calvin*, 263.

114. Calvin, *Institutes*, IV, 17, 33.

115. Barclay, *The Protestant Doctrine of the Lord's Supper*, 248-250 and McDonnell, *John Calvin*, 68.

116. Barclay, *The Protestant Doctrine of the Lord's Supper*, 248-250.

117. Heron, *Table and Tradition*, 80.

118. Ibid., 101.

119. Stone, *A History of the Doctrine*, vol. 2, 91.

120. Ibid., 88.

121. Niesel, *The Gospel and the Churches*, 104-105.

122. Ibid., 105.

123. Heron, *Table and Tradition*, 101.

124. Stone, *A History of the Doctrine*, vol. 2, 91.

125. Richardson, *Zwingli and Cranmer*, 11.

126. Heron, *Table and Tradition*, 152-153.

127. This section relies on the insights of Dix, *Shape of the Liturgy*, 622-625.

128. Ibid., 625.

129. This section relies on McDonnell, *John Calvin*, 289-292.

130. Ibid., 293.

131. Ibid., 36-37.

132. Calvin, *Institutes*, IV, 17, 26.

133. Brilioth, *Eucharistic Faith*, 286-287.

134. Maxwell, *An Outline of Christian Worship*, 72.

135. Brilioth, *Eucharistic Faith*, 96.

136. Martin Luther, *Blessed Sacrament of the Holy and True Body of Christ, And the Brotherhood, 1519* in *Luther's Works*, vol. 35, ed. Helmut T. Lehmann, trans. Jeremiah J. Schindel (Philadelphia: Muhlenberg Press, 1960), 58.

137. Elert, *Eucharist And Church Fellowship*, 39.

138. Brilioth, *Eucharistic Faith*, 134.

139. Joseph A. Jungmann, *The Sacrifice of the Church*, trans. Cliffo (London: Challoner Publishers, 1961), 55.

140. Brilioth, *Eucharistic Faith*, 131-134.

141. Ibid., 158.

142. Ibid., 157.

143. Heiko A. Oberman, "Reformation, Preaching, and *Ex Opere Ope.* in *Christianity Divided: Protestant and Roman Catholic Theological Issues,* Daniel J. Callahan, Heiko A. Oberman, and Daniel J. O'Hanlon (New Yc Sheed and Ward, 1961), 227.

144. McDonnell, *John Calvin*, 90.

145. Brilioth, *Eucharistic Faith*, 161-162.

146. Ibid., 162-163.

147. See Gerrish, *Grace and Gratitude*, 182-190.

148. McDonnell, *John Calvin*, 190.

149. Calvin, *Institutes*, IV, 17, 38.

150. Ibid., IV, 18, 7.

151. Ibid., IV, 17, 39.

152. Ibid., IV, 18, 7.

153. Ibid., IV, 18, 8.

154. McDonnell, *John Calvin*, 146.

155. Brilioth, *Eucharistic Faith*, 278-279.

156. Dix, *Shape of the Liturgy*, 601.

CHAPTER FIVE

REITERATIONS OF REFORMATION MODELS

It would be an exaggeration to claim that there were no new developments in eucharistic theology from the time of the Protestant and Catholic Reformations of the sixteenth century to the Second Vatican Council and the subsequent ecumenical discussions of the twentieth century. However, it would not be an exaggeration to claim that most of the developments were shaped within the framework of the respective positions solidified in the Reformation period.[1] The truth of this statement is most clearly demonstrated by the paucity of references to these last four centuries in contemporary ecumenical documents.

We would be remiss, however, if we did not highlight the eucharistic topography of these centuries with the express purpose of underscoring the tremendous advances in eucharistic theology in the twentieth century. Since Roman Catholicism settled into a period of "frozen" sacramental theology as a result of the unprecedented unification and "clarification of liturgy" at Trent, this chapter will begin with a historical survey of Protestantism and will conclude with a historical survey of Roman Catholicism and the emergence of a new sacramental model, the "Interpersonal-Encounter Model."

Protestant Eucharistic Theology

Although the Church of England never developed a doctrine of the eucharist that bore the stamp of either a single great reformer or a common confessional agreement, Thomas Cranmer, the principal author of the Book of Common Prayer, blended Augustinian and Reformed thought.[2] Consequently, his eucharistic theology, though Zwinglian in content, contained elements of realism that were missing in Zwingli's theology. Attempting to connect sacramental realism with the faithful believer, and not with the consecrated elements, Cranmer's "doctrine can best be described as a doctrine of the real partaking of the body and blood in the eucharist rather than as a doctrine of the real objective presence of Christ in the eucharist."[3] Anglican theologians through the seventeenth century continued to emphasize the faithful communicants and thereby shifted the focus of eucharistic theology and real presence from the medieval preoccupation with the elements (the production of real presence) to the nourishment of the Christian believers (presence related to the worthy receiver or "receptionism").

During the latter part of the seventeenth century and into the eighteenth century, Enlightenment theologians, with their exaltation of reason, attempted to strip mystery from the faith and to reduce Christianity to the rational. As a result, the doctrine of Christ's real presence in the eucharist was often denied and the Zwinglian theme of "simple remembrance" was championed. The eucharistic life in the Church of England reached its lowest ebb.

Ripe for renewal, the evangelical revival of John and Charles Wesley and George Whitefield stressed the necessity of frequent communion, and may properly be called a eucharistic revival. Uniting an evangelical and a sacramental vision of Christianity, the Wesleyan movement countered the spiritual lethargy of the age with, among other beliefs, a Calvinist doctrine of the real presence and a high church view of the centrality of the eucharist.[4]

In opposition to the dogmatic, propositional, orthodox religion of the continent in the seventeenth century, the pietism of Philip Jacob Spener and others introduced a shift in emphasis. The primacy of emotion in the religious experience replaced staunch scholasticism. "Sunday worship tended to be viewed by the Pietists as a kind of psychological experience."[5] Programmed to produce emotional and personal conversion, worship stressed the individual over the corporate experience. Celebration of the eucharist was minimal.

If most people in Europe communed four times a year under orthodoxy and pietism, that average declined even further under rationalism. Disgusted with the bitter religious wars, dissatisfied with the "narrow and naive biblicism of many Protestants," and disinclined "to the rigid anti-intellectual reaction of official Roman Catholicism," rationalists sought a faith of moderate reason in lieu of "primitive passions."[6] Consequently, most rationalists dismissed the sacraments "as anachronistic holdovers from an irrational and superstitious past."[7] The sermon, valued as a means of inculcating ideals and illuminating enduring truths, was the significant act of worship. Though diametrically opposed to pietism, rationalism's "tendency to reduce the Lord's Supper to a memorial service to celebrate Christ's struggle to the death for 'truth' (and) to encourage his disciples to lead lives of 'virtue'"[8] resulted in another era of the diminution of the corporate experience and the elevation of the individual conscience.

Paradoxically, the seventeenth and eighteenth centuries witnessed the gradual triumph of the European Free Church worship experience. Though the Free Church was persecuted by Lutheran, Reformed, and Anglican established churches, by the dawn of the nineteenth century its worship ideas dominated. The Sunday service became a "free preaching service." The sermon was central, while "congregational participation was limited to the singing of metrical psalms in the Reformed church and to German hymns in Lutheran churches."[9] Because the sacraments were rarely celebrated, when they were included in the worship service via a "fixed 'liturgical' text," they appeared as an "optional appendage" in the same way as they had been celebrated in the Zwinglian and Free churches.[10] The triumph was complete.

Several factors account for the fact that Lutheran and Reformed churches forsook their heritage and adopted Free Church worship patterns.[11] First and foremost, the Protestant accusation of works-righteousness leveled against Roman Catholicism came full circle. Afraid that their own worship services might degenerate into a form of works-righteousness, Protestants began to understand worship solely in terms of instruction and moral edification. The sermon, therefore, gained prominence.

Second, this emphasis on instruction proved compatible with both the pietist and rationalist emphasis upon education in the worship service. Whether the preacher was stressing conversion or inculcation mattered little; the sermon was functionally superior to the sacraments.

Third, the emphasis upon the individual in both pietism and rationalism not only severed the remaining ties to any semblance of corporate worship, but it also "complemented the rise of the capitalist spirit and new democratic, egalitarian ideals."

In conclusion, the seventeenth and eighteenth century European Protestant worship practice was a victim of the same fate that befell the Roman Catholic worship experience. However, the embryonic Protestant church had no liturgical tradition by which it could regenerate itself. Consequently, the absence of sacramentalism proved both appropriate and advantageous for the dawning of the age of secularism.

The American counterpart to the eighteenth century English revival was the Great Awakening. Under the capable leadership of Jonathan Edwards, the American awakening, not unlike its European parent, "emphasized the need for a transforming, regenerate change—a 'conversion.'"[12]

With the Second Awakening, which spread from New England through the Middle Atlantic States into the South and to the frontier, and with less than ten percent of the American population identified as church members at the turn of the nineteenth century, it is little wonder that the singular goal of this movement was the conversion of lost souls. Revivals such as Cane Ridge, Kentucky, in August of 1801, and revivalists such as Charles Grandison Finney, "the father of modern revivalism" who introduced the "anxious bench," guaranteed not only the numerical success of the American Awakening but, more important, also secured for the revival its prominence as the "greatest single 'liturgical' contribution of American Protestantism."[13] Without question it was both a creative and productive solution to the problem of the American unchurched populace.

Regrettably, the popularity of the revival far too easily overshadowed the inadequacies of that worship model. Though tailored to the needs of an uneducated and unchurched young nation, the institutionalization of the revival model exposed glaring weaknesses. More often than not it led to a "maudlin, subjective" religious experience which was "artificially induced, emotionally exploitive, simple-minded, and short-lived."[14] Since the primary goal of worship was to get people to the altar and to be "saved," the sermon became the vehicle for "passionate pleas." All other liturgical acts were merely the "preliminaries" to this central rite of motivation. Not surprisingly, "Baptism and the Lord's Supper took a back seat to the supreme 'sacrament' of the sermon."[15]

The evangelical Free denominations, like the Methodist, Baptist, and Presbyterian churches, benefited the most from the revival movement, while they concurrently deemphasized their eucharistic practices. However, several denominations, like the Lutheran and Anglican churches, retained their sacramental focus. Yet, they, too, were affected by the revival movement. In particular, the American Lutheran church experienced a dispute over the eucharistic presence of Christ.

Sympathetic to the pervasive Protestant belief that Christ is present only spiritually at the Lord's Supper and convinced that American Lutheranism had outgrown the superstition as reflected in the Augsburg Confession, revisionist Lutherans maintained that there did not exist a viable doctrine between transubstantiation and symbolic representation. As a result, these liberals abandoned Luther's conservatism and adopted a spiritualist doctrine.[16]

Yet, many Lutherans were willing neither to repudiate their tradition nor to concede that Lutheranism and Roman Catholicism were indistinguishable on the matter of Christ's eucharistic presence. Bent on retrieval and not abandonment, conservative Lutherans sought to "return to the ancient landmarks"—to retain the "peculiar" mode of divine presence that lay between Calvinist spiritual presence and Catholic transubstantiation.[17] In short, the conservatives viewed the mode of Christ's eucharistic presence as an essential, while the liberals viewed it as a nonessential (*adiaphoron*).

Surprisingly, neither revivalism nor rationalism could unravel the traditional Lutheran doctrine. By the middle of the nineteenth century, efforts to amend the confessions by purging them of their "irrational and superstitious elements" ceased.

The remainder of the nineteenth and twentieth centuries witnessed a most unusual phenomenon for the American religious experience. Although both liberal and conservative Lutherans agreed that the exact mode of Christ's presence had not been defined by the ancient confessions, they were almost in unanimous agreement in honoring the doctrine of real presence as stated in the Augsburg Confession and in declaring that "Christ is truly, substantially, corporeally, objectively, personally present; but not virtually, or merely spiritually."[18] Furthermore, they retained the traditional Lutheran emphasis on eucharistic fellowship. Despite the culture's exclusive emphasis on individualism, the dual foci of individual communion with God and with the fellowship of God's people were not lost on Lutheranism as they were in most American Protestant worship experiences.

Unlike the Lutherans, most Free Church Protestants of the nineteenth century were deeply suspicious, on the one hand, of old world "ritualism" and "formalism," and intrigued, on the other hand, with emotional "spontaneity" and "freedom" in worship.[19] With little to no liturgical tradition and with the growth of vibrant evangelical fervor, these American Protestant movements were easily seduced by the voluntaristic, democratic American environment. Corporate worship was sacrificed on the high altar of rugged individualism and the eucharist lost its focal point in corporate worship. In short, Zwinglianism had triumphed. The sermon reigned supreme.

Yet, the underside of emotionalism was soft and thin. Reinhold Niebuhr noted this truth when he observed that American Protestantism's

> protest against the various forms and disciplines (of worship) led to their destruction. It may be possible to have a brief period of religious spontaneity in which the absence of such disciplines does not matter. The evangelism of the American frontier may have been such a period. But this spontaneity does not last forever. When it is gone a church without adequate conduits of traditional liturgy and theological learning and tradition is without the waters of life.[20]

Few American Protestants possessed this clarity of vision in the nineteenth century. An exception was the Mercersburg Movement.

The Mercersburg Movement

The Mercersburg Movement, so-called because of the name of the small town of Mercersburg in the Appalachian foothills in Pennsylvania in which Marshall College and the Theological Seminary of the German Reformed Church were situated, is primarily identified with J. W. Nevin and P. Schaff. Two convictions motivated them. They believed that "the person of Christ is the ultimate fact of Christianity which makes Christology and the Incarnation the essential starting point of Christian theology" and that "the historical development of the Church" uncovers the richness and diversity of the Christian faith which both reveals and preserves its dynamic and adaptive quality.[21]

J. W. Nevin was attracted to eucharistic theology because it lay, for him, at the intersection of both Christology and ecclesiology. In *The Mystical Presence* Nevin observed:

> As the Eucharist forms the very heart of the whole Christian worship, so it is clear that the entire question of the Church, which all are compelled to acknowledge the great life-problem of the age, centers ultimately in the sacramental question as its inmost heart and core. Our view of the Lord's Supper must ever condition and rule in the end our view of Christ's person and the conception we form of the Church. It must influence at the same time, very materially, our

whole system of theology, as well as all our ideas of ecclesiastical history.[22]

Because the eucharist is the "most representative activity" of the church, James Hastings Nichols labels the Mercersburg Movement as primarily a "Eucharistic revival." Unlike the Oxford Movement, which arose as "a campaign for clerical prerogatives and authority," the Mercersburg Movement's essential concern was the Lord's Supper.[23] On October 8, 1845 in *The Weekly Messenger* Nevin wrote:

> To my own mind all that is great and precious in the gospel may be said to center in this doctrine (Lord's Supper). . . . Both for my understanding and my heart, theology finds here all its interest and attraction.[24]

At first sight John Williamson Nevin would hardly seem the candidate to lead a eucharistic revolt against American revivalism. Born into a Presbyterian home in Pennsylvania and educated at Princeton Theological Seminary where he studied under Charles Hodge, Nevin, by his own admission, was a conservative evangelical who actually experienced a conversion at a revival. In background and education, he was virtually indistinguishable from the prevailing model of American Christianity in the 1840s.[25] Yet, he differed at one point.

When Nevin came to Mercersburg in 1840 as professor of theology in the seminary, he brought with him a stout adherence to Calvin's doctrine of the Lord's Supper. In this respect he was "strangely at odds" with his religious environment. Both his new colleagues at Mercersburg, the German Reformed, and American Protestantism preferred Zwingli's doctrine of the Lord's Supper to Calvin's.[26]

Nevin was willing to challenge the dominant eucharistic theology of his time because of his adamant belief that Calvin's doctrine of the "mystical union" was essential if fallen humanity was to participate in salvation.

> In full correspondence with this conception of the Christian salvation as a process by which the believer is mystically inserted more and more into the person of Christ till he becomes thus at last fully transformed into his image, it was held that nothing less than such a real participation of his living person is involved always in the right use of the Lord's Supper.[27]

Nevin, who believed that he was merely affirming Calvinistic doctrine, considered the epitome of this union to be the Lord's Supper. And because this mystical union is "a real life union of Christ and the believer," Nevin maintained that "the Supper itself must involve no less than a real participation by the believer in the living energy of Christ's very life."[28] This was the basis for "Nevin's assault upon the host of Zwinglians in his own midst and in American Christianity at large."[29]

After attacking in 1843 the prevailing methods of revivalist preaching in *The Anxious Bench: A Tract for the Times*, Nevin penned his incomparable contribution to Reformed eucharistic theology in particular and to American theology in general, *The Mystical Presence*, in 1846. Succinctly, Nevin had three primary purposes for writing the book. First, he wanted to show that American Protestantism had fallen away from Calvin's doctrine of the Lord's Supper and adopted Zwingli's doctrine. Second, he desired to "re-establish and re-interpret Calvin's doctrine." Nevin's confidence in Calvin's eucharistic theology as the perennial standard is evident throughout the book.

> To obtain a proper view of the original doctrine of the Reformed Church on the subject of the Eucharist, we must have recourse particularly to Calvin. Not that he is to be considered the creator, properly speaking, of the doctrine. . . . (he,) however, was the theological organ by which it first came to that clear expression, . . . He may be regarded, then, as the accredited interpreter and expounder of the article for all later times.[30]

Third, he sought to "correct Calvin's 'psychology' or his 'sursum-corda' mechanics."[31] Our study will concentrate on the first purpose.

Nevin constructed a solid theological base by developing a historical argument that encompassed the patristic writings, Calvin, and specific official confessions of the Reformed Churches, as well as scripture. In particular, he sought to avoid two undesirable and opposite extremes which restricted the Reformed doctrine.

On the one side, he dismissed the error of Romanism. By identifying Christ's presence in the eucharist with the elements both transubstantiation of the Roman church and consubstantiation of the Lutheran church committed the error of "corporal presence" and thereby precluded a "*spiritual* only" participation of Christ's flesh and blood in the Lord's Supper.[32]

On the other side, he dismissed the error of rationalism. By articulating either a union of believers with Christ in a common humanity, a moral union, a legal union, or a spiritual union with the divine nature of Christ, the rationalists committed the error of spiritualizing the doctrine. Therefore, they precluded a union with the whole, living Christ—a union that was real, substantial, and essential.[33]

Nevin indicted those holding the prevailing American Protestant view as practitioners of this latter position. Disinterested in eucharistic theology in general, and in the old doctrine of the spiritual real presence of Christ at the Lord's

Supper in particular, the prevailing mentality espoused a "low" or anti-sacramental attitude. Citing such preeminent American theologians as Jonathan Edwards and Timothy Dwight, Nevin characterized them as "modern Puritans" in contrast to "old Reformers."

By distinguishing the Reformed eucharistic theology of Christ's presence from the extremism of Romanism and rationalism, Nevin was prepared to posit the "proper" view. He permitted the term "real" presence if it was understood to be synonymous with "true" presence, i.e., "a presence that brings Christ truly into communion with the believer in his human nature, as well as in his divine nature."[34] However, to guard against any identification of "real" presence with local or "corporal" presence, he prefixed the word "spiritual." He concluded:

> A *real* presence, in opposition to the notion that Christ's flesh and blood are not made present to the communicant in *any* way. A *spiritual* real presence, in opposition to the idea that Christ's body is in the elements in a local or corporal manner. Not real simply, and not spiritual simply, but real and yet spiritual at the same time. The body of Christ is in heaven, the believer on earth; but by the power of the Holy Ghost, nevertheless, the obstacle of such vast local distance is fully overcome, so that in the sacramental act, while outward symbols are received in an outward way, the very body and blood of Christ are at the same time inwardly and supernaturally communicated to the worthy receiver, for the real nourishment of his new life.... The living energy, the vivific virtue, as Calvin styles it, of Christ's flesh, is made to flow over into the communicant, making him more and more one with Christ himself, and thus more and more an heir of the same immortality that is brought to light in his person.[35]

Nevin firmly believed that his doctrine of "spiritual real presence" as articulated in *The Mystical Presence* was simply a retrieval of Calvin's authentic doctrine. Although it was necessarily recast in contemporary language, its content was equivalent to the Reformed doctrine that the "real life-union in the case of the believer with the whole person of Christ" was effected "by the power of the Holy Ghost."[36]

Yet, Nevin's version of Calvin's eucharistic doctrine provoked violent controversy. In general, his interpretation elicited charges from both anti-Catholic[37] and pro-revivalist groups. In particular, it elicited a refutation by Charles Hodge in the *Princeton Review* of April 1848.

Considered by Nevin "the only respectable or tolerable attempt" to disprove his exposition of Calvin, Hodge argued that there are three, and not one, as Nevin imagined, concurrent views in the Reformed confessions: "that of Zwingli, that of Calvin, and that which represents an amalgamation of the two, but which in the last analysis is patient of the Zwinglian interpretation."[38] To this third type Hodge assigned not only the Heidelberg Catechism but also the "reigning Puritan faith of the present time."[39] In addition, Hodge disputed any mystical union with the "glorified humanity" of Christ. Although our union with Christ was real, Hodge reasoned, it was effected by the Holy Spirit and could not, therefore, involve any participation in the "glorified humanity." To claim such a participation would diminish the role of the Holy Spirit in the Trinity.[40]

In his reply to Hodge, published under the title, "The Doctrine of the Reformed Church on the Lord's Supper," in the September 1850 issue of the *Mercersburg Review*, Nevin essentially expanded his section on the Reformation in *The Mystical Presence*. Concerning the charge of diminishing the role of the Holy Spirit, Nevin declared:

> The Princeton analysis finds in the intervention of the Holy Ghost, as constantly affirmed in the Reformed doctrine of the Eucharist, a full exclusion of Christ's proper presence, especially of his presence under any human view; the stress laid on the agency of the Spirit is taken to mean clearly that no communication is to be thought of in the case with the true and proper life of the Saviour himself. But this whole construction, we contend, is false and wrong. The intervention of the Spirit, in the old Reformed doctrine, stands opposed only to the idea of all action that falls within the sphere of mere nature, and was never designed to be set in this way over against the reality of Christ's presence. On the contrary, the mystery of the transaction is taken to lie especially in this, that in a mode transcending the experience of sense, by the mirifical power of the Holy Ghost, the life-giving virtue of his flesh and blood is made to be dynamically at hand, in a real and true way, for the use of his people.[41]

This reply, considered by many to represent one of the finest examples of theological polemics in American history,[42] silenced Hodge.[43] Nearly twenty years later Nevin commented that his essay was "an argument which no one has ever yet pretended to meet, and whose historical force, at least, never can be overthrown."[44]

Comprehensive in historical scope and brilliant in theological insight, Nevin's exposition of the Reformed Church's doctrine of the eucharist was unequivocally the climax of American nineteenth century eucharistic theology. He not only placed the sacrament of the eucharist into the larger context of tradition, but he also revived the significance of ecclesiology. Nevin was indeed ahead of his time.

The Oxford Movement

If we can claim the Mercersburg Movement as the single most significant Protestant liturgical movement on the American continent during the nineteenth century, its European counterpart would be the Oxford Movement. Centered at Oxford during the decades of the thirties and forties, the movement was primarily a scholarly effort to regain a high church theology and "redirect the Church of England away from the Protestant understandings of grace, salvation, and sacraments."[45] Although the movement was not directly a liturgical movement, its influence affected worship and the sacraments.

Perhaps the most expedient way to characterize the movement's views on the doctrine of Christ's eucharistic presence is to quote from article one of the 1867 memorial, which was presented to the Archbishop of Canterbury by twenty-one prominent clergy who accepted the teachings of the Oxford Movement. Among the signatories was Edward Bouverie Pusey, an eminent Tractarian leader.

> (1) We repudiate the opinion of a 'corporal presence of Christ's natural flesh and blood,' that is to say, of the presence of His body and blood as they 'are in heaven,' and the conception of the mode of His presence which implies the physical change of the natural substances of bread and wine, commonly called 'Transubstantiation.'
>
> We believe that in the Holy Eucharist by virtue of the consecration through the power of the Holy Ghost the body and blood of our Saviour Christ, 'the inward part or thing signified,' are present really and truly but spiritually and ineffably under 'the outward visible part or sign' or 'form of bread and wine.'[46]

As a *via media*, most Tractarian leaders who wrote on the eucharist positioned themselves between two extremes. John Keble viewed the two extremes as variations of rationalism. In his 1836 sermon, "Primitive Tradition," he chastised those who violated the rule of apostolic tradition and introduced novelty into religion.

> Had this rule (apostolic tradition) been faithfully kept, it would have preserved the Church just as effectually from the assertion of transubstantiation on the one hand, as from the denial of Christ's real presence on the other hand. The two errors in the original are perhaps but rationalism in different forms. . . .[47]

Edward Pusey underscored this same duality in his sermon, "The Presence of Christ in the Holy Eucharist."

I would then, once more, my younger brethren, set before you the doctrine of the Holy Eucharist on both sides. And this, both because some, looking for too much clearness in their intellectual conception of divine mysteries, are tempted to undue speculation in defining the mode of the sacred presence of our Lord; and others, practically, can hardly be thought to believe any real presence at all; else they would not approach, as they do, so unrepenting and so careless.[48]

Later in the same sermon Pusey pinpointed the Oxford Movement's main objection to the Roman Catholic doctrine of transubstantiation.

And yet Holy Scripture, taken in its plainest meaning, affirms both that the outward elements remain, and still that there is the real presence of the Body of Christ. And I may, in the outset, say, that when the Articles reject transubstantiation, they themselves explain what they mean to reject—a doctrine which 'is repugnant to the plain words of Holy Scripture,' i.e., those words in which our Lord and St. Paul speak of the natural substances as remaining.[49]

To the Oxford Movement the doctrine of transubstantiation, though correct in its advocacy of real presence, erred by attempting illegitimately to account for the "supernatural mystery of Christ's sacramental presence" and, thus, violated scripture.

In addition, the doctrine violated the theological necessity for the sign and the thing signified to remain connected. To annihilate the elements by having them transubstantiated into the body and blood of Christ is to vitiate the efficacy of a sacramental sign. Robert Isaac Wilberforce, in his 1853 monograph on *The Doctrine of the Holy Eucharist*, clearly affirmed this vital connection.

But that Christ's presence in the Holy Eucharist is a real presence . . . that consecration is a real act, whereby the inward part or things signified is joined to the outward and visible sign . . . these points it will be attempted to prove by the testimony of scripture and of the ancient fathers. . . . For there is a connection between the *sacramentum* and *res sacramenti*; and form and place belong to the first, though they do not belong to the second. So that, though the *res sacramenti* in itself has neither place nor form, yet it has them in a manner through the *sacramentum* with which it is united. Christ's body therefore may be said to have a form in this sacrament, namely, the form of the elements, and to occupy that place through which the elements extend. As the spirit may be said to be present in that place where the body is situated, and as light may be said to assume the shape of the orifice through which it passes, so it may be said that the *res sacramenti* borrows place and shape from the *sacramentum* with which it is united by consecration. . . . His will is to be present in the Holy Eucharist, not indeed as an object to the senses of the receiver, but through the intervention of consecrated elements.[50]

Thus, the Oxford Movement affirmed the real presence of Christ in the eucharist but in a sacramental and not a corporeal manner. Pusey was adamant.

The presence of which our Lord speaks has been termed sacramental . . . as opposed *not* to what is real, but to what is natural. . . . We know not the manner of his presence, save that it is not according to the natural presence of our Lord's human flesh, which is at the right hand of God; and therefore it is called sacramental.[51]

Reflecting its *via media* character, the Oxford Movement was quite comfortable, on the one hand, in appropriating traditional eucharistic language, while it was quite consistent, on the other hand, in advocating a spiritual interpretation. Again Pusey made the point.

In the Communion there is a true, real, actual, though spiritual (or rather the more real because spiritual), communication of the body and blood of Christ to the believer through the holy elements; . . . We see not why we need avoid language used by the fathers, as well as by the ancient liturgies, and quoted with approbation by great divines of our Church, that 'the bread and wine is made the body and blood of Christ,' seeing that its being spiritually the body and blood of Christ interferes not with its being still corporeally what the Apostle calls it, 'the bread and wine,' nor with the nature of a Sacrament, but rather the better agrees thereto.[52]

By conscientiously forging a middle route between the excessive rationalism of Roman Catholicism and Protestantism, the Oxford Movement, though not original contributors, rekindled interest in the question of the mode of Christ's eucharistic presence for nineteenth century Europe. Although their respective proposals retained an attachment to the elements, they avoided the dual dangers of either a corporeal or memorial (Zwinglian) interpretation.[53]

Albert Schweitzer

Although a reawakening of interest in liturgical and eucharistic theology informed the Church of England in the mid-nineteenth century, it was not until the turn of the century that continental theology evidenced any creative contribution. By that time Johannes Weiss and Albert Schweitzer had thematized the new "eschatological" interpretation of the teachings of Jesus. In its extreme form, which Schweitzer called "thorough-going eschatology," it struck like a bombshell and precipitated a "theological scandal."

> But it is an extraordinary fact that, while failing to make good in its extreme form in the field of New Testament exegesis, the eschatological idea overflowed its banks and watered all the land in a fruitful way, transforming the theological landscape, making the whole of theology in all its fields more eschatological than it had been for a long time.[54]

These perceptive words of John Baillie certainly held true for eucharistic theology. Schweitzer's book, *The Problem of the Lord's Supper according to the Scholarly Research of the Nineteenth Century and the Historical Accounts*, "recovered" eschatology as an important element not only in Jesus' thought but also in the Lord's Supper.

Fascinated by a reading of the *Glaubenslehre* in which Schleiermacher observed that neither Mark (14:22-24) nor Matthew (26:26-28) had any command to "do this" after the partaking of the bread and the wine, Schweitzer was startled by Schleiermacher's conclusion "that the Lord's Supper can never again be as Christ instituted it, and therefore it really could not have been ordained by him as an independent and permanent institution for the Church."[55] Although Schleiermacher did not follow up this potentially devastating observation, Schweitzer cited him as "the Hume of the question of causality in the problem of the Lord's Supper"[56] and credited him for "'awaken(ing) us out of our dogmatic slumber' in the Kantian sense."[57]

In his book, Schweitzer framed the problem by posing two questions:

> What were the motives which led the first congregation to observe a celebration of this kind which is associated with Jesus' last meal? Was that arbitrariness or necessity?

> There follows a second question, which Schleiermacher failed to take into account. If the first congregation repeated the celebration for definite reasons, are these reasons still valid for us?[58]

Bluntly and honestly, Schweitzer argued that there was no command by Jesus to repeat the meal. This conclusion was grounded in the belief that only the Marcan account was historically accurate, since the other accounts evidenced the trend toward paralleling the sayings over the cup and the bread.

Acceptance of Mark's version as historically authentic means (a) that there was no command from Jesus to repeat any rite, and that (b) he spoke the words 'this is my body' *while* they were eating and the words 'This is my blood' *after* they had all drunk of the cup, in neither case *before*.[59]

The interpretive key lay, then, not in focusing on the "sayings" about body and blood, but on both the "solemn proceedings" themselves and Jesus' impending passion and his expectation for an imminent reunion with his disciples, after his death, in the Kingdom of God (Mark 14:25). The church's preoccupation with the Words of Institution severed the eschatological emphasis from these events. Instead, demanded Schweitzer, Jesus' suffering and eschatological expectation should be linked.

> In the Marcan text, however, this eschatological saying assumes a principal position. It is the concluding saying of the celebration, spoken solemnly and impressively. At the same time it is closely and inseparably connected with the saying about the shed blood, so that it seems to form with it one single thought. This close connection between the ideas of death and return is characteristic of the second act in Mark.[60]

In spite of the absence of a command by Jesus to repeat the meal, Schweitzer affirmed "our Lord's Supper (as) authorized, imperative, and necessary," based on the actual celebration of the early church.

Yet, Schweitzer's unique contribution occurred in his declaration that there exists "no profit" in wrangling over the Words of Institution—whether Roman Catholic, Lutheran, Zwinglian, or Calvinist. After constructing an elaborate fourfold typology, which organized the multitude of views on the supper based on their affinity for emphasizing either the *Darstellungsmoment* ("the moment of presentation" or "the actions and words of Jesus during the historical celebration"), or the *Genussmoment* ("the moment of partaking" or "emphasis on the reception of the bread and wine in the act of communion"),[61] Schweitzer praised his own solution since it transcended both the typology and the dilemma which have "racked Christianity for most of its nineteen-hundred year history."

> Also here the true historical understanding brings freedom from this unnatural alternative. . . . The primitive Christian celebration is not based on the 'words of institution'—this is my body, this is my blood—though these words had been spoken during the historical celebration. Therefore our interpretation is independent of these puzzling figurative sayings.[62]

What exactly was Schweitzer's solution? It was to interpret the Lord's Supper "on the basis of the general pattern of the life of Jesus."[63] Since the current pattern was erroneous, eucharistic theology was likewise erroneous.

> The problem of the Lord's Supper is the problem of the life of Jesus! A new interpretation of the Lord's Supper can be built only upon a new interpretation of the life of Jesus, an interpretation which so contains the secrets of the messiahship and of the passion that his solemn action at the final meal becomes comprehensible and understandable. A new life of Jesus: that is the only way to the solution of the problem of the Lord's Supper.[64]

Although Schweitzer's bold retrieval of primitive Christian eschatology had been intended to transcend the old splits among the Reformation parties and to offer an ecumenical solution that would appeal to Protestants and Roman Catholics alike, in reality it neither convinced the experts nor solved the problems.[65] In fact, Schweitzer's work on the Lord's Supper has been virtually ignored by ongoing research. This is highly paradoxical in light of the resurgence of the eschatological theme in post-Vatican II Roman Catholic and Protestant liturgical writings. For instance, Geoffrey Wainwright's well-received book, *Eucharist and Eschatology*, gives prominence to Schweitzer "but only for his books beginning with *The Mystery of the Kingdom of God*."[66] Schweitzer's earlier and seminal work on the Lord's Supper is "unmentioned, and seemingly unknown."[67]

Regardless of the book's reception by the tradition, Schweitzer's recovery of the eschatological theme in the Lord's Supper, though ahead of its time, is now an accepted and common component in eucharistic study.

Conclusion

The Mercersburg Movement in America, the Oxford Movement in England, and Albert Schweitzer in Germany represent the significant Protestant eucharistic theologies of the nineteenth century. Yet, these three contributions are not innovative. The Mercersburg Movement simply recalled the insights of John Calvin. Although the Oxford Movement rekindled interest in the eucharist, it advanced no original proposal. Albert Schweitzer recovered the eschatological theme, but he did not address the mode of Christ's eucharistic presence. Post-Reformation Protestant theology merely reiterated the traditional eucharistic themes and models of the Reformation period.

There would emerge no other consequential Protestant eucharistic theologies until the growth of ecumenism in the mid-twentieth century. Neo-orthodoxy, the dominant theology of post-World War II mainline Protestantism, focused on the preached "Word" as the primary point of the divine-human encounter and, therefore, did not address the Lord's Supper.[68] "Existentialism, and its attendant theological formulations in the theologies of men like Paul Tillich and Rudolf Bultmann, manifested subjectivistic, individualistic tendencies which militated against renewal of corporate worship or sacramental emphasis."[69] Modern Pentecostalism, in part a rebellion against "lifeless forms" in Protestant worship, stressed the spirit and not the sacraments.[70]

In short, Protestantism of the last four centuries has basically lacked a comprehensive sacramental theology and been understandably suspicious of any attempts to revive or even emphasize liturgics. Concerns for the sacraments in general and for the mode of Christ's eucharistic presence in particular were essentially unrealistic until Protestants could overcome their prejudice against "popish traditions" and embrace the ecumenical spirit.

Roman Catholic Eucharistic Theology

In contrast to the virtual absence of liturgical and eucharistic renewal in Protestantism, Roman Catholicism evidenced a gradual trend toward liturgical renewal which culminated in the Second Vatican Council. Yet, the impetus for the Liturgical Movement was slow and deliberate.

Post-Tridentine Roman Catholic eucharistic theology tenaciously adhered to the decrees of that council and dared not deviate from the doctrine of transubstantiation. Not only did the Council of Trent serve as the "standard" for eucharistic expression, but in effect it placed authorized eucharistic pronouncements into a "deep freeze."[71]

One result of this solidification was the unconscious acceptance of what George S. Worgul calls the "Mechanistic-Physical Model" of sacramentology.[72] Combining a physical-quantitative notion of grace with a mechanical understanding of causality, i.e., an impersonal cause and effect relationship between grace and the sacraments, this model became the dominant Roman Catholic theory of sacramentology for the last four centuries.

However, the adoption of the "Mechanistic-Physical Model" in Roman Catholicism proved to be exceptionally costly. Not only did the sign/symbol character of the sacraments lie dormant, unable to secure any legitimacy among questions of "validity of performance" and "accumulation of graces," but this model also proved "inadequate for penetrating into the meaning of sacraments on three fundamental levels."[73] First, the understanding of grace as a free gift from God and of the sacraments as symbolic activities was greatly hindered by the consistent use of objective language. (Grace and sacraments cannot be described as "things" because the relation between God and humankind cannot be reduced to physical categories.) Second, this model, due to its dependence upon the late scholastic model, failed to refer to the essential links between sacraments, Christ, and the church. Without these expressed relationships it was possible to administer the sacraments without the community of faith. Third, this model ascribed a passive role to the recipients of the sacraments. Instead of being communal symbolic activities in which individuals participated, the sacraments became something private that individuals "attended" and "watched."

Because this model was concerned with safeguarding Christ's sacramental presence over against the unworthiness of both the priest and the recipient, objectivism dominated. This overemphasis on the "objective and gratuitous work of Christ" in the sacrament (*ex opere operato*) undermined, in turn, any development of the subjective dimension of the sacrament (*ex opere operantis*). Combine this concern with the inability of Aristotelian philosophical categories to depict personalist considerations, and it is relatively easy to account for the post-Tridentine Roman Catholic preoccupation with the objective dimension of the sacrament and the underdevelopment of the subjective dimension.

This one-sided emphasis in sacramental theology provides a partial explanation for the lack of ecclesial expression in Roman Catholic eucharistic theology. Not until the rise of the human sciences in the twentieth century could the intersubjective and the symbolic levels of the sacraments be properly restored.[74]

The Nineteenth and Twentieth Centuries

The gradual "thawing" of Roman Catholic sacramentology can be traced to two developments in the first third of the nineteenth century. In academics, the theological faculty at Tübingen placed "a strong emphasis on the communitarian life of the Church and on the critical study of the sources of the Church's traditions."[75] In liturgics, a French Benedictine monk, Prosper Louis Pascal Guéranger, began living at the abandoned priory at Solesmes and attracted others who wished to overcome the sins of "independence" and "individuality" by restoring a community based on corporate eucharistic worship.[76] Both the scholars of Tübingen and the monks of Solesmes prepared the way for the Liturgical Movement.

Additional precursors to liturgical renewal would include certain Modernists, especially Édouard Le Roy and Alfred Loisy. The former in his 1907 tome, *Dogma and Criticism*, pinpointed the hermeneutical problem of Post-Tridentine eucharistic theology.

> How is a plain man to behave in relation to a dogma which he is bound to hold, of which he ought therefore to know the meaning, if the formula in which the meaning is expressed has an aim which he cannot understand?[77]

Specifically, the problem resided, Le Roy continued, with scholastic philosophy.

> It is unquestionable that the fathers of the Council never dreamed of canonising one philosophy in opposition to another. The scholastic philosophy was the only philosophy with which they were acquainted, the only philosophy in vogue among them, one might almost say the only philosophy which existed in their time. They therefore made use of it, as they spoke the language of their time, but without their attention being fastened on it. We can say that the philosophy was not the point, that it was something else at which they were aiming.[78]

By distinguishing between the dogma itself and its expression, Le Roy located the key to the problem:

> Do not let us confuse the vehicle of the faith with its object. We must not fasten on the ideology any more than on the terminology of the definition. . . .[79]

And in a note he stated why the decrees of Trent are not binding:

> Neither the words nor the ideas are imposed on faith, but the reality which they signify and clothe in expressions which are human and therefore inadequate and incomplete.[80]

It comes as no surprise that in 1907 the Congregation of the Index placed Le Roy's book on the list of condemned and prohibited writings. Nevertheless, its hermeneutical insights into the relation of form and content could not be suppressed.

On November 22, 1903, Pope Pius X issued his *Motu proprio*. By providing official sanction to a movement for reform (though limited as the Le Roy condemnation indicated), by speaking of "returning to the fount" of liturgical life and restoring "active participation by the faithful," and by calling specifically for more frequent communion, this pronouncement dramatically changed the direction of Roman Catholic eucharistic theology and officially marked the beginning of the Liturgical Movement.[81]

Dom Lambert Beauduin, author in 1914 of *La Piété de l'Église*, which greatly popularized the aims of the Liturgical Movement, advanced liturgical renewal by translating the Roman Missal into the vernacular (for personal reading only) and by stressing the social character of the liturgy as a unifying factor for the church. In addition, many abbeys of Europe (Solesmes, Maredsous, Beuron, Maria Laach) contributed significantly to the work for liturgical reform by educating the laity.[82]

In the early decades of the twentieth century a "dialectical interaction between more creative elements of Eucharistic theology and the growing movement for liturgical reform" surfaced in the sacramental theologies of Maurice de la Taille and Odo Casel.[83] Although de la Taille's principal work, *Mysterium Fidei*, in 1921, argued for only one real immolation on the cross, to which the Supper looks forward and the Mass looks back, and against an immolation in the Mass, his book did emphasize the meal aspect of the eucharist.[84]

Trying to avoid the individualism and rationalism of scholasticism, Odo Casel, Benedictine monk at Maria Laach, envisioned the eucharist as a re-presentation of the mysteries of Christ by his church (*Mysterienlehre*) and, thus, developed a new eucharistic model, the "Mystery-Presence Model."[85] With the assistance of Husserl's phenomenological method, Casel sought to uncover "the Christian *Kult-eidos*, i.e., the core of Christian worship and the Christian sacraments."[86]

By initially examining the Greek mystery religions for their *Kult-eidos* (essence of cult), Casel concluded that "salvation was not a purely spiritual reality, but something tangible, audible, and perceptible in the context of their worship or cult."[87] Various elements coalesced to form the essence of worship, i.e., "Mystery-Presence." Through the cultic action or a specific rite, the mystery or divine reality was made present to the participants of the worshiping community. Casel proceeded, then, to apply these insights to Christian worship and the sacraments.

For the Christian community, God is revealed in the life of Christ and the mystery of God has become the mystery of Christ. Consequently, this mystery includes the person of Christ, and also involves the saving acts of the incarnate son, with their center in the passion. And if individual Christians are to relive the mystery of Christ, then they must share in these sacred events.[88]

At this point the liturgy becomes essential. Through worship, the historically unrepeatable past mystery of Christ is sacramentally re-presented. Casel explains:

> . . . the epiphany goes on and on in worship; the saving, healing act of God is performed over and over. Worship is the means of making it real once more. . . . The mystery is a sacred ritual action in which a saving deed is made present through the rite; the congregation, by performing the rite, takes part in the saving act, and thereby wins salvation.[89]

Understood as a mystery, the liturgy occupies the fundamental role in the Christian life and the eucharist assumes the highest form of worship.[90] Only through the liturgy can the divine reality, the mystery, be made present and the participants share in and be saved by the encounter:

> God has made it possible for us, even in this life, to enter into the divine present and the everlasting Today; this possibility is through

the sole door of the mystery of worship. There, for us too, there
is neither past nor future, only present. What is past in history, the
death of Christ for example, and what is in the future of history, his
parousia, are present in the mystery.[91]

Casel's "Mystery-Presence Model" proved advantageous for numerous
reasons.[92] It broke decisively with the individualistic and mechanistic tendencies
inherent in scholasticism, secured the freedom and gratuity of God's self-gift
in Christ, and reestablished grace as a participation in the redemptive acts of
Christ. Consequently, the interrelations among Christ, sacraments, grace, and
church were reaffirmed. (By moving in the direction of personalism, this model
helped pave the way for the "Interpersonal-Encounter Model" which was
developed in the mid-twentieth century.) The "Mystery-Presence Model" also
"rediscovered" the importance of the ritual element in worship as well as the
past-future dialectic. Finally, Casel's model grounded sacramentology and Christ's
eucharistic presence in the "'givenness' of God's presence." "Sacraments do
not conjure up God. They vividly make present, express, and deepen within
the sacramental participants the love of God which is already and always present
for his people."[93]

Yet, a devastating critique of the "Mystery-Presence Model" centers on
the explanation of how this "Mystery-Presence" occurs. Citing the genuine
historicity and bodiliness of the person of Jesus and, thus, the illegitimacy of
attributing to Jesus omnipresence, Edward Schillebeeckx notes a subtle form
of Docetism in Casel's model.

> For if God truly became man, then necessarily the sacrifice of the
> Cross in its historical manifestation is a reality belonging to the past
> and cannot be actualized anew in a sacrament. The historicity of
> the man Jesus and of his human acts of redemption shares inevitably
> in the irrevocability of temporal events. Should we wish to maintain
> the contrary, we would support a new form of Docetism; we should
> deny the genuine historicity of Jesus' existence as man. The
> omnipresence of God the Son takes on a human form in the man
> Jesus. . . . Because this human mode of being present is conditioned
> by bodily qualification, it remains limited and cannot be equated
> with omnipresence.[94]

Both de la Taille and Casel pioneered new interpretations in eucharistic
theology. Although Casel's insights contributed most significantly to our concern, both theologians, though bypassed by recent developments, advanced the
Roman Catholic Liturgical Movement.

These theological and liturgical reforms, however, were not always greeted with approbation. "Traditionalist" bishops opposed, for example, the celebrant facing the congregation and speaking to them during the celebration of the eucharist. This tension was profoundly evident in Pope Pius XII's monumental letter on the liturgy, *Mediator Dei*, in 1947. Although the letter strongly supported the continuing work of the Liturgical Movement by authorizing experiments in the vernacular, stressing participation in the eucharist, and calling all to a "priestly worship of God in Christ," it also invoked limits. Worshipers are not priests in the same way that the clergy are. Liturgical piety is not a substitute for personal piety and "the communion of the faithful is not absolutely necessary for the 'completion of the sacrifice of the mass.'"[95]

This budding liturgical crisis caused the formation of liturgical commissions in Germany, Austria, France, and Holland. In 1958, at the Benedictine priory of Saint-Croix d'Amay at Chevetogne, Belgium, an ecumenical conference attempted a fresh approach to Christ's real presence in the eucharist. A new sacramental model began to emerge.

The Emergence of the "Interpersonal-Encounter Model"

Theological dissatisfaction with eucharistic theology in general and the doctrine of transubstantiation in particular led to efforts at reinterpretation. Edward Schillebeeckx cites five factors that necessitated a new approach.

Although the liturgical reformists had no problem, on the whole, with the dogma of Trent, the term "substance," if equated with the substance-accident categories of the scholastics, created enormous difficulty. Schillebeeckx spoke for many eucharistic theologians when he exclaimed:

> The facts of modern physics had shaken the neo-scholastic speculations about the concept of substance to their foundations. This heralded the change from an approach to the Eucharist by way of natural philosophy to the anthropological approach.[96]

Due to the insights of scholars from Kant to Merleau-Ponty, both the idea of an objective reality behind and outside the world of phenomena, and the application of the category of "substance" to material reality, were seriously questioned.

The second factor that contributed to the development of a new approach was the "rediscovery of the principle '*sacramentum est in genere signi*' (the sacrament is in the category of 'sign')."[97] Although accepted by both Roman Catholics and Protestants and, therefore, not controversial, post-Tridentine theologians placed so much emphasis on the sacraments as instruments of grace that the sign-value of the sacraments was obscured.

This reaffirmation of the sign-value of the sacraments clarified greatly the issue of Christ's real presence in the eucharist. By situating this doctrine within the eucharistic sign-action, the false opposition between the *sacramentum-signum* and transubstantiation could be overcome. That is, by combining the second factor with phenomenological thought (the next factor), which situates the reality of the sign in an "anthropology" of the symbolic action, the location of the doctrine of real presence was shifted from a *gnoseological* theory of sign (scholasticism believed that the sign was an indication of an *absent* reality) to categories of "interpersonal dynamics." Instead of perceiving sacraments as objectified or static realities, the rediscovery of the category of "sign" enabled the sacraments to be perceived as "personal 'encounters' in which God and (humanity) reveal themselves effectively to one another, with all that this implies for the full realization of the reality of 'grace.'"[98]

The appropriation of modern phenomenology, the third factor, permitted sacramentology to disassociate itself "from the material sphere of things and (be) taken up into the personal sphere."[99] Since phenomenology's anthropology of the symbolic act is based on a view of *anthropos* that is not dualistic, reality can be experienced directly *in* human symbolic activity and not merely inferred *from* a sign that points to a different reality that may be signified but not really present. Schillebeeckx explained:

> Man can be in the world through self-revelation in the body only by orientating himself towards his fellow-men. It is only by directing itself outward towards other persons and the world that the human interiority is able to become fully a person. It is in his body that man reveals himself and becomes visible, perceptible and public. In this sense we may say—with no dualistic implications—that the human body does not refer to a soul situated *behind* it, it is not a *sign* of the spirit: it is, on the contrary, this interiority itself made visible. Thus human interiority is at the same time revealed and hidden. But this does not mean that it is hidden *behind* the bodily modes of expression. It is also revealed in a veiled manner, *in* the body.[100]

The concept of "embodiment" expanded the category of sign or symbolic activity to include "the visible presence of the spirit, however inadequate this disclosure may be."[101] Since the spirit is revealed in bodiliness, in human symbolic activity, sacraments become interpersonal encounters between the believer and Christ.

The fourth factor that inaugurated a new sacramental model was the realization that Christ's real presence should not be restricted to his presence in the eucharist. Stated positively, Christ's real presence is available in different modes—the Word, the sacraments, and the community (the encyclical *Mysterium Fidei*, to which we shall later refer, specifically identifies these modes). Schillebeeckx elaborated:

> Now one of the traits of the modern theological trend concerning the eucharist is to affirm that the real eucharistic presence cannot be isolated from the real presence of Christ in the whole liturgical mystery and in the souls of the faithful. In this manner it reappraises the biblical, patristic, and scholastic thought according to which the eucharistic presence in the consecrated bread and wine is ordered to the ever more intimate presence of Christ in the assembled community and in each member of the church.[102]

This acknowledgment of the many modes of Christ's real presence had a twofold gain. First, it shifted the focus of Christ's eucharistic presence from an individual context to an ecclesial context. Second, it meant that the dogma of transubstantiation did not restrict the real presence to the eucharist, although it did determine the proper mode of Christ's real presence in the eucharist.

Fifth and finally, the ecumenical movement generated new sacramental formulations as well as the realization by Catholics that Protestant experiences of the eucharist also constitute a *locus theologicus*. In particular, the contributions of F. J. Leenhardt and Max Thurian provided a non-Aristotelian interpretation of what they call a "real transubstantiation." Mutual sharing and dialoguing, then, enabled both communions to push beyond the traditional impasses.

Conclusion

These five factors, primarily, have contributed to the emergence of a new model of sacramentology—the "Interpersonal-Encounter Model." Dissatisfied with the Aristotelian scholastic framework of transubstantiation, and convinced of the value of the symbolic activity of the eucharist, of the insights of phenomenology, and of the appropriateness of the ecclesial context for the doctrine of eucharistic presence, advocates of this new model seek to overcome the shortcomings of the traditional "Mechanistic-Physical Model."

In short, the "Interpersonal-Encounter Model" emphasizes two new elements. First, the category of encounter underscores an "I-Thou" rather than an "I-It" relationship and, therefore, a mutual self-giving performed in equality and freedom.

Second, a new theology of grace is introduced in which God's action, accomplished in Christ and continued in the church, presupposes an ecclesial context.

The next chapter will highlight the historical development of this model, the official reaction of Rome to it, and the eucharistic theologies of its principal proponents.

Notes

1. John Reumann, *The Supper of the Lord* (Philadelphia: Fortress Press, 1985), 72-73 and Bernard J. Cooke, *Ministry to Word and Sacraments* (Philadelphia: Fortress Press, 1976), 591 & 624.

2. This section on the Church of England is greatly influenced by Crockett, *Eucharist*, chapter six.

3. Ibid., 170.

4. Willimon, *Word, Water, Wine and Bread*, 99.

5. Ibid., 96.

6. Ibid., 93-94.

7. Ibid., 95.

8. Theodore G. Tappert, "Meaning and Practice in Europe since the Reformation," in *Meaning and Practice of the Lord's Supper*, ed. Helmut T. Lehmann (Philadelphia: Muhlenberg Press, 1961), 121-122.

9. Willimon, *Word, Water, Wine and Bread*, 92-93.

10. Ibid., 93.

11. This section is indebted to Willimon, *Word, Water, Wine and Bread*, 93.

12. Ibid., 101.

13. Ibid., 102.

14. Ibid., 103.

15. Ibid.

16. Reginald W. Deitz, "The Lord's Supper in American Lutheranism," in *Meaning and Practice of the Lord's Supper*, ed. Helmut T. Lehmann (Philadelphia: Muhlenberg Press, 1961), 146-148.

17. Ibid., 148-149.

18. Ibid., 155-157.

19. Willimon, *Word, Water, Wine and Bread*, 112.

20. Ibid., 113.

21. Sydney E. Ahlstrom, *A Religious History of the American People*, vol. 2 (Garden City: Image Books, 1975), 56.

22. James Hastings Nichols, ed. with an Introduction, *The Mercersburg Theology*, A Library of Protestant Thought (New York: Oxford University Press, 1966), 199.

23. Ibid., Introduction, 13.

24. Ibid.

25. Bard Thompson and George H. Bricker, Preface to *The Mystical Presence and Other Writings on the Eucharist*, by John W. Nevin, Lancaster Series on the Mercersburg Theology, vol. 4, (Philadelphia: United Church Press, 1966), 7.

26. Ibid., 8.

27. Nichols, *The Mercersburg Theology*, 201.

28. Thompson and Bricker, Preface, *Mystical Presence and Other Writings*, 8-9.

29. Ibid., 9.

30. Nichols, *The Mercersburg Theology*, 200-201.

31. Jack Martin Maxwell, *Worship and Reformed Theology: The Liturgical Lessons of Mercersburg* (Pittsburg: The Pickwick Press, 1976), 31.

32. Nichols, *The Mercersburg Theology*, 204-205 & 243.

33. Ibid., 201-204.

34. Ibid., 205.

35. Ibid., 205-206.

36. Ibid., 200.

37. The decade of the 1840s in America was a period of widespread anti-Catholicism. Because of immigration and domestic problems, the charge of "Romanizing tendencies" was quite inflammatory. See Ahlstrom, *Religious History*, vol. 2, 57-58 and Nichols, Introduction, *The Mercersburg Theology*, 21.

38. Thompson and Bricker, Preface, *Mystical Presence and Other Writings*, 12.

39. Ibid.

40. Maxwell, *Worship and Reformed Theology*, 33-34.

41. Nichols, *The Mercersburg Theology*, 250-251.

42. See Maxwell, *Worship and Reformed Theology*, 35; Thompson and Bricker, Preface, *Mystical Presence and Other Writings*, 12-13; and Nichols, Introduction, *The Mercersburg Theology*, 246.

43. J. H. Nichols put it this way: "Hodge did not reply. He was beyond his depth and, whether he fully realized it or not, he had been demolished" (Maxwell, *Worship and Reformed Theology*, 35).

44. Nichols, Introduction, *The Mercersburg Theology*, 246.

45. Cooke, *Word and Sacraments*, 626-627.

46. Stone, *A History of the Doctrine*, vol. 2, 554-555.

47. Eugene R. Fairweather, *The Oxford Movement* (New York: Oxford University Press, 1964), 85.

48. Ibid., 372.

49. Ibid., 373.

50. Stone, *A History of the Doctrine*, vol. 2, 549-550.

51. Fairweather, *Oxford Movement*, 374.

52. Stone, *A History of the Doctrine*, vol. 2, 534.

53. This presentation of the Oxford Movement's doctrine of Christ's eucharistic presence did not utilize the writings of Cardinal John Henry Newman because his contributions were not unique during his Anglican or Catholic periods. See

John Tracy Ellis, "The Eucharist in the Life of Cardinal Newman," *Communio* 4 (Winter 1977): 324-325 & 339.

54. Donald M. Baillie, *The Theology of the Sacraments and Other Papers* (New York: Scribner's Sons, 1957), 67.

55. Albert Schweitzer, *The Problem of the Lord's Supper according to the Scholarly Research of the Nineteenth Century and the Historical Accounts*, ed. with an Introduction by John Reumann, trans. A. J. Mattill, Jr. (Macon: Mercer University Press, 1982), 46.

56. Ibid., 48.

57. Ibid., 47.

58. Ibid., 50.

59. John Reumann, Introduction, *Problem of the Lord's Supper*, 17.

60. Schweitzer, *Problem of the Lord's Supper*, 136.

61. Reumann, Introduction, *Problem of the Lord's Supper*, 22-23.

62. Schweitzer, *Problem of the Lord's Supper*, 51-52.

63. Although it is not our intention to resolve the question "of whether *Abendmahl* was Schweitzer's central theme out of which his life-of-Jesus studies emerged (Reumann); or whether a new concept of the life of Jesus was his driving passion from student days on, in which study of the *Abendmahl* was but a starting point for his thesis (Groos; Picht; Grässer)" (Reumann, Introduction, *Problem of the Lord's Supper*, 33); it must be acknowledged that it stands as "an integrative factor" in his work around the turn of the century.

64. Schweitzer, *Problem of the Lord's Supper*, 137.

65. Reumann, Introduction, *Problem of the Lord's Supper*, 33.

66. See Wainwright, *Eucharist and Eschatology*, 155, n. 6.

67. Reumann, Introduction, *Problem of the Lord's Supper*, 35-36.

68. Reumann, *Supper of the Lord*, 74 and Willimon, *Word, Water, Wine and Bread*, 115.

69. Willimon, *Word, Water, Wine and Bread*, 115. See chapter one of Dietrich Ritschl's *Memory and Hope* for a detailed analysis of the failure of modern Protestantism to espouse a "corporate consciousness" of the church.

70. Willimon, *Word, Water, Wine and Bread*, 115.

71. See Reumann, *Supper of the Lord*, 74; Cooke, *Word and Sacraments*, 604 & 627; and Stone, *A History of the Doctrine*, vol. 2, Post-Tridentine Roman Catholic writers, 356-442, especially his section on eucharistic presence, 412-442.

72. Although George S. Worgul, *From Magic to Metaphor: A Validation of the Christian Scraments* (New York: Paulist Press, 1980), 204, provides this label, both Powers, *Eucharistic Theology*, 79-80 and Schillebeeckx, *Christ the Sacrament*, 3, concur with the description.

73. This description is dependent upon Worgul, *Magic to Metaphor*, 204-205.

74. Regis Duffy, *Real Presence: Worship, Sacraments, and Commitment* (San Francisco: Harper and Row, 1982), 23-25.

75. Powers, *Eucharistic Theology*, 43.

76. Ibid., 44 and Willimon, *Word, Water, Wine and Bread*, 106-107.

77. Stone, *A History of the Doctrine*, vol. 2, 435.

78. Ibid.

79. Ibid.

80. Ibid.

81. Powers, *Eucharistic Theology*, 44 and Willimon, *Word, Water, Wine and Bread*, 107.

82. Ibid.

83. Cooke, *Word and Sacraments*, 632.

84. Reumann, *Supper of the Lord*, 75.

85. Worgul, *Magic to Metaphor*, 206.

86. Ibid.

87. Ibid., 207.

88. Charles Davis, Preface to *The Mystery of Christian Worship, and Other Writings*, by Odo Casel, ed. Burkhard Neunheuser (Westminster, MD: The Newman Press, 1962), x.

89. Odo Casel, *The Mystery of Christian Worship, and Other Writings*, ed. Burkhard Neunheuser, with a Preface by Rev. Charles Davis (Westminster, MD: The Newman Press, 1962), 53.

90. Ibid., 157.

91. Ibid., 142.

92. The following comments are dependent upon Worgul, *Magic to Metaphor*, 208-209.

93. Ibid., 209.

94. Schillebeeckx, *Christ the Sacrament*, 56.

95. See Powers, *Eucharistic Theology*, 45 and Willimon, *Word, Water, Wine and Bread*, 108.

96. Edward C. F. A. Schillebeeckx, *The Eucharist*, trans. N. D. Smith (New York: Sheed and Ward, 1968), 94.

97. Powers, *Eucharistic Theology*, 147.

98. Ibid., 148. Also see Edward C. F. A. Schillebeeckx, "Transubstantiation, Transfinalization, Transignification," in *Living Bread, Saving Cup*, ed. R. Kevin Seasoltz, trans. David J. Rock (Collegeville: The Liturgical Press, 1982), 177-178.

99. See Schillebeeckx, *The Eucharist*, 99-101.

100. Ibid., 100.

101. Ibid.

102. Schillebeeckx, "Transubstantiation," 179-180.

CHAPTER SIX

THE "INTERPERSONAL-ENCOUNTER MODEL"

By the middle of the twentieth century, widespread dissatisfaction with the Aristotelian scholastic framework of transubstantiation assured both the refinement of and the reaction to the new "Interpersonal-Encounter Model" of sacramentology. Our final chapter will chronicle these events in four steps. First, the historical development of the new model will be highlighted; second, the reaction of Rome to this new model will be recounted; third, the influential proponents of the "Interpersonal-Encounter Model" will be examined; and fourth, two principal criticisms of the new model will be posited.

Historical Development of the New Model

Explicit criticisms of the Aristotelian scholastic formulation of the doctrine of transubstantiation were voiced publicly by the Belgian priest, A. Vanneste,[1] in 1956 and by the Dutch priest, Joseph Möller, in 1960.[2] Vanneste, who is the more germane to our study, tried to make transubstantiation intelligible without referring to either philosophy or phenomenology. He wished to draw a distinction "between what things are for God (and for the believer) and what they are for our secular experience as men."[3] This differentiation, he hoped, would ensure that transubstantiation would be perceived as a religious and not a natural phenomenon. Thus, there would exist no contradiction between what bread means for God and what it means for humans.[4]

Jean de Baciocchi's work, however, was the first attempt by a Catholic theologian "to synthesise 'realism' (transubstantiation) and 'the sacramental symbolism in its full depth of meaning.'"[5] In a 1955 article,[6] and repeated at the Chevetogne Conference in 1958, he emphasized that the real presence is not an isolated reality but one which must be interpreted within the context of Christ's gift of himself to the church in the form of a sign—the sign of bread and wine. The key question for de Baciocchi, says Schillebeeckx, was the question of reality: what is "real"?

> The ultimate reality of things is not what they are for our senses or for the scientific analysis that is based on this, but what they are for Christ. Christ's power as Lord makes all things be for him. If, therefore, Christ really gives *himself* in bread and wine, God's good gifts, then an objective and fundamental change has taken place, a transubstantiation—bread and wine become *signs* of Christ's real gift of himself. De Baciocchi was reacting here against the concept of a substance situated *behind* the phenomenal world.[7]

Christ, whose will expresses ultimate reality, gave new meanings to created things. "Thus, transsubstantiation and the real presence are not opposed to the symbolism of the sacraments, but rather are deeply rooted in it."[8] By appropriating this new concept, de Baciocchi was the first to use the term "transfinalization."[9]

Desiring to retain the *conversio entis* (change of being itself) as expressed by transubstantiation but seeking to reinterpret it, Bernhard Welte placed this dogma on the "level of giving meaning." Since "personal and spiritual relationships are more real than physical and material relationships," the being itself of things changes when relationships change. For example, colored fabric is purely decorative until a national government decides to elevate it to the level of a national flag. Although the physical fact of the cloth has not changed, its significance has definitely changed. It has undergone a "historical transubstantiation." In the case of the eucharist, Christ has granted a new meaning to the bread and wine.[10]

Protestant Contributions

Concurrently, three Protestants contributed to the eucharistic discussions. By accepting the concept of transubstantiation, but in a non-Aristotelian sense, F. J. Leenhardt, Max Thurian, and Charles Davis greatly influenced Roman Catholic reformulations.

The Geneva Reformed theologian, F. J. Leenhardt, in his pamphlet *Ceci est mon corps*, espoused a particularly strong Protestant realistic theology by stressing the transformative meaning of Jesus' words, "This is my body."

When Christ first uttered these words and when we continue to invoke the Words of Institution, a real change in the reality of the bread occurs. Yet, the bread remains bread. Leenhardt explained:

> Enfolded and, as it were, immersed in the will of Jesus Christ, this bread remains bread; that is quite certain. Physico-chemical analysis will continue to find in it the same elements. There is no *transmutation* of matter in it. Christianity has always reacted against an interpretation of the words of Jesus which ends by saying that the bread is materially the body.[11]

However, Leenhardt insisted on a real change. Consequently, this change, if not operative on the material level, must occur on a different level of reality. This introduced the issue of ultimate reality. Leenhardt concluded that:

> the true reality of things is to be found in what God wishes them to be for His creatures. . . . Things are what God makes of them:

they are what they realize of His active will; their reality depends
upon the creative will of His Word. . . . Things have a vocation, and
they acquire their final reality from the fulfillment of this vocation.[12]

What Christ intended for the bread and the wine was different from the
intentions of the baker and winegrower.

What is essential in this bread, which Christ gives, declaring that it is
His body, is not what the baker has made of it, but what Jesus Christ
has made of it when He gives it and declares that it is His body.[13]

Thus, the word "transubstantiation" was essential for the real presence of
Christ in the eucharist.

It is useful because it preserves two affirmations which are essential
to faith, in which everything can be summed up: (1) The substance
of things is not in their empirical data, but in the will of God who
upholds them. (2) Jesus Christ declares in the upper room, in a
sovereign manner, His will that the bread should be His body; He
transforms the substance of this bread.[14]

The key category for Leenhardt, and all theologians who wish to retain yet
reinterpret the doctrine of transubstantiation, was the category of "substance."
Knowing the bankruptcy of the Aristotelian usage, Leenhardt declared that
"substance is the final reality of things as faith recognizes it in God's Creation
and in His ordinance to His creatures."[15]
Though marginal to his actual reformulation, Leenhardt also acknowledged
the importance of the church.

The presence of Christ is not an individual affair . . . but it is truly objective
because it is 'for many', . . . It relates to the *ecclesia* in its totality. . . .[16]

When Christ distributes the bread, this offering which He makes
of His body is addressed to the totality of believers—that is certain.
Each has his place at the table only in virtue of his membership of
the *ecclesia* which Christ gathers together.[17]

It is necessary *to be gathered together in His name* for Christ to be present;
that is of the order of faith.[18]

The bread is the body of Christ only because it is Christ who gives
this bread. He can give it only if there is someone to take it, if the

church is there, if two or three are gathered together in His name, if faith welcomes this word.[19]

By introducing the issue of ultimate reality and by redefining the category of "substance," F. J. Leenhardt was able to reinterpret as well as retain the doctrine of transubstantiation.

Max Thurian of the community of Taizé in his earlier work, *The Eucharistic Memorial*, as well as in his later work, *The Mystery of the Eucharist*, placed all theological questions about the eucharist into the broader context of memorial event. Memorials are significant because God is present in them renewing continually the covenant between God and God's people. Thus, the eucharist, as a memorial, does not merely recall the past event of Christ's sacrifice. Rather, Thurian interpreted Christ's words, "Do this for my remembrance," as the fulfillment of a new covenant given by God in Christ in which the eucharist acts as the "real 're-presentation' of the unique sacrifice which Christ accomplished once and for all."[20] Through the eucharistic memorial, "Christ renders his sacrificial reality sacramentally present" in order that the church may participate in it.

By closely connecting Christ's sacrifice and real presence, Thurian affirmed the theology of the real presence in Tridentine terms. He argued that the three adverbs, "truly, really, substantially," retained by the Council of Trent to qualify the mode of Christ's eucharistic presence, are found not only in the texts of Calvin and Luther but that they also express the eucharistic mystery for Protestants.[21]

In opposition to a purely symbolic interpretation, Thurian declared the value of the adverb "truly."

> The first adverb refers to the *truth* of the gift of God in the Eucharist: when Christ says that here he gives us his body, it is because in truth his Risen Body is present and is given. Truth is there in opposition to the image, the simple figure the purely external sign which would send us back to a distant reality, absent from us now.[22]

Assured by Jesus in the Words of Institution and empowered by the Holy Spirit, the second adverb addresses the objective character of Christ's eucharistic presence.

> The second adverb refers to the *reality* of God's gift in the Eucharist ... it is present objectively, independently of the subjectivity and even of the faith of the celebrants. . . . faith receives him in the Eucharist and allows this communion to bear fruit. It is the Word of God and the Holy Spirit that bring the real and objective presence

of the risen body of Christ under the signs of the bread and the wine they sanctify.[23]

The third adverb connects the reality level of Christ's presence with the sacramental signs of bread and wine. The body of the risen Christ:

> is present *substantially*, that is to say according to a particular mode, unique to the eucharistic mystery. The consecrated bread and wine are no longer ordinary food and drink, they have become the outward signs of a profound new reality which is the risen body of Christ, truly and really present.[24]

In order to ensure a viable interpretation of Trent which is also compatible with Calvin and Luther, Thurian must, like the others, redefine the term "substance."

> The substance means here, in the etymological sense of the word 'what stands underneath,' it is the profound reality of its being which causes it to be what it is and not something else. Being can change its substance, or its profound reality, and become something else. . . .

> The conversion of the bread into the sacrament or presence of the body of Christ, who has become the substance of profound reality of this consecrated bread is . . . irreversible because of the work of the Word of God and the Holy Spirit.[25]

By reinterpreting the Tridentine language and by redefining the term "substance," Max Thurian bridged Roman Catholic and Protestant eucharistic theology.

The use of interpersonal relationship categories to explain eucharistic presence also appeared in the theological writings of England's Charles Davis.[26] Like de Baciocchi, Davis argued that Christ's eucharistic presence constitutes a "substantial presence" since the term "substance" indicates "the intimate or basic reality of the bread as opposed to the appearances."[27] When the bread is identified with Christ, the reality of the bread undergoes a change. For this reason, there is no "consubstantiation," but there is a "real transubstantiation."

Yet, the identity between bread and Christ is not complete. The change alters neither the appearance nor the chemical composition. Rather, the change occurs at a non-empirical level—the level of human meaning. In a summary of Davis' *Sophia* article, H. Benedict Green observed:

> What seems to be the truth of the matter is that bread and wine are knowable only in relation to man. They are realities of human

life—material things with a human significance. Their unity depends upon the finality imposed upon them by man. It is the human meaning, not the physical make-up, which matters.[28]

Because bread has its reality as a "human object" and because the unity we call bread is unintelligible without human relation, transubstantiation gives to bread a "new human unity." The real ontological meaning of bread is radically changed from physical bread to the sacrament of Christ's body. Christ's real presence in the eucharist finds its completion "in the reciprocal encounter that takes place between Christ and ourselves."

With the assistance of interpersonal categories, Davis suggested that the basic meaning of the doctrine of transubstantiation includes an "ontological 'transfinalization' and 'transsignification.'" Although he did not employ these exact terms,[29] his theological emphasis on interpersonal relations implies that transubstantiation involves a change in the final meaning or significance of the "human object" of bread and wine.

Roman Catholic Contributions

While these three Protestants enhanced eucharistic discussions, Roman Catholic theologians were not idle. Although Karl Rahner discussed the mode of Christ's eucharistic presence and affirmed that Christ is present under the words of consecration,[30] his real contribution occurred in his book, *The Church and the Sacraments*, where he advanced the "Interpersonal-Encounter Model." By setting the doctrine of Christ's eucharistic presence within the ecclesial framework and by emphasizing the importance of signs, Rahner gave legitimacy to the new model.

Acknowledging the confusion that exists over the connection between church and sacraments, Rahner rejected any mechanistic image:

> In general, the sacraments are regarded as means of grace for the salvation of the individual, which they certainly are, of course, but as nothing else. If the sacraments are viewed in that way, the church can only appear as the dispenser of these means of grace for the individual's salvation . . . but from whom one turns away as soon as they have been supplied.[31]

Instead, Rahner envisioned the church as the "primal and fundamental sacrament." That is, Christ, as the incarnate one, "is the primal sacramental word of God." Now that Christ is physically absent the church becomes the locus of Christ's salvific presence.

> The church is the abiding presence of that primal sacramental word
> of definitive grace, which Christ is in the world, effecting what is
> uttered by uttering it in sign. By the very fact of being in that way
> the enduring presence of Christ in the world, the church is truly the
> fundamental sacrament. . . .[32]

Rahner started with the presupposition that the church is the source of all
the sacraments. Then he argued that the "efficacy of sacraments is precisely
that of signs." The sacraments are the cause of grace because they are signs
of God's presence. Just as the sacraments are acts fundamentally expressive
of the nature of the church, so the church experiences her own nature when
she recognizes that those particular acts that flow from her are sacraments.[33]
Rahner reinforced the "Interpersonal-Encounter Model" by laying the
groundwork for the connection between Christ and church as sacraments, and
for the understanding of sacraments as signs.

Conclusion

It was necessary to detail the historical development of the "Interpersonal-
Encounter Model" and to highlight its early proponents in order to demonstrate
that the new model inaugurated a "quantum leap" in sacramental theology.
Not surprisingly, many Catholic theologians interpreted these deviations
from the scholastic formulation as tantamount to a deviation from the doctrine
of transubstantiation itself. The proponents of the new model countered by
declaring that the presentation of the dogma in relational categories accomplished
not only an ontologically more profound expression but also a more intelligible
expression. And behind these often heated exchanges stood the irreconcilable
presuppositions of two rival models—the old "Materialistic-Physical Model"
and the new "Interpersonal-Encounter Model." A historical example illustrates.
In one sense the impetus toward a new model can trace its origins to Italy.[34]
Although few Catholics have ever heard of the debate, from 1949-1960, between
Professor Carlo Colombo of the Milan Major Seminary and Professor Filippo
Selvaggi of the Gregorian University, it underscores the clash between these
two sacramental models.
Professor Colombo, advocate of the new model, argued that transubstantiation
constitutes an ontological and not a physical change, while Professor Selvaggi,
advocate of the old model, identified the Tridentine dogma with a physical and
even chemical change. This classic alignment pinpoints the critical issue of
ontology versus cosmology. Selvaggi, like some conservative theologians,
interpreted the dogma through terms of chemical theories of atoms and molecules.
Reacting against this physical change theory, Colombo emphasized the ontological

dimension of the *conversio substantialis*. The debate was hopelessly deadlocked because their presuppositions were antithetical and incompatible.

The subsequent debate of the 1960s was even more complex since the Italian polemic neglected totally the category of *sacramentum-signum*. In this sense, Schillebeeckx observed, "the eucharistic controversy has entered into a truly new phase." That is, the ontological conversion occurs only within the sacramental framework. Since "the ontological dimension is a *dimension* of 'sacramentum-signum,'" explanations of the mode of Christ's presence must stay within the eucharistic framework. To speculate on the physical composition of the bread or wine would violate this sacramental truth by venturing into the domain of the physicist or biologist. The realization that the ontology of physical reality operates on a different level than the ontology of eucharistic sacramentality constitutes the "quantum leap" in this new model.

The Reaction of Rome to the New Model

Unlike the more conservative theologians, the Roman Catholic hierarchy welcomed, with justifiable caution, the new eucharistic formulations. The two principal pronouncements of the 1960s, the "Constitution on the Sacred Liturgy" from the Second Vatican Council and Pope Paul's encyclical, *Mysterium Fidei*, illustrate the point.

Second Vatican Council

Vatican II's document on the sacred liturgy was in one respect the culmination of liturgical renewal. In this visionary, even radical, document the church leaders affirmed the connection between ecclesiology and sacramentology by situating Christ's eucharistic presence within the broader context of Christ's ecclesial presence. Paragraph seven summarized this thematic shift.

> To accomplish so great a work, Christ is always present in His Church, especially in her liturgical celebrations. He is present in the sacrifice of the Mass, not only in the person of His minister . . . but especially under the Eucharistic species. By His power He is present in the sacraments, so that when a man baptizes it is really Christ Himself who baptizes. He is present in His word, since it is He Himself who speaks when the holy Scriptures are read in the Church. He is present, finally, when the Church prays and sings, for He promised: 'Where

two or three are gathered together for my sake, there am I in the midst of them' (Mt. 18:20).[35]

In contrast to the extended tradition that once limited the discussion of Christ's eucharistic presence to the elements of bread and wine, this bold directive envisioned only one "real" presence of which eucharistic presence is but one among many modes of Christ's presence. Therefore, Christ's distinctive eucharistic presence can be properly understood only within the larger ecclesial context. At least three consequences follow.

First, the document indicts any theology "which attempts to isolate Christ's presence in bread and wine from the full pattern of symbolic actions by which God embraces the world (as) misleading at best and pernicious at worst."[36]

Second, it fosters the understanding that "the church makes the eucharist." Because the community in which Christ is present precedes the eucharist, any view that would image the church's celebration of the sacrament as the community's "pining" for its absent Lord is false. Christ is not in heaven first and then comes down to the altar in the manner of transubstantiation. Rather, Christ is already present in the church. Without Christ's prior ecclesial presence through faith and promise, the church would not be empowered to make Christ present in the eucharist.[37]

Since the church is "anterior" to the eucharist, it also constitutes the origin of the eucharist. Reflecting Rahner's influence, the church is esteemed as the primordial sacrament (the *Ursakrament*) of salvation. Thus, the church-as-sacrament is both "anterior" to and the origin of the eucharist-as-sacrament.[38]

Third, it recognizes that the presence of Christ in the worshiping community "preexists" any acknowledgment and acceptance by individuals. Worship is always communal and active—never private and passive. In paragraphs 26-30, the document affirmed these ramifications.

Liturgical services are not private functions, but are celebrations of the Church.... (They) pertain to the whole body of the Church. ...

It is to be stressed that whenever rites, according to their specific nature, make provision for communal celebration involving the presence and active participation of the faithful, this way of celebrating them is to be preferred, as far as possible, to a celebration that is individual and quasi-private. This rule applies with special force to the celebration of Mass. ...

By way of promoting active participation, the people should be encouraged to take part by means of acclamations, responses, psalmody, antiphons, and songs, as well as by actions, gestures, and bodily attitudes.[39]

Mysterium Fidei

In his 1965 encyclical, *Mysterium Fidei*, Pope Paul VI struck a profound note of caution concerning the new formulations. He thought it necessary both to reaffirm the Council of Trent's statements on the holy eucharist[40] and to set limits on the range of permissible expressions.

> ... it is not permissible to extol the so-called 'community' Mass in such a way as to detract from Masses that are celebrated privately; or to concentrate on the notion of sacramental sign as if the symbolism—which no one will deny is certainly present in the most Blessed Eucharist—fully expressed and exhausted the manner of Christ's presence in this Sacrament; or to discuss the mystery of transubstantiation without mentioning what the Council of Trent had to say about the marvelous conversion of the whole substance of the bread into the Body and the whole substance of the wine into the Blood of Christ, as if they involve nothing more than 'transignification,' or 'transfinalization' as they call it. . . .[41]

The first deviation, which Pope Paul VI discussed, is the preference for "'community' Mass" to the "derogation" of private Masses. Although his language may sound as if he is withdrawing support for Vatican II's statements on the social and public nature of the eucharist, that would be erroneous. A complete reading of the letter reveals that the pope rejected only the total devaluation of the private celebration. He wished to affirm both the ecclesial nature of the sacraments and the celebration of private Mass. However, the exact relationship between ecclesiology and sacramentology remains unaddressed.

The second deviation concerns the insistence that the sign-value of the eucharist constitutes the "total and exhaustive" explanation of Christ's eucharistic presence. Most important to our study, the pope did not reject all the new formulations that expound the sign-dimension of the sacraments; he rejected only those explanations that exclude the content of the traditional dogma.

The third deviation, which includes those formulations that supersede the doctrine of transubstantiation with transignification (transposition of the meaning) and transfinalization (transposition of the aim) exclusively, demands our full attention. Again, the pope did not dismiss automatically those theologies of eucharistic presence that use these concepts. Rather, he rejected the exclusive use of these terms and the corresponding neglect of the church's traditional formulation of transubstantiation.

Pope Paul's principal concern was that these new formulations include the reality of eucharistic conversion. That is, the encyclical insisted that the change occurring in the bread and wine is ontological.

> As a result of transubstantiation, the species of bread and wine undoubtedly take on a new significance and a new finality, for they are no longer ordinary bread and wine but instead a sign of something sacred and a sign of spiritual food; but they take on this new signification, this new finality, precisely because they contain a new 'reality' which we can rightly call *ontological*.[42]

The acknowledgment of a "new significance" and a "new finality" as well as the appropriation of the term "species" instead of "accidents" indicates that the encyclical's stress on the traditional Tridentine pronouncement did not preclude new expressions of the doctrine. Rather, the pope recognized the fundamental distinction between the dogma and its expression.

> These formulas . . . express concepts that are not tied to a certain specific form of human culture, or to a certain level of scientific progress, or to one or another theological school. . . . For this reason, these formulas are adapted to all men of all times and all places.[43]

Two points are indispensable. On the material level, the encyclical declared that nothing is changed and, therefore, a physical interpretation of the conversion is illegitimate. Consequently, scientific investigation into the molecular structure of the converted bread is unwarranted. On the sacramental level, the conversion of the bread and wine into the body and blood of Christ involves a metaphysical or ontological change. Expressing both the spiritualist tradition of Augustine and the realist tradition of Ambrose, the encyclical affirmed a real yet ontological conversion. These apparent contradictions can be united if the conversion is understood to take place within the sacramental framework. This dual concern prevents both the restriction of real presence to a symbolic explanation, since that would exclude an ontological change, and the affirmation of a material change, since that would deny the sacramental category. The reality, that the doctrine of transubstantiation affirms, operates on a sacramental level. Thus, transubstantiation can never be meant to transport the eucharist out of the sign category.

Within these mandatory guidelines, other formulations can exist alongside transubstantiation. Indeed, the utilization of transfinalization and transignification are required since greater clarity of expression is desired. Paragraph 25 stated this point clearly.

They (expressions) can, it is true, be made clearer and more obvious; and doing this is of great benefit. But it must always be done in such a way that they retain the meaning in which they have been used, so that with the advance of an understanding of the faith, the truth of faith will remain unchanged.[44]

Conclusion

Having completed our historical sketch of the development of the "Interpersonal-Encounter Model" and the reaction of the Roman Catholic hierarchy, it may be advantageous to summarize the model's essential elements before we examine its principal proponents.

Three fundamental presuppositions ground this new model. The first presupposition, a new theology of grace, makes it possible to avoid a materialistic interpretation of Christ's eucharistic presence. Instead of viewing grace as a thing which is the "adornment of the soul," grace is understood as the action which God has historically taken to disclose Godself to the world. Thus, the history of God's revelation accomplished in Christ, and continued in the church and her sacramental action, necessarily connects Christology and ecclesiology. As the primordial sacrament, Christ empowers the church to be the fundamental sacrament and, in turn, the church is "anterior" to and the origin of the eucharist. Clarified by this new theology of grace, this proper relationship of Christ, church, and sacraments undergirds a proper reinterpretation of Christ's eucharistic presence.

The second fundamental presupposition recognizes that the ontological dimension of the eucharist occurs within the sacramental dimension. That is, the real change of the bread and wine into the body and blood of Christ occurs on a metaphysical, and not a scientific, level. This simple yet profound acknowledgment prevents any return to the "Materialistic-Physical Model" as well as retains the intention of Trent.

The final presupposition involves the classical distinction between *res et sacramentum* and *res sacramenti*.[45] As the previous chapters reveal, the thinking of the patristic age and of medieval scholasticism gradually moved away from emphasizing *res sacramenti* (the "communio ecclesiastica" or unity of the mystical body, i.e., the life of the community and the individual in Christ) and began to emphasize *res et sacramentum* (the real presence of Christ under the consecrated bread and wine). In other words, the initial stress was not placed on the eucharistic presence, but upon the purpose of this presence—the presence of Christ in us. Forced by circumstances and by the momentum of scholastic tradition, post-Tridentine theology neglected *res sacramenti* and favored *res et sacramentum*.

This shift in emphasis caused popular piety to dislodge the celebration of the eucharist from its ecclesial context. Consequently, the sacrament was adored, but it was no longer eaten! Proponents of this new model wish, then, to restore the emphasis on the *res sacramenti* and to reinstate the active participation of the faithful in this communal rite.

Two implications arise from these presuppositions. Because of the third presupposition's emphasis on the presence of Christ in the community of Christians, "the eucharist must remain on the level of interpersonal relationship." The real presence of Christ in the eucharist, viewed as the saving act of Christ who gives himself to us under the sacramental elements, necessarily involves reciprocity. Christ offers himself, but in order for complete presence to occur, the offered presence must be accepted. Hence, Christ's eucharistic presence operates within the context of an interpersonal relationship.

Second, interpersonal presence is communicated by means of spatial, visible, and tangible presence. In the eucharist, Christ's presence is communicated by the bread and wine. Christ's spatial absence underscores the symbol-making activity of humanity and the importance of signs. Through the power of the Holy Spirit, the bread and wine become Christ's body and blood. Transubstantiation occurs.

The "Interpersonal-Encounter Model" affirms Christ's gift of himself by means of bread and wine. Although the elements undergo a transfinalization (transposition of the aim) or transignification (transposition of the meaning), the chemical composition of bread and wine does not change, since that would prevent eatable bread and drinkable wine from functioning as eucharistic signs. Only the ontological reality (the "substance") changes. The sacramental sign of bread and wine is no longer bread and wine, but the real presence of Christ offered to us under the sign of food and drink.

The next section will detail the exact meaning of transfinalization and transignification as found in the writings of the principal proponents of this new model.

Proponents of the New Model

We now examine four proponents of the "Interpersonal-Encounter Model": two American Roman Catholic theologians, Bernard Cooke and Joseph Powers, and two European Roman Catholic theologians, Piet Schoonenberg and Edward Schillebeekcx. The latter two are the most prominent advocates of this model and warrant the most attention.

Bernard J. Cooke

Bernard J. Cooke,[46] professor of systematic theology, acknowledges that Catholic sacramental theology has undergone a radical shift in the last half-century.

Undergirded by a mechanistic theology of grace, the sacraments served for centuries as "channels of grace" by which worshipers were freed from their sinfulness and were fortified against future failures. This instrumentalist view of the sacraments reinforced a corresponding emphasis on an individualistic interpretation of sacramental action. Sacraments were essentially conduits for a vertical flow of grace.

Cooke confirms that since the Second World War an increasing amount of attention has been directed to the communal dimension of Christian life, including the sacraments. This new appreciation for the interdependence of individual and community was augmented by additional liturgical insights, which, in turn, effected a comprehensive model shift in sacramentology.

Study of early Christian worship recovered for Cooke at least three significant themes. First, the risen Christ was understood as the principal agent of any sacramental action. Second, the "resurrection of Jesus" meant that Christ was still alive and in our midst as opposed to being "up in heaven." Finally, the community played an active role in sacramental liturgy.[47] The retrieval of these themes meant a corresponding realignment in the connection of Christology, ecclesiology, and sacramentology.

> The significance of that passover mystery, Jesus' passage through death into new spirit-life, is the new meaning that human life now bears. However, it is through the believing community, the church, that this significance is preserved and expressed in history. It is this community's faith that makes the risen Christ, himself the primordial sacrament of God's saving action, present in history. The church does this by living faith-fully and significantly, by expressing in its being and its activity the presence of Christ. The church is the sacrament of Christ, who himself is the sacrament of his Father.[48]

Because presence "takes place in terms of consciousness and personal communication,"[49] the mediation of God's presence in Christ requires the encounter model. Yet, the risen Lord, though living, is invisible and intangible. Therefore, the Christian community is needed as an "observable reality" that conveys to its members "the experience of the presence of the risen Lord." The absence of the physical Jesus requires that the church administer the sacraments. Cooke, again, affirms this triadic connection.

> Christ as a sacrament makes his Father present; the church as sacrament makes Christ present, and it does so most formally in those symbolic activities that have traditionally been called the sacraments.[50]

Although Cooke does not posit a specific formulation of Christ's eucharistic presence, his position is important for at least two reasons. First, his general understanding of the sacraments is set within the framework of the new model and second, he interprets the believer's encounter with the presence of the risen Christ as a transignification.

> Though the whole of Jesus' life was sacramental, special meaning attached to his death and resurrection. In experiencing death as the free acceptance of ultimate risk, as complete fidelity to truth and love, as supreme witness to his Abba, and as passage into new life, Jesus gave human existence its full and final significance. This is the Christ-meaning expressed by the Christian sacraments as they trans-signify human life. Jesus instituted these sacraments by being—in life, death, and resurrection—the primordial sacrament of his Father's saving presence.[51]

> Simply put, the presence of the risen Christ to a believer transforms the most fundamental meaning of that person; it is a basic 'transignification' and could also be called a 'transubstantiation.'[52]

Since humans both discover meaning in an event and impose meaning onto an event, religion, for Cooke, "provides us with an ultimate hermeneutic by which we can understand how our life experience is the 'Word of God.'"[53] In its more formal and most explicit fashion, a religious ritual conveys this "word." Sacraments grant, therefore, new meanings to life. The eucharist is no exception. Through the eucharistic celebration, a "Christ-meaning" is attached to the elements of food and drink. A transignification occurs and the gift of Christ himself is made available to the assembled worshipers.[54]

Joseph M. Powers

Joseph M. Powers, Jesuit professor of dogmatic and historical theology, employs a phenomenology of the sign-act in order to argue that the language and meaning of transignification are not only compatible with transubstantiation but, more important, they also move transubstantiation from the physical to the sacramental level.[55]

Like Cooke, Powers' theology of grace undergirds his understanding of Christ and the church as sacraments. Since "Jesus is *the* 'visible form of invisible grace'" and "is *the* sacrament," the church's sacramental character is grounded in Christ.[56] The action of Christ, which is sacramentally present to the world in the church, constitutes the power of the sacramental action of the church. "This is the meaning of the expression '*ex opere operato*,' an expression of the objective power of the sacraments which basically means that Christ is truly present in the action of the Church because of her sacramental identity with Him in being and action."[57]   Hence, the very essence of the church's reality, its "interiority," is that of presence—the "'real' presence of Christ to the world."[58]

Within this fundamental sacramental framework, Powers unfolds the basic meaning of a "sign-act." At the core of the "sign-act" lies a "pregnant alienation," as Schillebeeckx defines it. That is, the "sign-act" involves an act of self-communication in which the material object of the sign is robbed of its physical individuality by the very fact that it is taken up into a human sign-act.[59]

For example, a man gives his fiancée an engagement ring. Although the physical reality of the ring—it is of gold and contains a diamond set—is important, its physical reality is eclipsed by its human meaning. The ring conveys for the giver as well as for the recipient the embodiment of their love for each other and their intention to form a "love union."

The engagement ring is not assigned some abstract meaning because of the value of its material elements. Rather, these material elements incarnate a human meaning. It would be nonsense to concentrate exclusively on the physical realities of the ring—whatever its physical value. The human assigned meaning enhances and expands the physical value. Thus, the misplaced ring is frantically sought since the insurance company cannot replace its "human" worth![60]

Yet, Powers continues, the capacity of humans to assign meanings to material objects is limited by the capacity of that objective world of meaning to convey the precise human intention. For a human to mix water, yeast, and arsenic and assign it the meaning of food proves impossible because arsenic does not nourish, it kills.

Moreover, the ability of humans to assign meanings to material objects is severely limited on the level of God's relationship to humanity. On this level, God creates and humans receive. This limitation is particularly evident in the sacramental life of the church. Powers explains:

> The gift of the sacraments is always God's creative gift to man. The ritual does not charm grace out of heaven. It is God's absolutely free gift of God.[61]

As a sacramental presence, Christ's eucharistic presence is a presence in a sign-act. Yet, this is God's exclusive act. "The sacrament is an action of God performed in the visibility of the Church."[62] Through the spirit, Christ acts in the church. Through the worshiping community—the people, the celebrant, their sacramental action—Christ gives himself in the physical realities of bread and wine.

> This is not a meaning which is superimposed on the worshipping community by man's mind, or even by Christ's mind. It is rather the very inner reality of the action itself. The symbol, the sign-act

is not opposed to reality, it is rather the very incarnation of the deepest
reality. It is in this context that one can begin to understand what
is involved in the use of the expressions 'transsignification' and
'transfinalization.'[63]

Understood within the framework of a sign-act, transignification "basically
means the divine (not human!) act in which the substance (that is, the meaning
and power) of a religious sign is transformed in the personal revelation of
God."[64] Consequently, the language of transubstantiation, which states that
the substantial reality of bread and wine is changed into the substantial reality
of Christ, and the language of transignification, which states that the same
fundamental change occurs within the context of a sign-act of Christ, are not
only compatible but the latter is essential for the former.

At first sight the use of transignification seems to contradict the traditional
Tridentine affirmation of the real presence of Christ in the eucharist. That
is, transubstantiation affirms an "ontological" change in the substance of the
bread and wine, whereas transignification affirms only a change in the meaning
or the way one "looks" at the bread. On the natural level, the question is:
"Can a change in meaning involve a change of substance? Are 'transignification'
and 'transubstantiation' mutually exclusive or can one involve the other?"[65]

Arguing that the Cartesian dichotomy between the knower and the known
would have us believe that meaning is "psychic" (in the mind) and not "ontic"
(in the world around us), Powers acknowledges that only humans can perceive
meaning but insists that meaning is not a human invention. The "givenness"
of the world governs human meaning. Without question, humans can and do
"transignify" their world and in the process create, in a limited and human sense,
new "substances." But the "transignifying" power of humans "is limited by
the values which are 'pre-given' in the very objectivity of (the) world."[66] For
example, if humans mix the correct proportions of flour, water, yeast, and salt
and bake the ingredients properly, bread will be produced. Yet, gasoline cannot
be substituted for water if the final product is to be bread. Invoking his prior
argument, the limitation of humans to assign "transignifying" power on the natural
level translates into an impossibility on the supernatural level. Only God can
"transignify" the human world into a salvation-situation.[67]

The hermeneutical key to the institution of a sacramental rite is, then, the
"*institution* of the *meaning* of the rite." On the general level, the institution of Israel,
and the church and her sacraments, constitutes a transignification. For example,
the religious *substance* of Israel undergoes a transformation in its salvific meaning
and value for God, but not for humanity.[68] On the particular level, the institution
of the Seder meal undergoes a transignification by Jesus. The religious meaning
and power of the "unleavened bread" take on a new meaning. Jesus' words have
the power, then, to transform the bread into his body.[69] Powers summarizes:

The institution of the Eucharist, then, should not be seen so much as the institution of a ritual, but should rather be seen in the creative power of the word of Christ fulfilling and transforming-in-fulfillment the meaning of a ritual already given in the religious life of Israel. It should be seen, in other words, in a 'transignification,' in the fact that the creative word of Christ changes the meaning of Passover. The central meaning and religious value is no longer that of the paschal lamb, participation in whose sacrifice creates the unity of God's covenant people. The meaning of eating and drinking in the Eucharist now centers around the body and blood of Christ, the organ of the sealing of the new covenant, the creation of a new people, a people whose unity is in the unique reality of the body of Christ.[70]

To declare that the change, which occurs in the eucharist, is a transignification implies both a negative and a positive statement. Negatively, it means that humans cannot ascribe genuine salvific meaning to any religious rite. Thus, transignification conveys more than a change in the thinking or feeling level of the believer. Positively, it means that only God transforms the religious meaning of a rite. In the eucharist Christ gives to the bread and cup a new inner value distinct from, yet related to, the Hebrew meaning. Because of this transignification, Christ is really present in the eucharist.[71]

In conclusion, the use of transignification neither denies the real presence of Christ in the eucharist nor contradicts the traditional affirmation of an ontological change. Rather, this new language shifts the mode of Christ's eucharistic presence from a purely physical level to a specifically sacramental level. The body of Christ represents the central meaning of the eucharist, although it is not the material reality of the body that is central. Rather, the salvific meaning and power of Christ's body are central.

Thus, 'transignification' demands 'transubstantiation' because it is only in the body of Christ that God's gift of authentic worship is given to man and it is only in that body that the church is continuously gathered together by God in the gift of the Spirit.[72]

Fundamentally, then, Christ's eucharistic presence is an "ecclesial" presence: "the sign and the cause of the unity of the church."[73]

Piet Schoonenberg

The contributions to eucharistic theology of the Dutch Jesuit priest, Piet Schoonenberg, are invaluable.[74] Starting with the risen Christ's presence in the eucharistic community, Schoonenberg grounds his bold assertion that transignification and transfinalization are identical to transubstantiation through a phenomenology of personal presence. Our discussion will proceed in three stages. First, we shall examine Schoonenberg's phenomenological analysis of presence. Then, we shall highlight its importance for eucharistic presence. Finally, Schoonenberg's justification of his approach with respect to Trent and the encyclical, *Mysterium Fidei*, will be presented.

By distinguishing between the profession of faith, i.e., dogma, and the act of giving oneself over to God through Christ, i.e., trusting faith, and by declaring the latter as the ultimate end of the Christian faith, Schoonenberg places his eucharistic theology within the parameters of the "Interpersonal-Encounter Model." The most important thing about the eucharist "is not that we can accurately formulate the relationship of the species to Christ, but rather, that in the reception of this Bread we realize ourselves to be in the deepest community with Him who is our salvation."[75] Although the ultimate aim of faith is directed toward realities and not propositions, Schoonenberg is not reluctant to defend his understanding of Christ's eucharistic presence.

From the beginning, Schoonenberg insists that the presence of Christ in the eucharist must be situated within the larger context of the "whole presence" of the risen Lord in his church. Since both of these modes of presence (eucharistic and ecclesial) involve human beings, the starting point for theological reflection upon Christ's presence is a phenomenology of personal presence. This realization avoids the inclination to begin with ordinary spatial presence.

In its most general sense, the meaning of presence is the fact of one reality "being-in" or "being-next-to" or "being-in-front-of" another reality. Therefore, presence implies spatial nearness, but this spatial nearness also implies degrees of presence and absence. Books may be near at hand but their content may remain distant. Personal spatial nearness to another does not guarantee attentiveness, for example, in the classroom. The student may be absent "in mind."[76]

In addition, modern personalistic thought views presence as active. Applicable for inanimate as well as personal presence, though to a lesser degree for inanimate objects, presence involves an interplay of action and reaction. Presence is, therefore, communication. It consists of a communicating or a sharing that can either be received or rebuffed. As self-giving, personal presence is identical with communication. For Schoonenberg, "presence does not precede communication, but presence itself is brought into existence through communication."[77]

By contrasting spatial and personal presence, Schoonenberg clarifies their respective meanings. Considered purely in itself, spatial presence is a minimum or lowest form of presence. However, spatial presence can "go hand in hand with" personal presence. A precise understanding is crucial.

Succinctly, spatial presence is "being present in a spatial way." That is, a person is spatially present only if that person takes up a portion of the space that is bordered by other bodies.[78] Scholasticism called this "circumscribed presence" and declared that eucharistic presence is not circumscribed.

In contrast to being present in a spatial way, personal presence demands a real communication of one's "personal interior." The personal presence of one person to another requires more than the exchange of information and the passing of time together. It involves the "intuitive grasp of reality which defines one's personal relation and attitudes toward the real."[79] Thus, authentic personal presence demands "free self-determination" and a "spiritual openness" to one's world. Freedom is essential since persons must deliberately and willingly choose to "unlock" themselves for others—to share their personal reality in the presence of others. Spiritual openness is essential because personal presence is mutual. These two constitutive features of authentic personal presence, giving and receiving, can combine in different degrees and form endless variations of personal presence. However, genuine personal presence requires complete mutuality.[80]

Within this context, personal presence can be either immediate (face-to-face) or mediated (the presence of a person through some sign of personal relationship). Signs are, therefore, important for the mediated presence of someone who is physically absent. Yet, the physical reality of a sign, e.g., a letter, souvenir, or gift, can never bring about the reality of personal presence in an immediate sense. A sign's capacity to render someone present in a mediated way is contingent upon the existing level of the personal relationship and the connection of the sign to that relationship. To the degree that these physical objects invoke personal presence, thereby acquiring new meaning, Schoonenberg can say that they are "transubstantiated." Although their physical reality remains, they are no longer seen as physical objects, since they are so closely associated with the personal presence of the absent one.[81]

Building upon his previous discussion of spatial and personal presence, Schoonenberg reminds us that human presence involves both spatial and personal presence. We are embodied selves in space and our bodily relationships incarnate our self-communication. Thus, in the human being, spatial and personal presence summon forth each other. On the one hand, "the spatial presence of a human being is an invitation to personal presence" while, on the other hand, "our personal presence prefers to exist in a spatial being-together."[82]

Further, personal presence in humans is to a certain degree independent of space and time meetings. Obviously, personal presence "endures" spatial absence but, more important, it can be deepened by it. The loss of immediate presence can "purify" the relationship.

Yet, personal presence requires spatial presence for its commencement and its continuation. Although relationships can begin in spatial absence, spatial nearness is the normal ground for new relationships. Furthermore, mediated presence sustains itself in the hope of future meetings. The symbols of remembrance give promise of an expected reunion. Jesus' words at the eucharist reinforce this promise.[83]

However, the manner of Christ's reunion is necessarily unique. Life after death, and especially life after the resurrection, is different than earthly life. Personal presence with the risen Lord requires precise clarification.

When Schoonenberg discusses Jesus, he is quick to dismiss the importance of spatial (or local) presence. Although Jesus was obviously spatially present to his disciples and followers, spatial presence was significant only insofar as it was a vehicle of the personal presence of the Son of God. Now that Jesus is the gloried and risen Christ, his spatial presence is superfluous. Unlimited as his love, Christ's presence comes to fullness only when hearts are completely open in faith; otherwise, his presence is a judgment.[84]

A comparison between the presence of the glorified Christ and the personal presence of an absent loved one proves instructive. In one sense, Christ is less present because his existence can never be framed in earthly dimensions. But in another sense, it is the whole person of Christ who is glorified and not just his "body-less soul." Thus, the whole person of the Lord is present to those people who open themselves to him in faith by the power of the Holy Spirit.[85]

Only now can Schoonenberg address the issue of the presence of Christ in the eucharist. But he does not begin with the presence of Christ's body and blood under the elements. Rather, any discussion of Christ's presence must begin with his presence in the community that celebrates the eucharist. Echoing the encyclical, *Mysterium Fidei*, Schoonenberg affirms the various modes of Christ's presence and confirms that Christ is present in the community of believers prior to eucharistic presence. It is correct, therefore, to refer to Christ's presence under the species of bread and wine as a real presence but it is incorrect to understand that presence as either the only or even the primary real presence of Christ in the community.

Christ's eucharistic presence must also be distinguished from Christ's earthly presence. The former is neither a repetition of his spatial presence nor a "condensed" presence that is appropriate to the host or the chalice. Christ's eucharistic presence always remains in the category of personal presence. The host and the chalice mediate between the risen Lord (in his church) and the believer (in the same church). Eucharistic presence always involves, then, an interpersonal encounter in which the Lord offers himself to the believer.[86] Because Christ, in the eucharist, is the giver who gives himself, this sacrament represents the highest form of Christ's self-giving and "we have in the deepest way our union with him."[87]

This "actualizing presence" of Christ occurs because bread and wine are signs. Through the prayers of the community and the priest, the elements of bread and wine function as signs of his presence. This does not mean that Christ is "dragged out of heaven in a spatial way" nor does it mean that there occurs a "physical or chemical change in the bread and wine."

Rather, a change occurs in the sign-reality of the elements. The bread and the wine cannot change their physical reality if they are to continue as signs. However, in this eucharistic context, the elements "take on a greater meaning, so that, without any change in their physical reality, they come to be the signs in which Christ gives Himself as food."[88] Thus, the transubstantiation in the eucharist takes place in a transfinalization or a transignification, but in the depth that Christ alone can reach by means of his most real gift of himself.[89]

In conclusion, Schoonenberg's phenomenology of presence is especially useful in understanding both personal presence and eucharistic presence. Although real presence must have an objective basis, "the objective basis itself does not realize presence on the level on which it takes place."[90] This is true because action constitutes the essence of presence. On the level of personal presence, this action occurs through the "confrontation of subjectivities." Hence, genuine personal presence evolves to the extent that an authentic encounter "of two personal realities takes place in the mutual confrontation of the personal 'interior' of each person."[91]

Consequently, personal presence, though mediated by bodily presence, can and does move beyond spatial presence. This realization impacts directly on formulations of Christ's eucharistic presence. To say that genuine personal presence involves a "spiritual" reality is to affirm only the confrontation of free consciousness. To say that Christ's presence *is* "spiritual" affirms two assertions. First, it means that we cannot properly speak of Christ's presence in simple physical terms and still convey the religious reality. "Spiritual" presence does not nullify, however, true and objective presence. Second, it means that we cannot assume that Christ's eucharistic presence is not real. The reality in the eucharistic action is equivalent to the reality of Christ's gift of himself to the church and to believers. The eucharist consists, therefore, of Christ's action in which "He gives Himself really, truly and objectively to the Church in and by means of the sign-act in which He reveals Himself to the Church."[92] The sign is not opposed to reality because it is the incarnation of reality.

Finally, we present Schoonenberg's defense of his use of transignification in light of the Council of Trent and the encyclical, *Mysterium Fidei*.[93] His procedure is to address the dual questions of the extent to which Trent's teaching on transubstantiation is binding for Catholic eucharistic thought and to what extent its teaching is historically conditioned and, therefore, surpassable.

Schoonenberg posits three interpretations of the doctrine of transubstantiation. Because the first reflects assumptions from the "Materialistic-Physical Model," he dismisses it as "certainly not the official teaching of the Church." However, both the second and the third interpretations are taught by the church and, consequently, the determination of which one is the "real teaching" proves critical.

This is the pivotal question: does the official teaching of the church identify the term "substance" with the Aristotelian philosophical view in which it is opposed to "accidents" or with a broader, more general sense in which it is opposed to "outward appearances"? If the third more general interpretation depicts Trent's true position, then Schoonenberg believes that the concepts of transfinalization (transposition of the aim) and transignification (transposition of the meaning) would mean the same as transubstantiation.[94]

Schoonenberg argues that the Tridentine formulation was necessarily expressed in Aristotelian categories because there were no other categories available. Hence, the issue of real presence was tied to the categories of substance and accidents. Consequently, these concepts can be criticized without affecting real presence itself. This is possible because of the distinction Schoonenberg makes between the content of the doctrine and its historically conditioned expression. In order to preserve the truth of dogma through time, the vehicle of expression must adapt to the changing yet historically determinate situation. Hence, theologians must decide whether the new expression corresponds to the original intention and not merely whether it repeats the same language.[95] For Schoonenberg, the critical issue is whether the concept of transignification (he does not use the term transfinalization) affirms Trent's belief in the real presence.

Schoonenberg finds approval for the concept of transignification in *Mysterium Fidei*. Although the encyclical does not go far enough in acknowledging the hermeneutical role of historicity, paragraph 24 clearly states that the doctrine is "not tied to a certain specific form of human culture. . . ."[96] This pronouncement implies, then, that the Magisterium as well as Trent uses "substance" and "species" in the broad sense.

However, the encyclical clearly rejects the terms transfinalization and transignification as a "complete explanation." That is, one can refer to the eucharistic change of bread and wine as a transignification only if one adds the term transubstantiation.

At this point, Schoonenberg believes that the encyclical fails to distinguish sufficiently between two conceptions of transignification and, thus, between two conceptions of sign/symbol. In other words, the encyclical condemns a particular notion of transignification that is not held even by advocates of the new model.

Interpreting a sign as an action-sign, Schoonenberg identifies two kinds: "informative" signs and "communicating" signs. "Informative" signs "bring something to our knowledge" and, consequently, they instruct us, provoke feelings, or transmit commands. "Communicating" signs resemble "effective" signs and, consequently, reveal what at the same time they communicate or offer. A handshake or kiss, for example, visibly demonstrates what it also endeavors to convey.

When the encyclical maintains that the eucharist is a symbol but that it is also truly the body and blood of Christ, and that the eucharistic change is a transignification but also an ontological transubstantiation, the text understands "symbol," Schoonenberg says, as this second kind of sign. Failure to distinguish between "informative" signs and "communicating" signs results in treating all symbols alike and, therefore, in condemning eucharistic symbols as deficient of the reality of Christ's real presence.

Yet, the distinguishing characteristic of "communicating" signs is that the reality is already included. The eucharist is, therefore, the sign in which Christ "gives his body in order to make us into his body and in which he gives himself for us for communion in and with him."[97] Proponents of transignification do not have to add a real presence to the sign of the eucharist, since the eucharist, as a "communicating" and "effective" sign, already includes real presence. By declaring that the eucharist "realizes" what it symbolizes, Schoonenberg overcomes the traditional yet false dichotomy between symbol and reality, and restores a more adequate "symbolic consciousness" to eucharistic theology.

On the one hand, an "informative" sign is incapable of expressing Christ's real presence in the eucharist as well as the manner in which that presence is manifest, i.e., transubstantiation or an ontological change. On the other hand, a "communicating" sign includes Christ's real presence and "if we consider the finality and the significance themselves as 'substantial,' as given with the reality of bread and wine and co-constitutive of these elements, then transfinalization and transignification are identical with transubstantiation."[98]

Since the encyclical rejects as inadequate only that symbolism that excludes a real presence and a substantial change, and does not mention the possibility of a "substantial" transfinalization and transignification, Schoonenberg deduces that a transignification that maintains this realism is permissible. Because the encyclical leaves room for the broader, general interpretation and Schoonenberg's formulation meets the criteria of real presence and ontological change, the concept of transignification conveys the central elements of Roman Catholic eucharistic dogma.

Edward Schillebeeckx

Seeking to interpret the reality of Christ's distinctive and real presence in the eucharist in a manner that is both open to the experience of modernity and faithful to the Catholic tradition, the Belgian Dominican priest, Edward Schillebeeckx, has made the most significant contemporary contribution to eucharistic theology.[99] In separate yet interrelated sections we shall examine

Schillebeeckx's interpretation of the Tridentine doctrine, his formulation of the encounter model, and his constructive proposal for Christ's eucharistic presence.

The first requirement, Schillebeeck maintains, for an investigation into the mode of Christ's eucharistic presence, both theologically and methodologically, is to determine the "objective meaning of the Tridentine dogma."[100] That is, a Roman Catholic must be theologically faithful to the living tradition and methodologically aware of the primacy of Trent. A phenomenology of real presence that appeals only to a human giving of meaning is inadequate without inquiring initially into the meaning of Trent for today.

This emphasis on the present is critical. Hermeneutically astute, Schillebeeckx knows, on the one hand, that we cannot "bracket" our contemporary worldview and, on the other hand, that all expressions are historically conditioned. Hence, the distinction between the dogma (what is "really affirmed") and the form of the dogma (the way in which this affirmation is linguistically expressed) permits Schillebeeckx to propose a new contemporary formulation. His proposal is both true to the tradition and necessary for the present since it endeavors to make the "inviolable *dogma* itself once again relevant to the faithful of today by separating it from a framework of ideas within which faith can no longer thrive in the present age."[101] Although at the time of Trent a denial of that precise manner of presentation of the dogma was tantamount to a denial of the doctrine itself, that is no longer true. On the contrary, a change in the mode of expression is essential if the original meaning is to be preserved. Modernists are the ultimate traditionalists!

Having justified his approach, both theologically and methodologically, Schillebeeckx seeks the original meaning of the Tridentine dogma of Christ's eucharistic presence. Succinctly, the council wanted to safeguard the significance of real presence against "Zwingli, Oecolampadius and the Sacramentarians." Yet, the council did not say that Christ's eucharistic presence was the only real presence of Christ. Christ was also really present in the service of the Word and in the assembled community. However, the council was charged with the task of preserving the distinctive mode of Christ's real presence in the eucharist.[102] (The recognition of Christ's ecclesial presence will reappear in Schillebeeckx's constructive proposal.)

Schillebeeckx discerns three levels of affirmation in the Tridentine dogma. At the center of the doctrine resides the affirmation of Christ's specific and distinctive eucharistic presence: Christ's body and blood are "truly, really and substantially" present under the sacramental species of bread and wine; this is the level of faith. Second, this initial pronouncement can be affirmed only by declaring a change of the substance of bread and wine into the substance of Christ's body and blood; this is the ontological level. Finally, this change is suitably called transubstantiation; this is the level of natural philosophy.[103]

Two theological questions follow. First, what is the connection between eucharistic real presence and transubstantiation, i.e., does the latter add new content? Schillebeeckx answers in the negative since the council members perceived these as identical affirmations.

Second, "is this necessary connection between 'real presence' in the eucharist and 'transubstantiation' an *inner* necessity of the dogma itself or is it something that was necessary, in the spiritual and intellectual climate of the age, . . . the only way in which the dogma of the eucharistic real presence could, *at that time*, readily be established?"[104] This answer is vital because it will determine whether Catholics are forever bound to the "working" as well as to the content of Trent.

Initially, we must acknowledge that because the council's true intention was to safeguard Christ's eucharistic real presence, it had to insist on transubstantiation. This terminology was, after all, the only available manner of expressing this reality.

Schillebeeckx acknowledges, however, that the council's use of transubstantiation operates on two different levels. First, Trent wished to affirm the "substantial" (radical conversion) change in the bread and wine and second, the council employed the Aristotelian categories of substance and accidents. The crucial question now becomes: "does this mean that the council also sanctions the Aristotelian philosophy in whose terms this change is stated?"[105]

Rejecting the interpretation of modern historians that the council disassociated itself from the Aristotelian philosophy of nature because, for example, the council employed the word "accidents" instead of the word "species," Schillebeeckx contends that the words "species" and "accidents" are virtually identical. Furthermore, he recognizes that the Aristotelian framework was the only thought-category available to the council at that time. Since Trent had to discuss and convey their thoughts within a given comprehensive system of thought, it would be inconceivable that they would not have used the existing Aristotelian framework.

This does not imply, however, that the council sanctioned the Aristotelian philosophy. On the contrary, Schillebeeckx declares Trent's "wording" to be both historically determined and unmistakably relative. He substantiates this bold claim by the even bolder assertion that the Aristotelianism employed by the Catholic theologians of Trent was in fact a radical transubstantiation of the authentic, historical Aristotelianism! In essence, the transubstantiation of Trent had been transubstantiated!!

The case of John Wyclif illustrates. Wyclif was condemned by the Council of Constance in 1415 because he posited, like the subsequent Reformers, a purely symbolic interpretation of Christ's eucharistic presence. Yet, Wyclif justified his interpretation on Aristotelian grounds. Since authentic Aristotelianism insisted that accidents cannot continue to exist without their corresponding substance and, therefore, any division between substance and accidents was metaphysically impossible, the dogma of transubstantiation was incorrect. Only a symbolic interpretation fits the facts. No "corporeal presence" means symbolic presence.

Ironically, yet inevitably, both Wyclif and the Roman Catholic Church appropriated Aristotelian categories; there were no other options in the Middle Ages. However, Wyclif was faithful to the authentic, historical Aristotelianism, while the church's use of Aristotle's philosophy of nature amounted to a transubstantiation of Aristotelianism. Thus, the Tridentine expression was historically determined and unmistakably relative.[106] Catholics are not bound to it.

Yet, Catholics are bound to an expression of ontological conversion. At the heart of the modern problem, for Schillebeeckx, is the question of whether the change of substance is also an aspect of the "wording" of the Tridentine dogma.

Schillebeeckx utters an emphatic "no." Although the Aristotelian wording of transubstantiation is relative, its content is not. The basic patristic intuition was a "real transubstantiation," but it was obviously not conceived in Aristotelian terms. Consequently, the reality of a substantial change was affirmed by both the early church and the Council of Trent. An ontological change is requisite to the faith.[107] Transubstantiation "as a formulation of a natural philosophy could be set aside . . . but insofar as it is an expression of an ontological conversion it must be retained."[108]

Only now is Schillebeeckx able to state the deepest meaning of the Tridentine dogma: transubstantiation has two dimensions of one and the same undivided reality. Because we live "between the times," i.e., between the resurrection and the parousia, we live in both the "old world" (the not yet) and the "new creation" (the already now). Therefore, the consecrated bread and wine also belong to both worlds. Schillebeeckx writes:

> . . . transubstantiation contains two dimensions—a *change of being* of the bread and wine (in which Christ's glorified body is really offered through the Holy Spirit), but *within the terrestrial, but now* (through this change of being) *sacramental form* of bread and wine, which remain subject, in this secular world, to the terrestrial laws of corporeality. . . .[109]

Thus, the ontological aspect is present in the eucharist through "a change of being" and "a sacramental symbolic activity on the part of Christ." Examination of the eucharist must, then, occur within the sphere of sacramentality.[110]

In conclusion, Schillebeeckx's analysis of the Tridentine dogma underscores at least two major points. First, the Aristotelian expression of transubstantiation is historically relative and requires reinterpretation if the Roman Catholic Church wishes to preserve the basic meaning of the dogma for contemporary believers. Simply repeating the doctrine word for word only introduces "unnecessary and unjustified" burdens and implies a *deus ex machina* hermeneutic. Second, the ontological change of the bread and wine into the body and blood of Christ is an indispensable datum of faith.

Since Schillebeeckx's examination of the Tridentine dogma reveals that one of the essential tasks of theology is to reinterpret the faith, he is, not surprisingly, responsible for a model shift in sacramentology. In opposition to the scholastic epistemology that treats all knowledge as analogous to the knowledge of things in the physical world, Schillebeeckx insists that "encounter" is the fundamental mode of human beings in the world. The model of encounter is not only appropriate for human relations but, more important, it is also the most appropriate model for religion and sacramentology.

At the heart of all religion, states Schillebeeckx, lies the human desire for a personal relationship with God. In its essence, then, religion is the "saving dialogue" between humanity and the living God. However, this intersubjective model of human encounter cannot be fully appropriated by religion. Although any human can initiate an encounter, only God can initiate religion. As divine encounter, religion consists of a modified dialogical structure. From God's side, this encounter is revelation but, from humanity's side, this encounter is a religious response.[111]

According to Schillebeeckx, this dialogical structure of revelation already appears in the Hebrew Bible. Yahweh, the God of the covenant, personally intervenes in favor of the chosen nation, Israel. Thus, the quintessence of divine revelation in Israel's history is the repeated phrase: "I will be your God, and you shall be my people."[112]

Yet, the complete fulfillment of this intersubjectivity occurs in the earthly Jesus. As the "one person in two natures," Jesus is God in a human way and humanity in a divine way. Jesus is the Christ because he is the "human embodiment of the redeeming love of God." The incarnation constitutes the completed revelation of God because in the person of Jesus both the invitation and the reply of faith are fulfilled. Our encounter with Jesus represents "a sacramental encounter with God."[113]

Christ becomes, for Schillebeeckx, the primordial sacrament (*Ursakrament*).[114] Since human encounter "proceeds through the visible obviousness of the body, which is a sign that reveals and at the same time veils the human interiority,"[115] and Jesus, the embodiment of redeeming love, is designated by God "to be in his humanity the only way to the actuality of redemption,"[116] the man Jesus is the primordial sacrament. "Human encounter with Jesus is therefore the sacrament of the encounter with God."[117]

Embodiment serves not only as "sign," but also as the interpretive key of the encounter model. Schillebeeckx elaborates:

> The point here is that dynamic personality constitutes itself in and through an activity which externalizes itself also in bodily form. In

the body the soul presents itself to another. 'What we in encounter call body is that through which we situate ourselves, express ourselves, and make ourselves known; in short, the form of man's being-in-the world. The person we encounter *has* this form, but he also *is* this form!' It is through the body and in the body that human encounter takes place.[118]

But a problem persists. If encounter is possible only in and through human bodiliness and Jesus, the human embodiment of God, has died and departed from earth, how are we who have not encountered Christ in the flesh to obtain salvation through a personal encounter with the man Jesus? Not only has the very means of our encounter vanished (because of the resurrection), but Jesus himself has declared that bodily mediation is meaningless: ". . . it is to your advantage that I go away. . ." (John 16:7). The corporeal absence of Christ seems to nullify the encounter model!

It is true that the fundamental posture of the Christian life is one of waiting for the parousia and Christ's return. Yet, Christ's death and resurrection are good, not because of his disappearance, but because of his glorification. Although Christianity is the religion of *maranatha* and is markedly eschatological, this is not the final word. Our expectation of the ultimate, perfect encounter with Christ is grounded in and sustained by the fact that we have already in some way had an encounter with the glorified Lord.

This future expectation breaks into the present via the sacraments. Not merely a spiritual encounter but a sacramental encounter with the living Lord undergirds the pledge and anticipation of the eschatological and perfect encounter with Christ. Christ maintains contact with us not through his own bodiliness, but by extending among us on earth in visible form the function of his bodily reality which is in heaven. The sacraments are, then, the earthly extension of the "body of the Lord."[119]

To speak of the sacraments, says Schillebeeckx, is to first speak of the sacramental church herself. As the *sacramentum humanitatis Christi* (sacrament of the humanity of Christ), the church's primary action is the administration of the sacraments. That is, the visible action of the church in the sacraments is in fact the action of Christ in heaven. Consequently, visible contact with the church through the reception of her sacraments constitutes an encounter with Christ. In this sense, the church can also be called the primordial sacrament.[120]

As Christ's action through the church, the sacraments confer no new or additional meaning. Resting on a Christological foundation, the sacraments bring us, in their own way, into living contact with the "perennial Christ." Because of Christ's ascension, permanent sacraments represent an intrinsic requirement of Christianity. Sacramentality bridges the gap between the glorified Christ in heaven and the unglorified humanity on earth. The sacraments make possible an encounter with Christ.[121]

> The Church's sacraments are, therefore, our quasi-bodily encounters with the transfigured man Jesus, a veiled contact with the Lord but, nonetheless, one which is concretely human in the full sense because both body and soul are involved.[122]

In conclusion, religion, for Schillebeeckx, is intersubjective. God encounters humanity in revelation and humanity responds in faith. For the Christian, Christ is the embodiment and fulfillment of this intersubjectivity. Consequently, an encounter with the earthly Jesus, the primordial sacrament, is equivalent to an encounter with God.

If, however, the divine plan of salvation requires an encounter with Christ, the death and resurrection of Jesus present a massive stumbling block. How can we still encounter the man Jesus?

The church and the sacraments represent God's salvific solution to the problem of Christ's corporeal absence. By embodying the action of the glorified Christ in heaven, the church is the locus for Christ's presence on earth. By using earthly, untransfigured elements as visible symbols, the sacraments of the church are the earthly extension of Christ's glorified body. In order for the conferral of grace to continue after the ascension, both the sacramental church and the sacraments are necessary. In the church and in the sacraments, we encounter Christ in a bodily way, though bodily absent.

Schillebeeckx's adoption of the encounter model allows him to connect Christology, ecclesiology, and sacramentology, and to hold in tension the dialectics of absence-presence and past-future. We have already discussed how the problem of Christ's absence, as a result of the ascension, can be fully resolved only at the parousia. Yet, Christ's glorified body may be encountered in the present through the church and the sacraments. As "media," they permit a real and present encounter between "living people"—the eternal living Lord and believers.

Though indirect, this immediate (since in the body subjectivity immediately and directly expresses itself) encounter with Christ in the sacraments also incorporates the past-future dialectic. The eucharist, for example, constitutes an *anamnesis* or a commemoration of the past sacrifice of Jesus on the cross because it connects us through the Words of Institution to the historical moment when Christ died for us. The eucharist also constitutes an anticipation of the future parousia because it renders through transubstantiation "the sacramental presence of Christ the *Eschaton*." The sacramental encounter of humanity with Christ in the church and in the sacraments is based, therefore, on the past redemptive act of Christ on the cross and a pledge of eschatological salvation.[123]

We now turn to Schillebeeckx's formulation of the crowning point of this actual encounter with Christ, the eucharist.

We recall that the goal of Schillebeeckx's formulation of Christ's eucharistic presence is the reinterpretation of the "inviolable" datum of the Catholic dogma so that it is both faithful to the tradition of the church and intelligible to contemporary believers. Enroute to his proposal, two methodological foci guide him and one overarching question confronts him. The two foci are the witness of the apostles and the phenomenological approach; these are the vehicles by which he can both preserve the original meaning of the church and remain relevant to modernity. The overarching question is the proper relationship between transignification and transubstantiation.

Schillebeeckx's analysis of the witness of the apostles reveals that the original emphasis of the eucharist was not on interpreting the meal, but on celebrating and experiencing it. The early church experienced themselves as the eschatological community of the New Covenant and celebrated their personal relationship with Jesus—before and after his departure—through table fellowship. Although Christ's real presence in the assembled community was focused in his real presence under the forms of bread and wine, the primary emphasis was always the special relationship realized in community about the table.

Yet, Schillebeeckx already detects in the New Testament a shift of emphasis away from the ecclesiastic community of grace in Christ (the *res sacramenti*) to the real presence of Christ in the eucharist under the species of bread and wine (the *res et sacramentum*). Regrettably, the tradition continues to subordinate the importance of the eschatological community. The recovery of this theme is both essential for his reinterpretation and necessary for his phenomenological synthesis.[124]

In order to determine the distinctive eucharistic meaning of real presence, Schillebeeckx interprets the eucharist in its broadest context. That is, the basic principle of life is that reality is not a human construct. Although humans interpret reality, they neither create the world nor assign its true meaning. Humanity is the subject in which God's revelation finds an answer. God initiates encounter; humanity responds.

The world, then, has a "general quasi-sacramental significance" since God is present to humanity in the world. This deepest reality—the revelation of God to humanity—is, however, a mystery. The world both discloses and conceals this foundational truth and only the eyes of faith discern this "for us" character of the world.[125]

This phenomenological analysis of the basic principle of reality uncovers a most significant find: human consciousness is referential. Everything that is explicit in our consciousness is referential; we know reality only in signs. The world is a sign of God to humanity. Applying this principle to the eucharist, bread and wine are, then, signs of a deeper reality since God's personal presence is always the "deepest relationship in everything."[126]

As signs, bread and wine can take on a variety of human meanings. They can nourish, seal a friendship, or activate a memory. In no way do these human meanings deny the biological utility of eating and drinking. Rather, bread remains physical bread while it is "transignified" or "humanized." Consequently, bread possesses different levels of meaning for humanity.

It is critical, then, that discussions operate on the same level. For example, an inquiry into the physical nature of the bread after consecration is legitimate, but it seeks a physical answer to a sacramental reality. This confusion of levels has plagued the theology of the eucharist almost from inception. For this reason, an examination of eucharistic transubstantiation must operate on the level of sacramental signs. The levels of physics and the philosophy of nature are inappropriate since transubstantiation is an establishment of meaning in which food, meal, and the community of believers about the table come together in a religious symbolic activity.[127]

The peculiarity of Christ's real eucharistic presence must be approached on the sacramental level. Only on the sacramental level do we realize that the basis of the entire eucharistic event is Christ's gift of himself to humanity (I Timothy 2:6). The eucharist is both the sacramental visibility of this continuous self-giving and an *anamnesis* of his historical death on the cross. In the context of this commemorative meal, the bread and wine are endowed with a new establishment of meaning. The living Lord in the church, not the worshiping recipient, bestows upon the elements the sacramental meaning of the sacrificial gift of himself. The "given-ness" of the eucharist is the very proclamation of the Lord's death. As a religious symbolic activity, the meal becomes a sacramental memorial of the death, resurrection, and glorification of Christ.[128]

Recalling the ecclesial theme of the apostolic church, Schillebeeckx insists that the reality of Christ's eucharistic presence presupposes his real ecclesial presence. The scholastic understanding, that the *res sacramenti* is a product of Christ's presence "in heaven" and "in bread and wine," should be reversed. There is ultimately only one real presence of Christ, although there exist different modes. Hence, the elements of bread and wine by virtue of Christ's designation become signs of Christ's presence, which is already "really and personally present for us." Christ's presence in the church is, therefore, "co-constitutive" of the eucharist itself. Without this proper ordering of Christology, ecclesiology, and sacramentology there lurks the danger, which scholasticism evidences, that transubstantiation merely gives "something" to us.

On the contrary, transubstantiation operates on a much deeper level. The gift of the eucharist is not a thing, but a person. When Christ declares that the bread is his body and the wine is his blood, the gift is Christ Himself.

What the sacramental forms of bread and wine signify, and at the same time make real, is not a gift that refers to Christ who gives himself in them, but Christ himself in living, personal presence. The signifying function of the sacrament (*sacramentum est in genere signi*) is here at its highest value.[129]

Furthermore, the eucharistic elements of bread and wine are not only the sign of Christ's gift of himself to the church, but they are also the sign of the church's gift of itself to Christ. As an encounter with the living Lord, the eucharist signifies the "reciprocity" of real presence. "The 'body of the Lord' in the christological sense is the source of the 'body of the Lord' in the ecclesiological sense."[130] The Apostle Paul conveys the quintessence of this reciprocity:

Because there is one bread, we who are many are one body, for we all partake of the one bread (I Corinthians 10:17).

An important consequence follows. The presence of Christ in the eucharist does not hinge upon the belief of the recipient, since Christ's presence precedes an individual's acceptance of his presence. As an offered reality, Christ's presence is independent of a worshiper's positive or negative response. However, the "reciprocity" of real presence means that eucharistic real presence is realized only when, in faith, consent is given to the sacramental meal.

The eucharistic presence is therefore not dependent on the faith of the individual, but the sacramental offer cannot be thought of as separate from the community of the Church.[131]

As the rite of the church and of the real presence of Christ residing in the church, the eucharist receives its new establishment of *meaning* only from the living Lord. Therefore, this giving of meaning occurs within the context of the community of faith. This limitation neither reduces transubstantiation to a purely subjective event nor makes it less real. It does mean, however, that the eucharistic reality of Christ's presence can be apprehended only by faith and is not valid as a reality for non-believers. Disbelief does not "nullify the reality of the Eucharist," it merely rejects the "offered reality."[132]

Only within the context of this entire eucharistic event can our final question of transignificaton's proper relationship to transubstantiation be addressed. Yet, this question is ultimately a question of the reality to which the eucharistic rite refers. Before Schillebeeckx can determine whether transignificaton is identical to transubstantiation, he must uncover the general structure of humanity's knowledge of reality. To neglect this route would be tantamount to making human faith "into a kind of 'superstructure,' built on top of our human knowledge" and thereby undermining an intelligible formulation.[133]

Human perception, for Schillebeeckx, is neither pure nor simple. Since perception cannot be separated from the subjects who perceive, people "humanise" what they encounter. Elevated above the purely sensory, perception is always tinged with human meaning. Thus, humans fashion the content of reality into signifying functions and thereby convert their perceptions into referential signs. In this manner humanity opens itself up to the mystery of reality—to the metaphysical being which is prior to the perception itself, and to God's creation.[134]

Because the understanding of the reality of salvation necessarily parallels humanity's general knowledge of reality, human perception in faith comprises an active openness to what is objectively communicated to us as reality, which is accompanied by a giving of meaning in faith.[135] In the eucharist, then, the projective act of faith must be open to the "distinction between the reality itself and this reality as a phenomenal appearance." Without this "openness," the phenomenal appearance would suggest that bread is only bread. Yet, faith, open to reality as God's gift, perceives the change from bread and wine to the body and blood of Christ.

> Thus, there is a change in the signifying function of these appearances, but that change (a 'transignification') is a change precisely because the reality which is contained in these appearances is no longer the reality of bread and wine, but Christ's bodily reality.[136]

Transignification, the giving of a new meaning or new sign, presupposes transubstantiation. Because the metaphysical change of the reality of bread and wine into the body and blood of Christ, to which transubstantiation refers, has priority, transignification cannot be identical to transubstantiation. Yet, because what is signified through the appearance is changed objectively and, therefore, the significance of the appearance itself is also changed, the two are "indissolubly connected." By "allowing" the form of bread and wine experienced phenomenally to refer to Christ's body and blood, the real presence of Christ in the eucharist involves a projective act of faith by the believer that does not bring about the real presence, but presupposes it as a metaphysical priority.[137] The ontological change, effected by God, is necessarily accompanied by human recognition of this changed meaning. Transubstantiation requires transignification.

Schillebeeckx's contributions to the reinterpretation of the mode of Christ's eucharistic presence are profound and immense. The soundness of his theological method is evident in at least three ways: in his insistence that the original datum of Trent be reinterpreted for modernity, in his hermeneutical principles that guide his interpretation of Tridentine dogma, and in his rejection of a purely phenomenological interpretation of real presence that appeals to a human giving of meaning alone without "metaphysical density." Moreover, his development and refinement of the "Interpersonal-Encounter Model" permit him to integrate the eucharistic elements and the worshiping community, while avoiding the limitations of Aristotle's natural philosophy.

As the sacrament of God, Christ is the person by whom God more openly encounters humanity. As the sacrament of God and the risen Lord, the church is the locus of Christ's presence in the world. Both sacramental efficacy and causality result from the encounter with the risen Lord in and through the church. Eucharistic emphasis is shifted away from *res et sacramentum* (real presence of Christ under the sacramental elements) and back to *res sacramenti* (life of the community in Christ).

Conclusion

Not since the Reformation has eucharistic theology in general and the mode of Christ's eucharistic presence in particular been the object of such attention. The need for a new Roman Catholic sacramental model seemed obvious. Modern physics called into question the Aristotelian category of substance and the scholastic doctrine of transubstantiation, while post-Kantian philosophy called into question the idea of an objective reality behind and outside the world of phenomena. The old "Mechanistic-Physical Model," in which a physical-quantitative notion of grace and a mechanical understanding of causality led to an impersonal cause and effect relationship between grace and the sacraments, became suspect. Transubstantiation, as a medieval answer to the specific question of how Christ was present under the elements of bread and wine, was unsatisfactory. Indeed, some theologians questioned whether this was even the proper eucharistic question, while others voiced displeasure with spatio-temporal models of presence. The general opinion in modern Roman Catholicism was that the ontological change of the bread and wine into the body and blood of Christ occurred on a sacramental level. The clear trend was "away from substantialistic views and toward relational interpretations of Christ's presence."[138]

The emergence of the "Interpersonal-Encounter Model" was inevitable, since the objectification of the eucharist, particularly through the category of substance, proved inadequate for and unintelligible to modernity.[139] "The category of substance (originated) as an answer to the question 'What is that out there?'"[140] Applied to the empirical level of questioning, it explained the nature of things like rocks, plants, animals, and humans—even angels. A sacrament, however, is relational and not reducible to an object. Thus, the medieval appropriation of the category of substance, though used analogously, "objectified" the sacraments.

Proponents of the "Interpersonal-Encounter Model" realized that the practical consequence of applying an empirical category to a relational or symbolic being was "ambiguity." The doctrine of transubstantiation states that a "change" occurs under the elements of bread and wine. Although our experience of physical change provides an analogy by which we can understand non-physical changes, we seldom employ the word in that way. "When we use it of *exterior objects*, we normally mean some sort of physical change: the weather changes, chemical substances change, traffic lights change."[141] Therefore, at best, ambiguity is built into the doctrine of transubstantiation and, at worst, the sacraments and their cause and effect relationship are "objectified."

The "Interpersonal-Encounter Model" overcomes both the objectification of the eucharist and the fixation on the elements there on the altar by declaring that personal presence takes place in terms of human consciousness and personal communication. Hence, the mediation of God's presence in general and of Christ's eucharistic presence in particular requires an encounter model.

Advantages of the New Model

The advantages of this new model are numerous. First, a new theology of grace, in which grace is understood as the actions that God has historically taken to *disclose* Godself to the world, avoids a materialistic interpretation of Christ's eucharistic presence.

Second, the new model replaces the category of efficient causality with symbolic causality, i.e., divine self-communication through symbol.[142] Because symbols are self-expressions and necessary for communication, and because human mutual availability occurs only through bodiliness, "the primary form of bodily communication is symbolic." Consequently, the incarnation is God's definitive self-communication, since it is in the mode of human bodiliness. Christ is, therefore, the primordial sacrament (*Ursakrament*) and the sacrament of God. Yet, Christ's ascension creates a problem. Spatially absent, Christ no longer mediates redemption. God's encounter with humanity in Christ now occurs through the church and the sacraments. The linkage of Christology, ecclesiology, and sacramentology is achieved.

Third, the new model asserts that the "real change" of the bread and wine into the body and blood of Christ occurs on a metaphysical, and not a physical, level. Hence, the ontological change in the eucharist, which the encyclical, *Mysterium Fidei*, insists on retaining, happens on a sacramental, and not a scientific, level. Christ's eucharistic presence is presence in a "sign-act."

Fourth, by employing a phenomenology of personal presence to explain this "sign-act," which is called transignification (transposition of the meaning) or transfinalization (transposition of the aim), the new model retains the term transubstantiation. Involving an act of self-communication in which the material objects of the sign (bread and wine) are robbed of their physical individuality by the very fact that they are taken up into a human sign-act, transignification (the preferred term) refers to the divine (not human) act in which the substance (or meaning) of a religious sign is transformed in the personal revelation of God.[143] Consequently, the language of transubstantiation, which states that the substantial reality of bread and wine is changed into the substantial reality of Christ, and the language of transignification, which states that the same fundamental change occurs within the context of a sign-act of Christ, are compatible.

Fifth, and most important for our thesis, the new model restores the emphasis on the *res sacramenti* (the life of the community in Christ) and reinstates the concept of ecclesial presence. The "Constitution on the Sacred Liturgy" from the Second Vatican Council offers the most persuasive argument that Christ's eucharistic presence should be situated within the broader context of Christ's ecclesial presence. Without Christ's prior ecclesial presence through faith and promise, the church would not be empowered to make Christ present in the eucharist. Both Schoonenberg and Schillebeeckx concur.

These five advantages of the "Interpersonal-Encounter Model" make possible the replacement of the medieval concept of substantial presence with the patristic concept of ecclesial presence.

Three Requisite Features

Before we cite our principal criticisms of the new model, we need to comment on the three requisite features of the eucharist. Although the "Interpersonal-Encounter Model" has not directly addressed these features, general observations are possible.

In contrast to Trent's insistence that Christ's substantial presence be essentially related to the consecrated elements, the new model is the result of a complete rethinking of the connection of ritual and material elements. By understanding personal presence to take place in terms of human consciousness and personal communication, the objectification of the eucharist and the fixation on the consecrated elements are overcome. The mediation of God's presence and of Christ's eucharistic presence requires an encounter model and a "sign-act" in which a "pregnant alienation" characterizes the giving of human meaning to material objects. Significantly, the eucharistic "sign-act" occurs within the larger context of the worshiping community. Hence, the people, the celebrant, and their sacramental action enable Christ to give himself under the physical realities of bread and wine. Thus, the new model values both the ritual and the material elements of the eucharistic rite since they facilitate the reception of new religious meaning—a transignification.

Although Schillebeeckx affirms the past-future dialectic by stating that the eucharist constitutes both an *anamnesis* of the past redemptive act of Jesus on the cross and an anticipation of the future return of Jesus, the new model gives the impression that the present time mode is exclusively important. Since God and Christ are encountered in the present, the "now" is overemphasized to the detriment of the past and future.[144] Advocates of the "Interpersonal-Encounter Model" should expand their investigation into human consciousness to include both memory (the backward referent) and hope (the forward referent).

Unlike the medieval and Tridentine eucharistic theologies, which were preoccupied with Christ's local presence to the virtual exclusion of Christ's absence, the new model embraces the presence-absence dialectic. Since encounter is possible only in and through human bodiliness, and Jesus, the human embodiment of God, has died and departed from earth, Christ's absence is taken seriously. Yet, the redemptive function of Christ's bodily reality is continued through the church and the sacraments. Sacramentality bridges the gap between the glorified Christ in heaven and the unglorified humanity on earth. The physical absence of Christ does not, therefore, preclude our encounter with him. The "Interpersonal-Encounter Model" retains the tension in the presence-absence dialectic.

Two Principal Criticisms

We now turn to our two principal criticisms of the new model. Our first criticism will present a Protestant critique of the Roman Catholic concept of transignification that intentionally reflects traditional Roman Catholic-Protestant differences. If these differences can be resolved, the establishment of common ground for an ecumenical proposal will be greatly advanced. Our second criticism will locate a methodological inconsistency in the new model, the correction of which will require a social phenomenology of ecclesial presence.

First Criticism

Our first criticism has a dual purpose. Most important, we must pose the questions that any intelligent and self-conscious Protestant would ask about transignification. Yet, a second purpose looms on the horizon. Any attempt to formulate an ecumenical proposal must overcome the obstacles which attend the definitions that are built into the concepts we employ. By responding satisfactorily to a Protestant critique, a common ground of understanding can emerge. We now offer our Protestant critique of the Roman Catholic concept of transignification.

Our initial observation may startle modernists: transignification is not a radical departure from traditional transubstantiationist doctrine! If this is true, Protestants may be reluctant to endorse transignification.

Clearly, the Council of Trent did not claim that the physical accidents of the elements changed—only their metaphysical substance; and for good reason. There is no empirical evidence for a physical change. Likewise, the concept of transignification does not posit a physical change. Rather, the metaphysical change is one of signification, or meaning, rather than one of substance. To the Protestant, the only difference between transubstantiation and transignification seems to be that the metaphysical substance is considered in relational instead of substantialist terms. In short, a modern ontology is inserted into an old dogma, which otherwise remains intact. If this observation is correct, and we believe Roman Catholics would agree, then Protestants are justifiably nervous.

Furthermore, the possibility that the concept of transignification can bridge the differences between Roman Catholic and Protestant eucharistic theologies and thereby provide a common ground for an ecumenical proposal is problematic. In other words, it appears that the shift in language from transubstantiation to transignification represents a small step for many Roman Catholics but a giant leap for most Protestants. That is, the concept of transignification signals a reinterpretation of the traditional doctrine of Trent but not an abandonment of the affirmation of an ontological change. Consequently, the perennial obstacle for most Protestants remains: the insistence upon a metaphysical change.

A Protestant critique of the concept of transignification clusters around three sets of interrelated questions. First, Protestants want to know what exactly is a "metaphysical change"? By insisting on an ontological change in the eucharist, is not modern Roman Catholic thought really holding onto the "core conviction" of transubstantialist dogma and is not this the precise point that Protestants find most problematic?

Second, if the personal presence of God really occurs in terms of human consciousness and personal communication, why is any change whatsoever required in the eucharistic elements? Do not the elements, together with the eucharist, signify divine saving presence without having to undergo an ontological change? And if a change is requisite, why is God required to bring it about? The signification of objects in the world changes all the time without any particular divine intervention.

Finally, Schoonenberg and Schillebeeckx appear to disagree on the exact relationship between transignification and transubstantiation. Schoonenberg affirms an identity between the two, while Schillebeeckx only claims that they are "indissolubly connected." Which, if either, is correct?

Second Criticism

Our second criticism addresses a methodological inconsistency in the "Interpersonal-Encounter Model." Cognizant of the inherent danger in any encounter model to deteriorate into "privatized individualism" or a "me and God" attitude, which would distort the true dialogical character of any encounter as well as deny the encounter of God in and through the community of the church,[145] proponents of this new model stress ecclesiology. Reflecting the insights of the encyclical, *Mysterium Fidei*, both Schoonenberg and Schillebeeckx agree that Christ is present in the community of believers prior to eucharistic presence.

Schoonenberg states:

> Now this brings to mind the fact that the whole presence of the Lord in his Church—in the celebration of the Eucharist—is important, even more important than his presence in the sacred species alone. Only when we try to plumb the depths of the riches of this presence in community do we find therein the meaning of the real presence under the sacred species—at least, that is the point of view from which we start.[146]

> Finally, we can speak about the presence of Christ in the Eucharist, his Eucharistic presence. But by this we do not mean in the first place the presence of Christ's body under the species, *but his presence in the Eucharistic community*. This Eucharistic presence is in existence when we come together to listen to his Word and to proclaim his death in the Holy Meal. . . . The Eucharistic celebration begins with a 'presentia realis,' a real presence of the Lord among us, and has as its aim the making of this presence more intimate, and this happens in the symbols of the word and of the bread and wine.[147]

Schillebeeckx concurs when he writes:

> In this commemorative meal, bread and wine become the subject of a new *establishment of meaning*, not by men, but by the living Lord *in* the Church, through which they become the *sign* of the real presence of Christ giving himself to us. This establishment of meaning by Christ is accomplished in the Church and thus presupposes the real presence of the Lord in the Church, in the assembled community of believers and in the one who officiates in the Eucharist.

> I should like to place much greater emphasis than most modern authors have done on this essential bond between the real presence

of Christ in the Eucharist and his real presence as Lord living in the Church. After all, there is ultimately only one real presence of Christ, although this can come about in various ways.[148]

Despite these affirmations of Christ's ecclesial presence, neither theologian carries his respective program to its logical conclusion. While both Schoonenberg and Schillebeeckx correctly frame the doctrine of the mode of Christ's eucharistic presence in terms of human consciousness, they are locked into individualism: Schoonenberg undertakes a phenomenology of personal presence and Schillebeeckx pursues a phenomenology of human meaning. By failing to move beyond individualism to a social phenomenology of ecclesial presence, both Schoonenberg and Schillebeeckx are methodologically inconsistent with their stated objectives. Their respective theologies of Christ's eucharistic presence remain incomplete until a social phenomenology of ecclesial presence is conducted.

Notes

1. A. Vanneste, "Bedenkingen bij de scholastieke transsubstantiatieleer," *Collationes Gandavenses et Brugenses* 2 (1956): 322-335.

2. J. Möller, "De transsubstantiatie," *Nederlandse Katholieke Stemmen* 56 (1960): 2-14.

3. Schillebeeckx, *The Eucharist*, 111.

4. Powers, *Eucharistic Theology*, 116.

5. Schillebeeckx, *The Eucharist*, 109.

6. Jean de Baciocchi, "Le mystère eucharistique dans les perspectives de la bible," in *Nouv. Rev. Théol* 87 (1955): 561-580.

7. Schillebeeckx, *The Eucharist*, 109.

8. Powers, *Eucharistic Theology*, 115.

9. Jean de Baciocchi, "Présence eucharistique et transsubstantiation" *Irénikon* 32 (1959): 139-161.

10. Schillebeeckx, *The Eucharist*, 112-114.

11. F. J. Leenhardt, "This is My Body," in *Essays on the Lord's Supper*, Oscar Cullmann and F. J. Leenhardt, trans. J. G. Davies (Richmond: John Knox Press, 1958), 46-47.

12. Ibid., 47.

13. Ibid., 48.

14. Ibid., 49-50.

15. Ibid., 50.

16. Ibid., 73.

17. Ibid., 73-74.

18. Ibid., 75.

19. Ibid., 76.

20. Powers, *Eucharistic Theology*, 119.

21. Thurian, *Mystery of the Eucharist*, 55.

22. Ibid.

23. Ibid., 56.

24. Ibid., 57.

25. Ibid., 57-58.

26. Charles Davis, "Understanding the Real Presence," in *The Word in History: The St. Xavier Symposium*, ed. T. Patrick Burke (New York: Sheed and Ward, 1966), 154-178, and "The Theology of Transubstantiation" *Sophia* (University of Melbourne) 3 (1964): 12-24.

27. H. Benedict Green, "The Eucharistic Presence: Change And/Or Signification," *The Downside Review* 83 (1965): 46.

28. Ibid., 47.

29. Schillebeeckx, *The Eucharist*, 116-117.

30. See Karl Rahner, *The Church and the Sacraments*, trans. W. J. O'Hara (New York: Herder and Herder, 1964), 84. In his article, "The Presence of Christ in the Sacrament of the Lord's Supper," *Theological Investigations*, vol. 4, trans. Kevin Smyth (London: Darton, Longman & Todd Ltd, 1966), 287-311, Rahner provides an excellent summary of Trent's interpretation of real presence and identifies key issues that need further clarification. However, he does not posit a specific proposal.

31. Rahner, *Church and Sacraments*, 9.

32. Ibid., 18.

33. For more detail see Rahner's section on "signs" in *The Church and the Sacraments*, 34-40.

34. The following discussion is based on Schillebeeckx, "Transubstantiation," 184-186.

35. "Constitution on the Sacred Liturgy" in *The Documents of Vatican II*, ed. Walter M. Abbott, trans. Joseph Gallagher (New York: The American Press, 1966), 140-141.

36. Mitchell, *Cult and Controversy*, 351.

37. Lucien Deiss, *It's the Lord's Supper*, trans. Edmond Bonin (New York: Paulist Press, 1976), 116.

38. Ibid., 116-117.

39. "Constitution on the Sacred Liturgy," 147-148.

40. Paul VI, *"Mysterium Fidei," The Pope Speaks* 10, no. 4 (1965): 309-310.

41. Ibid., 313-314.

42. Ibid., 321.

43. Ibid., 314.

44. Ibid.

45. This third presupposition is dependent on Schillebeeckx's insights, "Transubstantiation," 186-189.

46. Three of his books are directly related to our study. They are: *Christian Sacraments and Christian Personality* (New York: Holt, Rinehart and Winston, 1965), *Ministry to Word and Sacraments* (Philadelphia: Fortress Press, 1976), and *Sacraments and Sacramentality* (Mystic, CT: Twenty-Third Publications, 1985).

47. Cooke, *Sacraments and Sacramentality*, 76-77.

48. Ibid., 77.

49. Cooke, *Word and Sacraments*, 640.

50. Ibid.

51. Cooke, *Sacraments and Sacramentality*, 66.

52. Cooke, *Word and Sacraments*, 639.

53. Cooke, *Sacraments and Sacramentality*, 40.

54. Cooke, *Word and Sacraments*, 648.

55. His two principal works on the eucharist are: *Eucharistic Theology* (New York: Herder and Herder, 1967), and "*Mysterium Fidei* and the Theology of the Eucharist," *Worship* 40 (1966): 17-35.

56. Powers, *Eucharistic Theology*, 88.

57. Ibid., 88-89.

58. Ibid., 89.

59. Ibid., 165-166 & 85.

60. Ibid., 166-167.

61. Ibid., 168.

62. Ibid., 169.

63. Ibid.

64. Ibid., 171.

65. Powers, "*Mysterium Fidei*," 20-21.

66. Ibid., 22.

67. Ibid.

68. For an expanded explanation see Powers, "*Mysterium Fidei*," 25-26.

69. For Powers' treatment see "*Mysterium Fidei*," 26-28.

70. Ibid., 28.

71. Ibid., 30.

72. Ibid., 29.

73. Ibid., 35.

74. Only three of Schoonenberg's articles on the eucharist are translated into English: "Presence and the Eucharistic Presence," trans. Sr. Mary Pierre Ellebracht, *Cross Currents* 17 (Winter 1967): 39-54; "Transubstantiation: How Far is this Doctrine Historically Determined?" in *Concilium*, vol. 24, *The Sacraments: An Ecumenical Dilemma*, ed. Hans Küng, trans. Theodore L.

Westow (New York: Paulist Press, 1966):78-91; and "The Real Presence in Contemporary Discussion," *Theology Digest* 15 (Spring 1967): 3-11.

75. Schoonenberg, "Presence," 40.

76. Ibid., 41.

77. Ibid., 43.

78. Ibid., 44-45.

79. Powers, *Eucharistic Theology*, 136.

80. Schoonenberg, "Presence," 45-48.

81. Powers, *Eucharistic Theology*, 136-137.

82. Schoonenberg, "Presence," 48-49.

83. Ibid., 49-50.

84. Ibid., 52.

85. Ibid.

86. Ibid., 52-53 and Powers, *Eucharistic Theology*, 138.

87. Schoonenberg, "Presence," 54.

88. Powers, *Eucharistic Theology*, 139.

89. Ibid.

90. Ibid., 160.

91. Ibid.

92. Ibid., 160-161.

93. The following argument of Schoonenberg is taken from his article "Transubstantiation: How Far is this Doctrine Historically Determined?".

94. Schoonenberg, "Transubstantiation," 80-82.

95. Ibid., 83-85.

96. Pope Paul VI, "*Mysterium Fidei*," 314.

97. Schoonenberg, "Transubstantiation," 90.

98. Ibid.

99. Schillebeeckx's seminal works on the eucharist are *Christ the Sacrament of the Encounter with God*, trans. Paul Barrett (New York: Sheed and Ward, 1963) and *The Eucharist*, trans. N. D. Smith (New York: Sheed and Ward, 1968).

100. This discussion is based on *The Eucharist*, 25-86.

101. Ibid., 28.

102. Ibid., 43-44.

103. Ibid., 44-45 & 63-64.

104. Ibid., 47.

105. Powers, *Eucharistic Theology*, 142.

106. Schillebeeckx, *The Eucharist*, 58-60.

107. Ibid., 65-70 & 75-76.

108. McDonnell, *John Calvin*, 314.

109. Schillebeeckx, *The Eucharist*, 83.

110. Ibid., 83-84.

111. Edward Schillebeeckx, "The Sacraments: An Encounter with God," in *Christianity Divided: Protestant and Roman Catholic Theological Issues*, ed. Daniel J. Callahan, Heiko A. Oberman, Daniel J. O'Hanlon, trans. John L. Boyle (New York: Sheed and Ward, 1961), 245-246.

112. Leviticus 26:11-12; Jeremiah 7:23, 11:4, 24:7, 31:33; and Ezekiel 11:20, 14:11, 37:27.

113. Schillebeeckx, *Christ the Sacrament*, 13-15.

114. Schillebeeckx, "The Sacraments," 241-249.

115. Schillebeeckx, *Christ the Sacrament*, 15.

116. Ibid.

117. Ibid.

118. Schillebeeckx, "The Sacraments," 250.

119. Schillebeeckx, *Christ the Sacrament*, 40-41.

120. Schillebeeckx, "The Sacraments," 255-257.

121. Schillebeeckx, *Christ the Sacrament*, 43-44.

122. Schillebeeckx, "The Sacraments," 253.

123. Ibid., 262-263 and *Christ the Sacrament*, 62.

124. Schillebeeckx, *The Eucharist*, 122-124.

125. Ibid., 127-129 and Powers, *Eucharistic Theology*, 149-150.

126. Schillebeeckx, *The Eucharist*, 129.

127. Ibid., 130-132.

128. Ibid., 137.

129. Ibid., 139.

130. Ibid., 140.

131. Ibid., 141-142.

132. Ibid., 142-143.

133. Ibid., 148.

134. Ibid., 145-148.

135. Ibid., 148.

136. Powers, *Eucharistic Theology*, 153.

137. Schillebeeckx, *The Eucharist*, 149-150 and Powers, *Eucharistic Theology*, 153.

138. Robert L. Browning and Roy A. Reed, *The Sacraments in Religious Education and Liturgy: An Ecumenical Model* (Birmingham, AL: Religious Education Press, 1985), 5-6.

139. These comments are indebted to Guzie, *Jesus and the Eucharist*, 67-68.

140. Ibid., 67.

141. Ibid., 68.

142. David N. Power, *Unsearchable Riches: The Symbolic Nature of Liturgy* (New York: Pueblo Publishing Co., 1984), 196-197.

143. Powers, *Eucharistic Theology*, 171.

144. Worgul, *Magic to Metaphor*, 212.

145. Ibid.

146. Schoonenberg, "Presence," 40.
147. Ibid., 52-53.
148. Schillebeeckx, *The Eucharist*, 137-138.

EPILOGUE

Our historical survey of the eucharist confirms a profound yet ironic truth: the one rite of the church that is both creative and expressive of our unity as the one body of Christ has in practice been one of the most controversial and divisive. Furthermore, the doctrine of Christ's eucharistic presence, which has received virtually unanimous assent from the church, has been a center of controversy that has divided not only Roman Catholicism and Protestantism but also the churches of the Reformation themselves. Now the emergence of the "Interpersonal-Encounter Model" and its concept of transignification, although developed primarily by Roman Catholic theologians, commends itself to the universal church as an ecumenical vehicle for articulating Christ's eucharistic presence. In this epilogue we shall offer six reasons that justify our assertion as well as make recommendations that address both the two principal Protestant criticisms and ways to develop further the model's ecumenical promise.

First, the "Interpersonal-Encounter Model," by focusing on the structures of human consciousness and personal communication, identifies the constitutive features of personal presence that transcend historically determinate forms of presence. Consequently, this model respects and encompasses diverse theological expressions of Christ's eucharistic presence and thereby allows greater acceptance.

Second, the concept of transignification commends itself to the church because it is a new—and thus neutral—term. Since its meaning is grounded in a phenomenological analysis of personal presence and human meaning, it avoids traditional Roman Catholic-Protestant differences. On the one hand, "transignification" is free from most of the negative connotations that attend the Roman Catholic term "transubstantiation" and, on the other hand, it places the change in a religious context and, thus, becomes more acceptable to Protestants.

Furthermore, the tradition has continuously expressed the intention of transignification. In the fifth century, Augustine asserted that beneath the appearance of the sign lay the unseen reality of Christ's eucharistic body which is evoked by the consecration. In the eleventh century, Berengar argued that the consecration provided the abiding bread and wine with a religious value. In the thirteenth century, Thomas Aquinas claimed that the sacrament signified Christ's eucharistic presence through the sensible realities of bread and wine.

Even the Reformers concur. Ulrich Zwingli insisted that Christ's words "This is my body" should be changed to "This signifies my body." And John Calvin believed that the integrity of the sacraments is preserved when the sacraments communicate what they signify.

When these voices from the past are joined with the contemporary Protestant and Roman Catholic advocates of the "Interpersonal-Encounter Model," a chorus of endorsements can be heard across the tradition for the intention of transignification.

Third, by refining the category of substance to denote the intimate or basic reality of a thing, the new approach both avoids the dangers of the Aristotelian scholastic substance-accident categories and broadens its appeal to Protestants. In particular, this redefinition of substance recalls John Calvin's efforts to dissociate altogether the category of substance from dimensional space.

Both Martin Luther and Ulrich Zwingli, when referring to the substance of the body of Christ, had in mind something extended in space—Luther to affirm it, Zwingli to deny it. Calvin detoured the problem by linking substance to power. Wherever anything acts, there it is. Thus, Calvin's connection of substance and presence foreshadowed the connection of action and presence for the new model. By reinterpreting the category of substance, the "Interpersonal-Encounter Model" stands in the tradition of the Reformers.

Fourth, the concept of transignification preserves the notion of divine initiative in salvation, a priority for both Roman Catholic and Protestant theologians. Thomas Aquinas held that all sacraments are instrumental causes of a grace that requires, yet does not stem from, the faith of the recipient and the intention of the celebrant. The efficacy of the sacrament is due solely to the will of the one who has instituted it, Jesus Christ. Hence, Thomas' formulation of transubstantiation, which received ecclesiastical endorsement, articulated an elaborate and eloquent explanation of how matter could be changed into the holy through the exercise of sheer divine power.

The Reformers were equally adamant in protecting God's initiative. Luther's opposition to both the Roman Catholic doctrine of transubstantiation and the Enthusiasts' expression of symbolic presence arose in response to what he perceived as the one great human heresy—the refusal to accept the external means of grace and the attempt to replace divine activity with human initiatives.

Calvin countered what he perceived as the Roman divinization of ecclesiasticism and sacramentalism by constructing his theology of the church upon the foundation of union with Christ and upon the secondary supports of Christology and pneumatology. This interior norm guarantees that the sovereign God initiates the call to community. Neither the enjoyment of fellowship nor even the perceived need for repentance can account for the church. Rather, Christ himself calls his members into his body through the work of the Holy Spirit. This reliance upon the inwardness of the Spirit, and thus upon the initiative of God, is carried through in Calvin's eucharistic doctrine.

Although the formulations have varied, the seminal thinkers in both the Roman Catholic and the Protestant communions have emphasized God's initiating activity. Both traditions can recognize in the concept of transignification a positive assertion of the divine initiative in salvation.

Fifth, this new model reestablishes the symbolic dimension of life. By shifting from the category of efficient causality to symbolic causality, i.e., divine self-communication through symbol, the "Interpersonal-Encounter Model" overcomes the polarization that evolved from the eucharistic controversies of the ninth and eleventh centuries in which "symbolic" and "realist" positions emerged. Although the current debate is usually couched in terms of the "objective" presence of Christ in the elements on the altar and the "subjective" presence of Christ in the hearts of the believers, defenders of this new model establish common ground by arguing that Christ is present in a sacramental mode that does not imply a local presence, a physical change, or an interior presence alone.

Sixth, and highly significant, the "Interpersonal-Encounter Model" affirms the ecclesial context of Christ's eucharistic presence. From its inception, the Christian tradition has conveyed the interrelationship of ecclesial community and eucharist through the imagery of the many grains of wheat coming together to form the single loaf of bread. This bipolar relationship, where "the *assembled community* is the necessary presupposition for actualizing the salvific presence and communion with Jesus . . . while at the same time the *presence of Christ* in the community is the necessary presupposition for the efficacious gathering of the community,"[1] grounds the early church's eucharistic theology. However, the gradual erosion of the communal context of the liturgy during the first millennium severed this vital connection. Consequently, attention shifted to the material elements and the moment of consecration. By retrieving the ecclesial context of worship, the "Interpersonal-Encounter Model" restores to eucharistic theology the communal context, which this book has argued is a necessary and constitutive feature of eucharistic celebrations.

Despite these reasons, obstacles to rapprochement remain. If the "Interpersonal-Encounter Model" is to fulfill its promise as a vehicle by which the church may establish common ground for an ecumenical interpretation of Christ's eucharistic presence, its advocates will need to respond satisfactorily to our Protestant critique.

In particular, the issue of a "metaphysical change," our first criticism, must be resolved. Many Protestants perceive the shift in language from transubstantiation to transignification as a Catholic "Trojan Horse" that merely exchanges substantialistic categories for relational ones. Although a modern ontology has been inserted into an old dogma, Roman Catholicism has not abandoned Trent's "core conviction"—the affirmation of an ontological change.

Proponents of this model may wish to overcome this Protestant "stumbling block" by showing that a "metaphysical change" conveys a truth to which Protestants can also agree. But before that can occur, the relationship between transignification and "metaphysical change" needs clarification. For the "Interpersonal-Encounter Model," a "metaphysical change" constitutes a change in the intrinsic or constitutive meaning of an object without denying or altering its biological composition. Is this change in *meaning* equivalent to what the tradition has normally meant by a "metaphysical change"? That is, does this new interpretation adequately capture the sense of a "metaphysical change" in the eucharist by which the very reality of bread and wine is changed into the body and blood of Christ?

In addition, supporters of this new model will want to address the questions of why any change whatsoever is required in the eucharistic elements and, if a change is requisite, why God is needed to bring it about. Both Catholics and Protestants agree that God initiates *all* redemptive changes. But why single out the eucharist as requiring a special and unique kind of divine activity?

Our second criticism claimed that neither Schoonenberg nor Schillebeeckx moved beyond individualism to a social phenomenology of ecclesial presence and were, therefore, methodologically inconsistent with their stated objectives. In short, the new model, with all of its promise, had not been fully developed.

This criticism pinpoints the strength of this new model—that Christ's eucharistic presence should be situated within the broader context of Christ's ecclesial presence. Both the "Interpersonal-Encounter Model" and our method of discernment call for a social phenomenology of Christ's eucharistic presence. Because human beings are constituted by both subjectivity and intersubjectivity, human meaning operates within a social world of meaning. As a particular way humans relate to each other, the church is a corporate historical existence that shares a determinate intersubjectivity (redemptive consciousness) and a specific structure of cointentions that unifies its participants. Hence, the ecclesial dimension is indispensable to both the meaning of the eucharist and Christ's eucharistic presence.

Our criticism, therefore, does not constitute an intrinsic flaw in the model itself. On the contrary, the fact that the model can integrate a phenomenology of personal presence with the ecclesial context may be its most important contribution to eucharistic theology.

Advocates of this model can fully develop its potential by undertaking a social phenomenology of ecclesial presence along the same lines as the phenomenology of personal presence. Specific questions to guide the study would include: How does redemption occur, and how does this relate to intersubjectivity and ecclesial consciousness? How is redemption related to the eucharist in general and to Christ's eucharistic presence in particular?

Satisfactory responses to our concerns will significantly advance the prospects for formulating a viable ecumenical interpretation of Christ's eucharistic presence as well as further the cause of the oneness of Christ's church.

Notes

1. Aune, "The Presence of God in the Community," 457-458.

SELECTED BIBLIOGRAPHY

Baptism, Eucharist And Ministry. Faith and Order Paper 111. Geneva: World Council of Churches, 1982.

Barclay, Alexander. *The Protestant Doctrine of the Lord's Supper: A Study in the Eucharistic Teaching of Luther, Zwingli and Calvin*. Glasgow: Jackson, Wylie and Company, 1927.

Bettenson, Henry. *Documents of the Christian Church*. New York: Oxford University Press, 1972.

Bouyer, Louis. *Eucharist*. Translated by Charles Underhill Quinn. Notre Dame: University of Notre Dame Press, 1968.

Brilioth, Yngue. *Eucharistic Faith and Practice: Evangelical and Catholic*. Translated by A. G. Hebert. London: Society for Promoting Christian Knowledge, 1934.

Bromiley, G. W., ed. *Zwingli and Bullinger*. Philadelphia: Westminster Press, 1953.

Browning, Robert L. and Roy A. Reed. *The Sacraments in Religious Education and Liturgy: An Ecumenical Model*. Birmingham, AL: Religious Education Press, 1985.

Buescher, Gabriel N. *The Eucharistic Teaching of William Ockham*. New York: Paulist Press, 1951.

Calvin, John. *Institutes of the Christian Religion*. Edited by John T. McNeill. Translated by Ford Lewis Battles. The Library of Christian Classics, vols. xx & xxi. Philadephia: The Westminster Press, 1960.

Casel, Odo. *The Mystery of Christian Worship, and Other Writings*. Edited by Burkhard Neunheuser. With a Preface by Rev. Charles Davis. Westminster: The Newman Press, 1962.

Cirlot, Felix L. *The Early Eucharist*. London: Society for Promoting Christian Knowledge, 1939.

Clements, R. E., Austin Farrer, G. W. H. Lampe, C. W. Dugmore, Alf Härdelin, John Wilkinson, and C. B. Naylor. *Eucharistic Theology Then And Now*. London: SPCK, 1968.

"Constitution on the Sacred Liturgy." In *The Documents of Vatican II*, edited
    by Walter M. Abbott, translation editor, Joseph Gallagher. New York:
    The American Press, 1966.

Cooke, Bernard J. *Christian Sacraments and Christian Personality*. New York:
    Holt, Rinehart and Winston, Inc., 1965.

_____. *Ministry to Word and Sacraments*. Philadelphia: Fortress Press, 1976.

_____. *Sacraments and Sacramentality*. Mystic: Twenty-Third Publications, 1985.

Crockett, William R. *Eucharist: Symbol of Transformation*. New York: Pueblo
    Publishing Company, 1989.

Cullmann, Oscar. *Early Christian Worship*. Translated by A. Stewart Todd and
    James B. Torrance. London: SCM, 1953.

Deiss, Lucien. *It's the Lord's Supper*. Translated by Edmond Bonin. New York:
    Paulist Press, 1976.

Delling, Gerhard. *Worship in the New Testament*. Translated by Percy Scott.
    Philadephia: Westminster Press, 1962.

Dix, Dom Gregory. *The Shape of the Liturgy*. New York: Seabury Press, 1982.

Duffy, Regis A. *Real Presence: Worship, Sacraments, and Commitment*. San
    Francisco: Harper and Row, 1982.

Dugmore, Clifford W. *The Mass and the English Reformers*. London: Macmillan
    and Company, 1958.

Elert, Werner. *Eucharist And Church Fellowship in the First Four Centuries*.
    Translated by N. E. Nagel. St. Louis: Concordia Publishing House, 1966.

Ellis, John Tracy. "The Eucharist in the Life of Cardinal Newman." *Communio*
    4 (Winter 1977): 321-340.

Fahey, John F. *The Eucharistic Teaching of Ratramn of Corbiey*. Mundeleim,
    IL: St. Mary of the Lake Seminary, 1951.

Fairweather, Eugene R. *The Oxford Movement*. New York: Oxford University
    Press, 1964.

Fischer, Robert H. "Luther's Stake in the Lord's Supper Controversy." *Dialog* 2 (Winter 1963): 50-59.

Gerrish, B. A. *Grace and Gratitude: The Eucharistic Theology of John Calvin.* Minneapolis: Fortress Press, 1993.

_____. *The Old Protestantism and the New.* Chicago: The University of Chicago Press, 1982.

_____. *Tradition and the Modern World: Reformed Theology in the Nineteenth Century.* Chicago: The University of Chicago Press, 1978.

Gray, Donald. "The Real Absence: A Note on the Eucharist." In *Living Bread, Saving Cup*, edited by R. Kevin Seasoltz. Collegeville: The Liturgical Press, 1982.

Green, H. Benedict. "The Eucharistic Presence: Change And/Or Signification." *The Downside Review* 83 (1965): 32-48.

Grislis, Egil. "The Manner of Christ's Eucharistic Presence According to Martin Luther." *Consensus* 7 (January 1981): 3-15.

_____. "The Manner of Christ's Eucharistic Presence in the Early and Medieval Church." *Consensus* 6 (October 1980): 3-14.

Guzie, Tad W. *Jesus and the Eucharist.* New York: Paulist Press, 1974.

Hamman, André, comp. *The Mass: Ancient Liturgies and Patristic Texts.* Translated by Thomas Halton. Staten Island: Alba House, 1967.

_____, ed. *The Paschal Mystery: Ancient Liturgies and Patristic Texts.* Translated by Thomas Halton. Staten Island: Alba House, 1969.

Heick, Otto W. "Consubstantiation in Luther's Theology." *Canadian Journal of Theology.* 12 (January 1966): 3-8.

Heron, Alasdair I. C. *Table and Tradition.* Philadelphia: Westminster Press, 1983.

Higgins, Angus J. B. *The Lord's Supper in the New Testament.* Chicago: Henry Regnery Company, 1952.

_____. "The Origins of the Eucharist." *New Testament Studies* 1 (February 1955): 200-209.

Hill, William J. "The Eucharist as Eschatological Presence." *Communio* 4 (Winter 1977): 306-320.

Hinson, E. Glenn. "The Lord's Supper in Early Church History." *Review and Expositor* 66 (Winter 1969): 15-24.

Hitchcock, F. R. Montgomery. "Tertullian's Views on the Sacrament of the Lord's Supper." *Church Quarterly Review* 267 (April-June 1942): 21-36.

Hoffmann, George R. "The 'Real Presence' of Christ in the Eucharist According to Roman Catholic Theology." *Canadian Journal of Theology* 9 (October 1963): 263-270.

Jeremias, Joachim. *The Eucharistic Words of Jesus*. Translated from the 3d German edition by Norman Perrin. New York: Scribner, 1966.

_____. "The Last Supper." *The Journal of Theological Studies* 50 (1949): 1-10.

Jones, Cheslyn, Geoffrey Wainwright, Edward Yarnold, and Paul Bradshaw, eds. *The Study of Liturgy*. Revised ed. New York: Oxford University Press, 1992, 184-338.

Jungmann, Joseph A. *The Mass of the Roman Rite: Its Origins and Development*, vol. 1. Translated by Francis A. Brunner. New York: Benziger Brothers, 1951.

_____. *The Sacrifice of the Church*. Translated by Clifford Howell. London: Challoner Publishers, 1961.

Kelly, J. N. D. *Early Christian Doctrines*. New York: Harper and Row, 1978.

Kilmartin, Edward J. *The Eucharist in the Primitive Church*. Englewood Cliffs, NJ: Prentice-Hall, 1965.

Kilpatrick, George Dunbar. *The Eucharist in Bible and Liturgy*. New York: Cambridge University Press, 1984.

Lash, Nicholas. *His Presence in the World*. Dayton: Pflaum Press, 1968.

Leenhardt, F. J. "This is My Body." In *Essays on the Lord's Supper*, Oscar Cullmann and F. J. Leenhardt, translated by J. G. Davies. Richmond: John Knox Press, 1958.

Lehmann, Helmut T., ed. *Meaning and Practice of the Lord's Supper*. Philadelphia: Muhlenberg Press, 1961.

Lietzmann, Hans. *Mass And Lord's Supper: A Study in the History of the Liturgy*. Translated by Dorothea H. G. Reeve. Leiden: E. J. Brill, 1979.

_____. "The Liturgical History of the Eucharist." In *Twentieth Century Theology in the Making*, vol. 1, edited by Jaroslav Pelikan and translated by R. A. Wilson. London: William Collins Sons and Company, 1969.

Luther, Martin. *Admonition Concerning the Sacrament of the Body and Blood of our Lord, 1530*. In *Luther's Works*, vol. 38, edited by Helmut T. Lehmann, translated by Martin E. Lehmann. Philadelphia: Fortress Press, 1971.

_____. *Against the Heavenly Prophets in the Matter of Images and Sacraments, 1525*. In *Luther's Works*, vol. 40, edited by Helmut T. Lehmann, translated by Bernhard Erling and Conrad Bergendoff. Philadelphia: Fortress Press, 1975.

_____. *Babylonian Captivity of the Church, 1520*. In *Selected Writings of Martin Luther*, vol. 1517-1520, edited by Theodore G. Tappert, translated by A. T. W. Steinhaeuser. Philadelphia: Fortress Press, 1967.

_____. *Blessed Sacrament of the Holy and True Body of Christ, And the Brotherhood, 1519*. In *Luther's Works*, vol. 35, edited by Helmut T. Lehmann, translated by Jeremiah J. Schindel. Philadelphia: Muhlenberg Press, 1960.

_____. *Brief Confession Concerning the Holy Sacrament, 1544*. In *Luther's Works*, vol. 38, edited by Helmut T. Lehmann, translated by Martin E. Lehmann. Philadelphia: Fortress Press, 1971.

_____. *Confession Concerning Christ's Supper, 1528*. In *Luther's Works*, vol.37, edited by Helmut T. Lehmann, translated by Robert H. Fischer. Philadelphia: Fortress Press, 1961.

_____. *The Disputation Concerning the Passage: "The Word Was Made Flesh" (John 1:14), 1539.* In *Luther's Works*, vol. 38, edited by Helmut T. Lehmann, translated by Martin E. Lehmann. Philadelphia: Fortress Press, 1971.

_____. *The Large Catechism of Martin Luther.* Translated by Robert H. Fischer. Philadelphia: Fortress Press, 1959.

_____. *The Sacrament of the Body and Blood of Christ - Against the Fanatics, 1526.* In *Luther's Works*, vol. 36, edited by Helmut T. Lehmann, translated by Frederick C. Ahrens. Philadelphia: Muhlenberg Press, 1959.

_____. *A Short Explanation of Dr. Martin Luther's Small Catechism.* Saint Louis: Concordia Publishing House, 1943.

_____. *That These Words of Christ, "This Is My Body," etc., Still Stand Firm Against the Fanatics, 1527.* In *Luther's Works*, vol. 37, edited by Helmut T. Lehmann, translated by Robert H. Fischer. Philadelphia: Fortress Press, 1961.

_____. *A Treatise on the New Testament, that is, The Holy Mass, 1520.* In *Luther's Works*, vol. 35, edited by Helmut T. Lehmann, translated by Jeremiah J. Schindel. Philadelphia: Muhlenberg Press, 1960.

MacDonald, Allen J. *Berengar and the Reform of Sacramental Doctrine.* Merrick, NY: Richmond Publishing Company, 1977.

Marshall, I. Howard. *Last Supper and Lord's Supper.* Grand Rapids: Eerdmans Publishing Company, 1981.

Maxwell, Jack Martin. *Worship and Reformed Theology: The Liturgical Lessons of Mercersburg.* Pittsburgh: The Pickwick Press, 1976.

Maxwell, William D. *An Outline of Christian Worship.* London: Oxford University Press, 1936.

McCue, James F. "The Doctrine of Transubstantiation from Berengar Through Trent: The Point at Issue." *Harvard Theological Review* 61 (July 1968): 385-430.

McDonnell, Kilian. *John Calvin, the Church, and the Eucharist.* Princeton: Princeton University Press, 1967.

Meyer, Boniface. "Calvin's Eucharistic Doctrine: 1536-1539." *Journal of Ecumenical Studies* 4 (Winter 1967): 47-65.

Michell, G. A. *Eucharistic Consecration in the Primitive Church*. London: SPCK, 1948.

Mitchell, Nathan. *Cult and Controversy: The Worship of the Eucharist Outside Mass*. New York: Pueblo Publishing Company, 1982.

Montclos, Jean de. *Lanfrance et Bérenger: La Controverse Eucharistique Du XIe Siècle*. Leuven: Spicilegium Sacrum Lovaniense, 1971.

Moule, Charles Francis Digby. *Worship in the New Testament*. Richmond: John Knox Press, 1961.

Nevin, John W. *The Mystical Presence and Other Writings on the Eucharist*. In Lancaster Series on the Mercersburg Theology, vol. 4, edited and with a Preface by Bard Thompson and George H. Bricker. Philadelphia: United Church Press, 1966.

Nichols, James Hastings. *Corporate Worship in the Reformed Tradition*. Philadelphia: Westminster Press, 1968.

_____, ed. *The Mercersburg Theology*. A Library of Protestant Thought. New York: Oxford University Press, 1966.

Oberman, Heiko A. "Reformation, Preaching, and *Ex Opere Operato*." In *Christianity Divided: Protestant and Roman Catholic Theological Issues*, edited by Daniel J. Callahan, Heiko A. Oberman, Daniel J. O'Hanlon. New York: Sheed and Ward, 1961.

O'Neill, Colman. "What is 'Transignification' All About?" *The Catholic World* 202 (January 1966): 204-210.

Paul VI. *"Mysterium Fidei." The Pope Speaks* 10 (1965): 309-328.

Piper, Otto A. "The Real Presence." *The Princeton Seminary Bulletin* 51 (October 1957): 16-23.

Porter, H. Boone, Jr. "The Eucharistic Piety of Justin Martyr." *Anglican Theological Review* 39 (January 1957): 24-33.

Power, David N. *The Eucharistic Mystery: Revitalizing the Tradition*. New York: Crossroad, 1992.

_____. *Unsearchable Riches: The Symbolic Nature of Liturgy*. New York: Pueblo Publishing Company, 1984.

Powers, Joseph M. *Eucharistic Theology*. New York: Herder and Herder, 1967.

_____. *"Mysterium Fidei* and the Theology of the Eucharist." *Worship* 40 (1966): 17-35.

Prenter, Regin. "The Doctrine of the Real Presence." *The Lutheran Quarterly* 3 (May 1951): 156-166.

Rahner, Karl. *The Church and the Sacraments*. Translated by W. J. O'Hara. New York: Herder and Herder, 1964.

_____. "The Presence of Christ in the Sacrament of the Lord's Supper." *Theological Investigations*, vol. 4. Translated by Kevin Smyth. London: Darton, Longman & Todd Ltd, 1966, 287-311.

Redmond, R. P. "The Real Presence in the Early Middle Ages." *Clergy Review* 8 (1934): 442-460.

Reumann, John. *The Supper of the Lord*. Philadelphia: Fortress Press, 1985.

Richardson, Cyril C. *Zwingli and Cranmer on the Eucharist*. Evanston: Seabury-Western Theological Seminary, 1949.

Rordorf, Willy, Georges Blond, Raymond Johanny, Maurice Jourjon, Adalbert Hamman, André Méhat, Victor Saxer, and Patrick Jacquemont. *The Eucharist of the Early Christians*. Translated by Matthew J. O'Connell. New York: Pueblo Publishing Company, 1978.

Sasse, Hermann. *This is My Body: Luther's Contention for the Real Presence in the Sacrament of the Altar*. Adelaide: Lutheran Publishing House, 1977.

Schillebeeckx, Edward. *Christ the Sacrament of the Encounter with God*. Translated by Paul Barrett. New York: Sheed and Ward, 1963.

_____. *The Eucharist*. Translated by N. D. Smith. New York: Sheed and Ward, 1968.

_____. "The Sacraments: An Encounter with God." In *Christianity Divided: Protestant and Roman Catholic Theological Issues*, edited by Daniel J. Callahan, Heiko A. Oberman, Daniel J. O'Hanlon, translated by John L. Boyle. New York: Sheed and Ward, 1961.

_____. "Transubstantiation, Transfinalization, Transignification." In *Living Bread, Saving Cup*, edited by R. Kevin Seasoltz, translated by David J. Rock. Collegeville: The Liturgical Press, 1982.

_____. *Vatican II: The Real Achievement*. Translated by H. J. J. Vaughan. London: Sheed and Ward, 1967.

Schmidt, Karl Ludwig. "The Eucharist in the New Testament and the Primitive Church." In Twentieth Century *Theology in the Making*, vol. I, edited by Jaroslav Pelikan, translated by R. A. Wilson. London: William Collins Sons and Company, 1969.

Schoonenberg, Piet. "Presence and the Eucharistic Presence," translated by Sr. Mary Pierre Ellebracht. *Cross Currents* 17 (Winter 1967): 39-54.

_____. "The Real Presence in Contemporary Discussion." *Theology Digest* 15 (Spring 1967): 3-11.

_____. "Transubstantiation: How Far is this Doctrine Historically Determined?" In *Concilium*, vol. 24, *The Sacraments: An Ecumenical Dilemma*, edited by Hans Küng, translated by Theodore L. Westow. New York: Paulist Press, 1966.

Schweitzer, Albert. *The Problem of the Lord's Supper according to the Scholarly Research of the Nineteenth Century and the Historical Accounts*. Edited with an Introduction by John Reumann. Translated by A. J. Mattill, Jr. Macon: Mercer University Press, 1982.

Schweizer, Edward. *The Lord's Supper According to the New Testament*. Translated by James M. Davis. Philadelphia: Fortress Press, 1967.

Sheedy, Charles E. *The Eucharistic Controversy of the Eleventh Century*. New York: AMS Press, 1980.

Snook, Lee E. "Consciousness and Contradiction: Luther's Doctrine of the Real Presence Reconsidered." *Dialog* 10 (Winter 1971): 38-48.

Stacey, John. "The Theology of John Wyclif." *The Expository Times* 69 (September 1958): 356-359.

Stone, Darwell. *A History of the Doctrine of the Holy Eucharist*, 2 vols. London: Longmans, Green, and Company, 1909.

Thomas Aquinas, Saint. "The Eucharistic Presence." In *Summa Theologiae*, vol. 58, translated by William Barden. New York: Blackfriars; McGraw-Hill Book Company, 1965.

_____. "Holy Communion." In *Summa Theologiae*, vol. 59, translated by Thomas Gilby. New York: Blackfriars; McGraw-Hill Book Company, 1975.

_____. "The Sacraments." In *Summa Theologiae*, vol 56, translated by David Bourke. New York: Blackfriars; McGraw-Hill Book Company, 1975.

Thurian, Max. *The Eucharistic Memorial*, 2 vols. Translated by J. G. Davies. Richmond: John Knox Press, 1960 & 1961.

_____. *The Mystery of the Eucharist*. Translated by Emily Chisholm. Grand Rapids: William B. Eerdmans, 1984.

_____. "The Real Presence." In *Christianity Divided: Protestant and Roman Catholic Theological Issues*, edited by Daniel J. Callahan, Heiko A. Oberman, Daniel J. O'Hanlon. New York: Sheed and Ward, 1961.

_____. "Toward a Renewal of the Doctrine of Transubstantiation." In *Christianity Divided: Protestant and Roman Catholic Theological Issues*, edited by Daniel J. Callahan, Heiko A. Oberman, Daniel J. O'Hanlon. New York: Sheed and Ward, 1961.

_____, ed. *Ecumenical Perspectives on Baptism, Eucharist And Ministry*. Faith and Order Paper 116. Geneva: World Council of Churches, 1983.

_____, and Geoffrey Wainwright, eds. *Baptism and Eucharist: Ecumenical Convergence in Celebration*. Geneva: World Council of Churches, 1983.

Tylenda, Joseph N. "Calvin and Christ's Presence in the Supper - True or Real?" *Scottish Journal of Theology* 27 (February 1974): 65-75.

Wainwright, Geoffrey. *Eucharist and Eschatology*. New York: Oxford University Press, 1981.

Wallace, Ronald S. *Calvin's Doctrine of the Word and Sacrament*. Edinburgh: Oliver and Boyd, 1953.

Warnach, Victor. "Symbol and Reality in the Eucharist." In *Concilium*, vol. 40, *The Breaking of Bread*, edited by Pierre Benoit, Roland E. Murphy, and Bastiaan Van Jersel. New York: Paulist Press, 1969.

White, James F. *A Brief History of Christian Worship*. Nashville: Abingdon Press, 1993.

_____. *Documents of Christian Worship: Descriptive and Interpretive Sources*. Louisville: Westminster/John Knox Press, 1992, 180-213.

Wiegand, Friedrich. "The History of the Doctrine of the Eucharist." In *Twentieth Century Theology in the Making*, vol. 1, edited by Jaroslav Pelikan, translated by R. A. Wilson. London: William Collins Sons and Company, 1969.

Willimon, William H. *Word, Water, Wine and Bread*. Valley Forge: Judson Press, 1980.

Worgul, George S., Jr. *From Magic to Metaphor: A Validation of the Christian Sacraments*. New York: Paulist Press, 1980.

Zwingli, Ulrich. *On the Lord's Supper*. In *Zwingli and Bullinger*, edited and translated by G. W. Bromiley. Philadelphia: Westminster Press, 1953.

SCRIPTURE INDEX

INDEX OF NAMES